I0821866

THE SCANDAL OF HAVING SOMETHING TO SAY

THE SCANDAL OF HAVING SOMETHING TO SAY

Ricoeur and the Possibility of Postliberal Preaching

Lance B. Pape

BAYLOR UNIVERSITY PRESS

Cover Design by Nita Ybarra

Library of Congress Cataloging-in-Publication Data

Pape, Lance B., 1970–
The scandal of having something to say : Ricoeur and the possibility of postliberal preaching / Lance B. Pape.
176 p. cm.
Includes bibliographical references and index.
ISBN 978-1-60258-528-7 (alk. paper)
1. Ricœur, Paul. 2. Preaching. 3. Postliberal theology. I. Title.
B2430.R554P355 2013
251—dc23
2012028966

Printed in the United States of America on acid-free paper with a minimum of 30% post-consumer waste recycled content.

for my parents

Contents

Acknowledgments

This book owes much to my days in the Graduate Division of Religion at Emory University, and, in more ways than I know how to name, its ideas are a product of the teachers and colleagues I enjoyed there. Among the latter, Matthew Flemming was especially influential. Among my teachers, I wish to acknowledge a debt both intellectual and personal to Thomas Long, Gail O'Day, David Bartlett, and Joy McDougall. To Tom, especially, the debt is deep. I also wish to thank and acknowledge the help of my editor at Baylor University Press, Carey Newman, and my research assistant, Douglass Anne Cartwright. Naturally, none of these people are to blame for what I have made of their good advice and influence, but they are to praise for what is best in it.

I also wish to acknowledge the constant help and support of the finest working preacher I know, the Rev. Dr. Katie Hays, who took on more than her share of the work of the household, and the parenting, and the bread-winning while I did this work. Thanks, Kate. Finally, I want to express my gratitude to my parents, Jack and Sylvia Pape, to whom this book is dedicated. When, after more than a decade in ministry, I went back to school, they moved across the country to help with the grandkids. Their help with the kids was all I had hoped, but getting a chance to know them well as an adult has been an unexpected wonder and a blessing.

Chapter One

The Scandal of Having Something to Say

This book explores how scriptural language and sermonic language participate in God's free act of self-communication. I begin with some theological reflections on the contemporary context that motivates this project.

The Scandal of Preaching after Christendom

The North American pulpit has been in decline for decades.[1] Of course, worries about the decline of preaching are not entirely new.[2] But if this is not

[1] For a classic articulation, see Fred B. Craddock, *As One without Authority*, rev. and with new sermons (St. Louis: Chalice Press, 2001), 3–20. Originally published in 1971, Craddock's opening chapter, titled "The Pulpit in the Shadows," names many factors motivating detractors of the pulpit in his context, including one that often escapes less astute observers: "[T]hese critics have heard us preach" (3).

[2] A generation before Craddock, W. E. Sangster employed the same image of the shadow to express concerns about the state of preaching at mid-century. William Edwin Sangster, *The Craft of Sermon Construction* (Philadelphia: Westminster, 1951), 11. Looking even further back, Clyde Fant compiled a remarkable list of nineteenth-century citations mourning the state of the discipline, and so chastised, "We do not need to dispute the very real problems preaching has today, but we do need to lay to rest once and for all the unrealistic 'Golden Age' myth and we do need to know that pulpit criticism was not born in our generation." Fant, *Preaching for Today* (San Francisco: Harper & Row, 1987), 26–27.

the first generation of homileticians to wrestle with the challenges faced by preaching in the North American context, this cultural moment does represent a fundamentally new challenge.

The indifference of the twenty-first-century mainstream North American context to Christian preaching is the popular culture endgame of centuries-old intellectual developments. Christianity is entering a season in which it must strive to reclaim its rightful vocation as a religion and renounce the false vocation of underwriting Western culture generally.[3] The most helpful and hopeful way of framing the current crisis in homiletics is that the cultural fatigue surrounding Christian proclamation is a clue about a wrong turn and an opportunity for self-correction. If Christianity is finally exposed in its failed bid to supply the conceptual framework capable of exhaustively funding the many and diverse projects of Western civilization, then Christian preaching is set free to explore its true vocation with new focus.

Claiming this freedom depends upon coming to terms with loss. However real the hostility toward preaching, forty years ago when Fred Craddock gamely requested his "stay of execution" for preaching,[4] the Protestant pulpit in the United States was in fact a comfortably ensconced public fixture just as the church's cultural enfranchisement was assumed. Things have changed.[5] It now seems increasingly unlikely that preaching will ever again reclaim its place in the pantheon of respected North American cultural institutions. Homiletical reflection now can and must work free from such privilege and distraction.[6] The challenge is to claim this new freedom and trust that it is as real as the loss the church has endured. One need not regard the cultural

[3] "[T]he most fateful issue for Christian self-description is that of regaining its autonomous vocation as a religion, after its defeat in its secondary vocation of providing ideological coherence, foundation, and stability to Western culture." Hans W. Frei, "The 'Literal Reading' of Biblical Narrative in the Christian Tradition: Does It Stretch or Will It Break?," in *The Bible and the Narrative Tradition*, ed. Frank McConnell (New York: Oxford University Press, 1986), 74.

[4] Craddock, *One without Authority*, 3.

[5] Mainline Protestant cultural disenfranchisement has occurred at an astonishing pace, but due to the sheer scope of such a realignment it has taken a generation. As late as 1987, William H. Willimon could characterize the situation of the church in the West as "awkward" because "having once been culturally established, [Christians] are not yet clearly disestablished." Willimon, "Answering Pilate: Truth and the Postliberal Church," *Christian Century* 104, no. 3 (1987): 84. Willimon's "yet" shows that he had no illusions about the trend, which has continued and accelerated since his observation.

[6] Richard Lischer has rightly discerned the opportunity at hand: "We cannot . . . rescue the profession of the ministry from social decline, but we can embrace our vocation. We can preach." Lischer, *The End of Words: The Language of Reconciliation in a Culture of Violence*, Lyman Beecher Lectures in Preaching (Grand Rapids: Eerdmans, 2005), 41.

decline of the Protestant churches as an unambiguously welcome development in order to appreciate that it should now be possible to ask the old question "What is Christian preaching?" with new clarity and so embrace our true vocation with new seriousness.

If homiletics is to meet the challenge and opportunity of this new situation, it must attend with fresh urgency to the scandal of the church's original commission to preach. Such a turn toward what is offensive and strange in the call to preach is fraught with risks—and not only those proper to faith. A renewed focus on the scandal of what we preach must not be allowed to degenerate into a baptized sensationalism calculated to satisfy the seemingly endless appetite for spectacle that characterizes much of popular culture; nor should it be allowed to mask a retreat into the survivable holding pattern of a cautious sectarian ghetto. It must grow, rather, out of the distant and humbling memory that the church is really and always a "nothing" that is continually called into existence by the One upon whom it completely depends (Rom 4:17, 1 Cor 1:26-28).

Of course this beginning is itself a scandal in our context because it is precisely the authenticity of this vocation, this *vocatio*, that is contested by the heirs of Feuerbach, Marx, Nietzsche, and Freud. The challenge of these "masters of suspicion" makes us acutely aware of two possibilities, between which a chasm has been fixed.[7] If the summoning the church heeds is not the voice of Another—if it is merely a human projection arising predictably from so many wishes, needs, resentments, and drives—then the church has no real existence, no authentic commission to preach, but only a habitual and unwarranted longing to speak back to the world its own fears and hopes, filtered through the images and idioms of a very old book. In this case, the world shows great forbearance by benignly ignoring our "preaching," which surely deserves worse than indifference. On the other hand, if the voice that calls us is real—that is, if it is somehow God—then the church has a true and vital existence and may preach as an echo of that prior word of summons. Indeed, in this case it would be truer to say that we must preach (1 Cor 9:16). There is simply no place to stand in the chasm between these two possible worlds. Within a generous orthodoxy there can and should be space

[7] Paul Ricoeur included Marx, Nietzsche, and Freud under this description and regarded their iconoclastic hermeneutics as necessary to "clear the horizon for a more authentic word." Ricoeur, *Freud and Philosophy: An Essay on Interpretation* (New Haven: Yale University Press, 1970), 33. For the thought of the earlier Feuerbach in this connection, see Paul Ricoeur, *The Rule of Metaphor: Multi-Disciplinary Studies of the Creation of Meaning in Language*, trans. Robert Czerny, University of Toronto Romance Series 37 (Toronto: University of Toronto Press, 1977), 318.

for supple minds to explore subtle distinctions in sorting out the "somehow God" of the second possibility; but the difference between these two broadly conceived positions is absolute.

It is this absolute difference—this absolutely significant difference—that frames the contemporary scandal of preaching. The hermeneutical stances that correspond to these two positions are mutually inscrutable, so that not only are interpretations vigorously contested, but there is and can be no broadly accepted forum for the adjudication of such divergent construals of reality. The result is that although Christian preaching is grounded in the conviction that a divine commission has authorized a most urgent, winsome, and demanding kind of talk, such talk is not only not warranted to the satisfaction of all those implicated in its claims, but unwarrantable according to any generally accepted public standard. It is, therefore, scandalous talk. It boldly gives offense. This is the situation of preaching not only in the eyes of those most intentionally and mindfully committed to the hermeneutic of suspicion that dismisses Christian faith as false consciousness but also in the eyes of the many late moderns who have been formed in a cultural climate of pervasive suspicion and radical autonomy, albeit without much explicit grounding in the profound thought that generated it. Furthermore, if preaching is a scandal for the many in our context, then its offense ought to be appreciated also by those who believe, as it surely is by those of us who believe and yet must pray constantly for help with unbelief (Mark 9:24).

Naming the scandal of preaching after Christendom motivates fresh consideration of the scandal of preaching before Christendom. We are reminded again that Christian preaching was born steeped in the storied scandal that was both the content of its proclamation and (as I will argue below) the circumstances of its transmission. From within our new situation of accelerating disestablishment, the perspective shifts and it becomes possible to imagine that the middle centuries of Constantinian establishment were anomalous for preaching. The startling prospect emerges that the communicative situation most proper and "native" to preaching is perpetually one of audacity and jeopardy. The most promising path to reconnecting with the implications of this essential quality of preaching in a post-Christian context is to consider again those who preached to the pre-Christian world.

The Scandal of Preaching before Christendom

Arguably the earliest evidence pointing to the existence of communities that confessed faith in Jesus of Nazareth is a letter written from a Hellenized Jew to his Gentile converts in Thessalonica, circa 51 C.E. The author was Paul of Tarsus, who, after a profound religious experience (Gal 1:13-17, 1 Cor 15:8-10), understood himself to be the recipient of an unlikely divine commission to proclaim the Lordship of the Jewish messiah among the Gentiles (Gal 2:7, Rom 11:13). The oddness of this fact builds in layers upon reflection. That a former persecutor of the Jesus movement (Gal 1:13) should be commissioned as one of its apostles is no more remarkable than the notion that its offer of salvation—founded, bizarrely, upon the shameful public execution of this Jesus in a manner previously construed as a sign of God's curse (Deut 21:23, Gal 3:13)—should be extended to those outside the chosen race. The letters of Paul reflect this improbable confluence: a message of salvation claiming continuity with Jewish history and faith, radically reinterpreting that history and faith in light of the crucifixion/resurrection, and proffering its promise of relationship with Israel's God among Gentiles.

It is the cumulative "oddness" of the content and circumstances of the first proclamation that I am claiming as analogous to and instructive for the contemporary scandal of preaching. Note that, for Paul, the strangeness of his apostolic message and ministry was not an embarrassment to be downplayed. On the contrary, he embraced it as fundamental to a proper understanding of God's gracious new initiative in the world and sought to bring it into the clearest possible focus through the use of a symbol that neatly captured all that was offensive about this gospel: the cross.

In 1 Corinthians Paul's theological and ethical reasoning is dominated by the cross. In 1:18 Paul summarizes the content of his preaching in their midst as the "*logos* of the cross." In terms of the classical means of persuasion, this *logos* might more properly be classified as anti-*logos* in the sense that it stands in conspicuous contradiction to conventional plausibility structures.[8] But this is precisely the theological crux for Paul; it is because the message of the cross appears humanly foolish and weak that it is able to function as a sign of divine wisdom and strength. The gaping distance between the story of the cross and humanly plausible argument corresponds to the epistemological gap between God and humans. The world was unable to know God through its conventional ways of knowing (1:21a), but God took the initiative and made saving knowledge available by means of a proclamation that appears scandalous and foolish by human standards (1:21b-25). Christian preaching participates in God's self-disclosure only to the extent that it embraces and submits itself to this same scandal.

[8] This reversal of rhetorical expectations for rhetorical effect has also been explored by André Resner, who has drawn primarily on the Corinthian correspondence to build his case for Paul's use of a "reverse *ethos*." See Resner, *Preacher and Cross: Person and Message in Theology and Rhetoric* (Grand Rapids: Eerdmans, 1999).

For Paul, "Jesus Christ and him crucified" (2:2) is not an empty slogan; it has become the test of authenticity for any proclamation that claims to be Christian.[9] The shadow of the cross falls so heavily upon the preaching situation that the event of proclamation recapitulates its paradoxical power. Just as the story of the cross gives offense when it claims that God's Christ is revealed through a humiliating public execution, so the authentic bearers of this odd *logos* find that their own lives have been drawn into the pattern of scandal. Placed on exhibit as last of all, it is as if they, too, have been sentenced to death, and so become a spectacle in the eyes of all (4:9). Indeed, although some of the Corinthians wish to style themselves "rich," and worse, "kings" (4:8), it is truer to say that even the hearers of this strange good news fit the pattern perfectly: "Not many of you were wise by human standards, not many were powerful, not many were of noble birth" (1:26). At God's surprising initiative, the Christ was revealed in suffering, folly, and weakness; his saving story was disseminated by self-declared suffering, weak, and foolish messengers; and this most unlikely evangel was received as good news by an audience that Paul characterizes with troubling frankness as "things that are not" (1:28). Only when preaching is conformed to the scandal of the cross do God's wisdom and strength become manifest in it.

Is It Safe to Preach the Cross?

Before proceeding, it is appropriate to ponder some concerns about the cross as a theological resource for homiletics. The cross as a visual symbol has always been vulnerable to misuse. Cut off from its narrative, the cross is as malleable as any other visual artifact. The star-spangled cross of North American civic religion is part of a long and disturbing history of the cross' co-option as a utensil of empire. Set ablaze, the cross has been pressed into service as an instrument of intimidation by white supremacists. Countless armies have marched to victory and plunder under the sign of the cross. In its worst moments, Western civilization has supplied more evidence for supposing the cross the symbol of Mars than the God revealed as the Father of Jesus Christ.

[9] For this way of putting the matter, and for many of the ideas explored here, I am indebted to Jürgen Moltmann, who has inspired in many a renewed interest in Luther's maxim, *Crux probat omnia*. Moltmann, *The Crucified God: The Cross of Christ as the Foundation and Criticism of Christian Theology* (London: SCM Press, 1974), 7. I am especially conscious of a debt to Moltmann's explication of the church's many attempts to tame the cross' scandal, only to find such maneuvers defeated at every turn by its seemingly endless capacity to resist domestication (*Crucified God*, 32–81).

But increasingly, criticism of the cross is directed not toward these blatant misappropriations but toward theological interpretations of the cross long accepted as convincingly grounded in the New Testament. Feminist critics, for example, have argued that the word of the cross is often not good news for women and that Christian reflection on the cross has tended to glorify suffering—a message that is toxic for victims of abuse.[10] One study suggests that Christian talk about humility, forgiveness, and submission (along with the notion of God as an all-powerful father willing to sanction horrific mistreatment of his child in service of a greater good) contributed to a pattern of childhood sexual abuse in the lives of several women raised in Christian homes and served as a complication in their journey toward recovery.[11]

For some, such concerns have motivated a turn toward a radically revised Christology that attempts to reimagine the meaning of Christ's death not in terms of classic atonement theory but as an epoch-making event that has unmasked the "scapegoat mechanism," thereby exposing and dispelling a brutal and godless pattern of victimization that has plagued human culture from its beginning.[12] This Girardian approach to the significance of the cross rewards careful consideration, as when it suggestively elucidates certain features of the biblical narrative (e.g., Luke 23:12), but should not be embraced to the exclusion of other interpretations that enjoy more extensive textual grounding. It is better to recognize that the canonical witness itself models how a plurality of tensive images can work together to explicate the meaning of Christ's death.[13] The "scapegoat" approach to the cross may helpfully supplement other interpretations; but supplementation does not solve the problem.

The possibility that the word of the cross is a damaging word for the most vulnerable in our midst is a particular concern for preaching. Homiletician James Kay is not ready to become "an enemy of the cross" (Phil 3:18), but he acknowledges that "[w]here the cross remains the center of the church's proclamation it runs the risk of modeling and encouraging masochism,

[10] E.g., pastoral theologian Christie Neuger worries about any interpretation of the cross that suggests to victims of abuse that "there is divine meaning in their experience of abuse, that the abuse itself is salvific or a means to deeper spirituality, . . . or that it is a sign of deep Christian charity to tolerate being abused by a 'loved one.'" Neuger, *Counseling Women: A Narrative, Pastoral Approach* (Minneapolis: Fortress, 2001), 98.

[11] Annie Imbens and Ineke Jonker, *Christianity and Incest* (Minneapolis: Fortress, 1992).

[12] René Girard, *The Scapegoat* (Baltimore: Johns Hopkins University Press, 1986).

[13] For a helpful survey of this diverse imagery, see Paul S. Fiddes, *Past Event and Present Salvation: The Christian Idea of Atonement*, 1st American ed. (Louisville, Ky.: Westminster John Knox, 1989), 61–168.

victimization, and the abuse of children and women."[14] I find his choice of the word *risk* singularly instructive, for the cross undeniably involves risk. The pioneer of cruciform faith did not find the trail he blazed to be "safe" in any conventional sense of the word, and those followers who have attempted most courageously to conform their lives to the identity disclosed through the narrative of his betrayal, arrest, and brutal murder at the hands of those threatened by his way of being in the world have consistently found that the abundant life he offers is not the one they can secure for themselves.[15]

One of our cultural creeds is that life, and life abundant, is more or less a sure thing that can be forfeited only through exceptionally bad choices, or exceptionally bad luck. Or to put it another way, being careful is one of our culture's rare, shared virtues. If a happy and fulfilled life is really the default mode of human existence, then playing it safe makes perfect sense, and it would be the worst kind of folly to seek formation through engagement with narratives drenched in real human blood and echoing at turns with cries of dereliction and desperate prayers of hope against hope—narratives that primarily serve to render an identity distinguished by a radical wager of faith. Nietzsche balked at the New Testament's cowardice, its subversive mockery of classical nobility and valor. We are more inclined to worry that it all sounds rather dangerous.

This worry reminds us that the cross remains a particular scandal for us. In the current context, it does so by uncovering and contradicting a little gospel that we have made for ourselves; for it is by contrast to another narrative promising short odds on salvation writ small that the terrifying risks and sweeping promises of the gospel of Jesus Christ come into clear focus.

These observations are not intended to make a satisfactory answer to all the serious concerns raised by feminist theorists but rather to learn from the way such critiques serve to set in relief how odd the word of the cross preached

[14] James F. Kay, "The Word of the Cross at the Turn of the Ages," *Interpretation* 53, no. 1 (1999): 45.

[15] Opponents of the cross may counter that the New Testament attributes the murder of Jesus to the will of his divine Father. Close reading does not support this univocal claim, instead inviting the sympathetic imagination into a realistic interplay of causalities as diverse as the failure of his closest followers, the paranoid power of his secular enemies, the machinations of his religious enemies, the free act of his own self-giving love, and the mysterious intervention of "the rulers of this age." The theological claim that God was nevertheless at work through and behind these (and still other) causes is very different from the simplistic assertion that God the Father murdered his child, or casually sanctioned his brutal execution. The difference is that the latter (distorted) claim is so abstracted from the rich and complex web of agencies depicted in the biblical narratives as to be unrecognizable to someone formed through thick and sustained engagement with the world the biblical text displays.

by Paul remains in our context, how sorely the cross presses us to come to terms with what and whom we really trust, and especially how disastrous the cross can become in the hands of a community that dabbles in its imagery and rhetoric, but remains deeply invested in established power arrangements that contradict its deep logic.[16] The community that would speak the word of the cross rightly must practice it radically, for the cross in moderation is an unredeemed folly. This wager must be all or nothing, and half measures are sure to leave us beyond the conventional wisdom and comfort of one age, yet short of the divine wisdom and comfort of the next—a desert inhabited unhappily by those who are "of all people most to be pitied" (1 Cor 15:9). Christians have a responsibility to be vigilant against the ways superficial dabbling in the language of the cross can make us enemies of the very good news we claim to preach.

Yet despite the dangers of faithfulness to the cross, and the even greater dangers of faithlessly cloaking our own agendas in its rhetoric, the cross is not dispensable to us. We see by our own lights that the cross is not safe. But neither is there safety apart from it, for we also guess with Auden that nothing that is possible (for us) can save us.[17] In the late stages of cultural eviction anyway, the church may finally be ready to go willingly "outside" (Heb 13:13) to the homeless, crucified one. Disabused of faith in our own words, we may be ready at last to make our preaching conform to his scandalous word and no other (1 Cor 2:2).

Jürgen Moltmann has named the cross' claim on the late-modern Christian's imagination in a way that resonates with this analysis. The cross does not orient or edify, for the story it tells contradicts our shared intuitions about what is life producing.[18] In a world committed to the suppression of

[16] I am in agreement with James Kay, who warns that "any taking up of the cross as an ornamental symbol or rhetorical device whereby we can further promote our own status or stature is unworthy of the gospel" and "[i]nsofar as attacks on doctrines of the atonement by contemporary pastors and theologians are attacks on [such] *kata-sarka* construals of the cross, these attacks are faithful to the word of the cross." Kay, "Word of the Cross," 47.

[17] "We who must die demand a miracle. / How could the Eternal do a temporal act, the Infinite become a finite fact? / Nothing can save us that is possible: / We who must die demand a miracle." W. H. Auden, "For the Time Being: A Christmas Oratorio," in *Collected Poems*, ed. Edward Mendelson (New York: Modern Library, 2007), 353.

[18] "[The cross] does not bring man into a better harmony with himself and his environment, but into contradiction with himself and his environment. It does not create a home for him and integrate him into society, but makes him 'homeless' and 'rootless,' and liberates him in following Christ who was homeless and rootless. [It] does not elevate and edify in the usual sense, but scandalizes; and most of all it scandalizes one's 'co-religionists' in one's own circle. But by this scandal, it brings liberation into a world which is not free." Moltmann, *Crucified God*, 39.

vulnerability and mortality "there is nothing so unpopular as for the crucified God to be made a present reality through faith. It alienates alienated men, who have come to terms with alienation."[19] Moltmann goes on to say that an encounter with the authentic word of the cross brings us not just alienation, but pain. It is painful when our comforting illusions and idols are shattered upon the cross. This pain is an indication that space has opened up for an encounter with something beyond ourselves—something more than our own best efforts to control and make sense of our lives.[20]

The word of the cross comes to the Christian preacher as the voice of Another, and bids her preach as an echo of that prior word. It is the guarantee that the preacher has something more to say than her own best thoughts. And it is the test of what the preacher says when she claims to speak the word of God.

Embracing the Scandal of Having Something to Say

Of all the theological responses to the challenges of modernity—challenges arising from both the reasoned complaints of Christianity's cultured despisers and the subversive hermeneutics of the masters of suspicion—none has more convincingly conformed itself to the strange logic of the cross than Karl Barth's. Rather than seeking to show that the Christian gospel is not as odd as its critics have charged, Barth, like Paul, sensed that the proper response was not to make the message more conventionally plausible but to embrace the scandal.[21] Preachers can stand alongside those who wonder at the strangeness of our words. The gospel we preach is strange even to us, because it is not from us. By embracing the scandal of having something more to say, Barth has pointed the way forward for homiletics after Christendom.

Conversely, Barth shows us that when preaching is reducible without remainder to the saying of the best things we humans can think of to say to one another, it is an unredeemable embarrassment that should cease. It is precisely the many and varied attempts to carry on with "preaching" so

[19] Moltmann, *Crucified God*, 39.

[20] "In this pain we experience reality outside ourselves, which we have not made or thought out for ourselves." Moltmann, *Crucified God*.

[21] With special attention to the so-called "early" Barth of *Romans*, Stephen H. Webb has shown that Barth's peculiar brand of theological poetics was structured around a rhetorical one-two punch of first exacerbating the crisis of doubt (hyperbole), before twisting conventional assumptions in a surprising reversal (irony). Webb, *Re-Figuring Theology: The Rhetoric of Karl Barth*, SUNY Series in Rhetoric and Theology (Albany: State University of New York Press, 1991).

conceived—carry on in denial or concealment of the embarrassment—that have contributed to the pulpit's decline. Barth warns that even the most compelling (earnest, plausible, enlightened, pretty) human word is no substitute for the word of God.[22]

In the early essay "The Need and Promise of Christian Preaching," Barth articulates his theology of preaching not in terms of disembodied assertions about the self-authenticating Word of a Wholly Other God, but in the context of exegeting a Christian practice. Asks the young pastor at Safenwil, "Why do people come to church?" They do not come to hear even the best human words spoken well by a good person. When the minister discerns rightly—when she takes them (as they demand!) "more seriously than they take themselves"—she pries beneath the bourgeois veneer and arrives finally at the deep question that brings them expectantly on Sunday morning: "Is it true, this talk of a loving and good God, who is more than one of the friendly idols whose rise is so easy to account for, and whose dominion is so brief?"[23] They want to know if the preacher has something true to say—something more than the predictable aphorisms of the little gods of the age.

Barth's surprising practical judgment is that this is the people's question—a question that invites a most extraordinary kind of talk.[24] This is the deep human need presupposed in the expectancy of the preaching moment, and the people must not be put off with half measures, with preaching that stops short of addressing the ultimate concern they bring to the situation. One of the great dangers of the preaching situation is that people may be all too willing to be put off, at least for the moment, with a human word by which "they are touched, delighted, [and] gratified."[25] Indeed, Barth's charge is that they have really been put off, and that the modern decline of the church is not a symptom of its failure to engage the critiques of its cultured despisers persuasively, but rather an indication of how "unspeakably disappointed" people, both educated and uneducated, have become with an institution that

[22] "[O]ne can *not* speak of God simply by speaking of man in a loud voice." Karl Barth, "The Word of God and the Task of the Ministry," in *The Word of God and the Word of Man* (New York: Harper & Row, 1957), 196.

[23] Karl Barth, "The Need and Promise of Christian Preaching," in *The Word of God and the Word of Man*, 108. That Barth's theological project was born in the crucible of practice is too often overlooked. Barth is a practical theologian in the sense that his approach emerged from and remained engaged with the problems he encountered as a young preacher.

[24] They come "longing to have the *word* spoken, *the* word which promises grace in *judgment*, life in *death*, and the beyond in the *here and now, God's* word." Barth, "Need and Promise of Christian Preaching," 109 (emphasis in original).

[25] Barth, "Need and Promise of Christian Preaching," 109.

has refused to understand, to take seriously, and to respond courageously to their ultimate need.

And Barth insists that the very possibility of a preached word that speaks to, and not merely out of, this situation rests with the question of the Bible. The great need to know the truth about God is met in the promise of biblical preaching. This is where the notion of Christian preaching as a conventionally good human word offered earnestly and with great goodwill meets its crisis. For one can scarcely imagine a less likely resource for such well-intentioned human talk than the Bible. No wonder, then, that for many in the contemporary church it is the Bible that has become the embarrassment of preaching and not the reverse. The Bible has become an embarrassment for such "preaching" not only in the case of the occasional "text of terror," not only where its cultural remoteness is most acutely felt, but in its entirety. For the Bible opens relentlessly onto a vista that is bewildering to human eyes in every age, a "strange new world" that claims to be nothing less than "the world of God."[26] Only when the need of Christian preaching has been appreciated in all its raw urgency and the biblical world displayed in all its strangeness may such an awful resource be apprehended in all its proper embarrassment and promise. Indeed, so strange and awful is the promise of the Bible that it will speak to the people's question by first exacerbating it; it will probe the need and recast the question until it is truly a need for and a question about the God who speaks through the Bible.

So the word of the cross, corroborated by a deep understanding of the extraordinary practical situation presupposed in preaching, points toward a theology of preaching as a word (1) spoken to the human situation from beyond the human situation and (2) mediated by the Bible. These two aspects of Barth's theology of preaching are present in his definition of preaching and become explicit in his discussion of that definition:[27] "First, God is the one who works, and second, we humans must try to point to what is said in scripture. There is no third thing."[28]

[26] Karl Barth, "The Strange New World within the Bible," in *Word of God and the Word of Man*, 33.

[27] "Preaching is the Word of God which he himself speaks, claiming for the purpose the exposition of a biblical text in free human words." Karl Barth, *Homiletics*, trans. Geoffrey William Bromiley and Donald E. Daniels (Louisville, Ky.: Westminster John Knox, 1991), 44.

[28] Barth, *Homiletics*, 45.

The "Third Thing"

But there is a "third thing," and it is precisely the thing that is missing from Barth's own attempt at building a homiletic from this foundation. Based on lectures given at Bonn in 1933, Barth's *Homiletics* is a polemical work shaped by extraordinary circumstances.[29] It is forceful and clear about what preaching is not, but less helpful in advancing a detailed constructive proposal. Calling simply, perhaps simplistically, for the preacher to conform the sermon to the "distinctive movement of thought in the text,"[30] Barth launches a spirited assault against sermon introductions and conclusions, against contextual relevance, and against imaginative aesthetic evocation.[31] The resulting homiletic is inspiring in its clarion call for preaching that stays close to the biblical text; but it is also, ultimately, unworkable. Missing is an account of what is actually involved in identifying and then sermonically re-presenting the "distinctive movement of thought" in a biblical text.

Barth was suspicious of hermeneutical theory, which he understood within his own context as a misguided attempt to solve an illusory problem: the supposed gulf between the ancient text and the contemporary context. For Barth, such theorizing tends to recast the meaning taken from the biblical text as a human achievement, and ultimately represents yet another form of evasiveness before the God that addresses us in scripture. Following Kierkegaard, Barth insists that the gulf at issue in the preaching situation is of the infinite and qualitative variety—a distance and difference beyond the powers of any interpreter, and so traversable only from the other side by a miracle.

But if it is true that scripture is best approached as a word addressed to the present by a living God, it is nevertheless an address mediated by language that must be appropriated. In other words, the mandate for clear thinking about

[29] Barth was convinced that preaching in Germany had lost its grounding in the external authority of scripture and thus forfeited its leverage against a culture moving rapidly to the brink of ethical catastrophe. With Nazis beginning to surveil his lectures and the undistinguished and aging homiletics instructor at Bonn already firmly in the camp of the German Christians, he announced that he would be giving a series of lectures on homiletics. It should come as no surprise that these lectures, published from an admiring student's notes some thirty years later, are monomaniacal in their focus on exegesis and without nuance in their critique of rhetorical considerations that Barth associated with preaching's ineffectual and accommodationist past. See William H. Willimon, *Conversations with Barth on Preaching* (Nashville: Abingdon, 2006), 160.

[30] Barth, *Homiletics*, 49.

[31] Ironically, Barth's dismissal of such considerations is carried off forcefully and eloquently. A description first applied to Cicero and Augustine comes to mind: "the great rhetorician rhetorically dismissing rhetoric." Garry Wills, *St. Augustine* (New York: Penguin, 1999), 28.

hermeneutics, rhetoric, and poetics is not primarily a concession to the cultural distance at issue in Bible reading but rather a consequence of the nature of language itself, especially written language. Interpretation theory cannot truly be avoided in theology; when ignored it simply goes uncriticized.

Such is the case when Barth's zeal for a homiletic that practices uncompromising obedience to the objective text actually smuggles in a crucial hermeneutical assumption that is at odds with the character of the biblical text: a theoretical divorce between its ideational content and its rhetorical form. The thing toward which Barth would have his faithful preacher point is a "distinctive movement of thought," but the gospel is more than an idea to be thought.[32] As Amos Wilder argued so persuasively and influentially a generation ago, the gospel message is inextricably and essentially linked with its rhetorical form.[33]

The gospel is not some discrete ideational content deposited willy-nilly within the inert container of genre, but rather a linguistically mediated transformative meaning event that grows out of both the *what* and the *how* of its saying.[34] One need not question God's sovereign freedom to meet (or refuse to meet) us in the text in order to note that such encounters are borne by carefully chosen language through which something is both said and done. No

[32] The claim that Barth's understanding of the gospel is largely noetic need not hinge on a close reading of his wording here. See Willimon, *Conversations with Barth on Preaching*, 80–82. Heinz Zahrnt has highlighted Barth's tendency to suppose that the Bible's substantive ideational content exists independently of its rhetorical form and his related tendency to relegate concerns about language in preaching to the domain of (merely) practical theology. Zahrnt, *The Question of God: Protestant Theology in the Twentieth Century* (New York: Harcourt, Brace & World, 1969), 116–18. To cite just one example in Barth, "Theological speech is taught its content by exegesis and dogmatics, and it is given its form through the experiences of whatever psychology, sociology, or linguistics may be most trustworthy at a given moment. . . . Practical theology is studied in order to seek and to find, to learn and to practice, this speech." Barth, *Evangelical Theology: An Introduction* (New York: Holt, 1963), 183.

[33] Amos Niven Wilder, *Early Christian Rhetoric: The Language of the Gospel* (Peabody, Mass.: Hendrickson, 1999). For a homiletical appropriation of Wilder's basic insight, see Thomas G. Long, *Preaching and the Literary Forms of the Bible* (Philadelphia: Fortress, 1989).

[34] Even Paul's stark contrast between the word of the cross and human eloquence (1 Cor 1:17) cannot give comfort to those who would deny the centrality of rhetorical and poetical concerns in a theology of preaching; for it is obvious, and in any case it has been demonstrated with great care, that in the early chapters of 1 Corinthians Paul is engaged in a sophisticated rhetorical gambit even as he disavows concern for the niceties of language. See, e.g., Peter Lampe, "Theological Wisdom and the 'Word about the Cross': The Rhetorical Scheme in 1 Corinthians 1–4," *Interpretation* 44, no. 2 (1990), 117–31. James Kay is right to say that the word of the cross is not the end of rhetorical strategies, but the faithful preacher will see to it that such strategies are always "taken captive" (2 Cor 10:5) in service of the peculiar message she or he is commissioned to preach. Kay, "Word of the Cross," 48.

wonder then that the preacher who would truly conform her sermon to the text must wrestle with the question of how the gospel may best be brought to new language in both the *what* and the *how* of her saying.

Of course Barth could not really shun such considerations, even if he refused to integrate them explicitly into his approach to preaching. I am certainly not the first to note a discrepancy here between Barth's invective against rhetoric and his own practice as both preacher and prose author.[35] One of the most remarkable things about reading Barth is the sense that one is being drawn by the power of his rhetoric into the flow of that same biblical "river" to which he has "entrusted" himself.[36] And although he refuses to integrate the insight into his theology of preaching, Barth is perfectly aware of what is at stake in the quality of language the preacher brings to bear on her task. When he turns to practical advice about the actual writing of a sermon, he strongly admonishes his charges to attend in the minutest detail to how they go about saying what they say.[37] On some level Barth understood that there must be a "third thing," but he failed to appreciate its true significance for theology and preaching.

In brief, the "third thing" means thinking more about how scriptural and sermonic language participates in God's free act of self-communication. Such thinking is indispensible for those who want to understand Christian

[35] In spite of his theological misgivings about second-order reflection upon the use and appropriation of language, an important aspect of Barth's legacy is a vast, rhetorically sophisticated, and homiletically rich engagement with scripture, recorded primarily in the excursuses of the *Church Dogmatics*. Karl Barth, *Church Dogmatics*, 4 vols. (New York: T&T Clark, 2009).

In fact, not only his theology of the Word but also and especially the way of reading that grew out of that theology has served as a model for and inspiration to those exploring the hermeneutical options available to the church in the wake of modernity. Chief among these is Hans Frei, whose work on narrative can be understood as an attempt to explicate the hermeneutical assumptions at work in the kinds of readings displayed in the *Dogmatics*. For examples of rhetorical sophistication in his preaching, see Karl Barth, *Deliverance to the Captives* (New York: Harper, 1961). For an analysis of his rhetorically charged theological prose, especially in *The Epistle to the Romans*, see Webb, *Re-Figuring Theology*. Karl Barth, *The Epistle to the Romans*, translated by Edwyn Clement Hoskyns (London: Oxford University Press, 1957). Commenting on the extraordinary rhetorical force of Barth's prose, Langdon Gilkey has warned, "There is no arguing with this man *while* you are reading him. . . . If you wish to dispute with him, close the book, lock it in a closet and move away—preferably quite out of the house." Gilkey, "An Appreciation of Karl Barth," in *How Karl Barth Changed My Mind*, ed. Donald K. McKim (Grand Rapids: Eerdmans, 1986), 152.

[36] "There is a river in the Bible that carries us away, once we have entrusted our destiny to it—away from ourselves to the sea." Barth, "Strange New World," 34.

[37] A number of such strikingly *un*-Barthian admonitions can be found in a single remarkable paragraph. Barth, *Homiletics*, 120.

preaching more deeply and teach it more faithfully; and it is the central concern of this book.

So Barth's theology of preaching is the approach best attuned to the scandal of preaching after Christendom, but the task of expounding a homiletic consistent with his vision remains and depends upon the intermediate work of explicitly wrestling with issues of hermeneutics and poetics implicit in his practice, but absent from his homiletical theory. More specifically, the task is to venture an account of how the language of scripture (and in turn the language of the sermon properly conformed to scripture) does what Barth claims that it does: mediate a word from beyond the human situation to the human situation.

To be very clear, the theological claim that God speaks does not depend upon any theoretical demonstration that this is possible. God does not speak at the pleasure of the preacher, much less the homiletician. But preaching does seek to join itself at God's pleasure to the word of God not only possible, but always and already articulate in the church and in the world. Then in turn, it is the homiletician's desire and duty to think and say more about how preaching participates in God's living and active Word. Such are the theological understandings and commitments that motivate this project, and situate its appeal to the best theoretical resources available under the logical priority of the conviction that God speaks. Chief among these resources is the interpretation theory of Paul Ricoeur, whose humility before the possibility of Christian preaching suggests the deep affinity between his hermeneutical project and a theology of preaching grounded in the risks and rewards of hearing a call, and so having something to say:

> To confess that one is a listener is from the very beginning to break with the project dear to many, and even perhaps all, philosophers: to begin discourse without any presuppositions. . . . Yet it is in terms of one certain presupposition that I stand in the position of a listener to Christian preaching: I assume that this speaking is meaningful, that it is worthy of consideration, and that examining it may accompany and guide the transfer from the text to life where it will verify itself fully. Can I account for this presupposition? Alas, I stumble already. I do not know how to sort out what is here "unravelable" situation, uncriticized custom, deliberate preference, or profound unchosen choice. I can only confess that my desire to hear more is all these things, and that it defies all these distinctions. But if what I presuppose precedes everything I can choose to think about, how do I avoid the famous circle of believing in order to understand and understanding in order to believe? I do not seek to avoid it. I boldly stay within this circle in the hope that, through the transfer from text to life, what I have risked will be returned a hundredfold as an increase in comprehension, valor, and joy.[38]

[38] Paul Ricoeur, "Naming God," in Wallace, *Figuring the Sacred*, 217.

Chapter Two

Hans Frei on How to Read during an Eclipse

Behind every Christian sermon worthy of the name is a preacher reading the Bible.[1] Or, in the language of the previous chapter, the prospect of the Christian preacher "having something to say" to the human situation from beyond the human situation turns on the promise of the Bible as a resource for mediating such a Word. But the simple picture of the preacher in her study, diligently pouring over the language of the week's lection, is deceptive. The Bible on the desk appears open and inviting, but the serious options available for making sense of the scriptural text are constrained by manifold factors of great complexity. The task of understanding the dynamics implicit in the preacher's weekly act of theological interpretation on behalf of a community of faith in our post-Enlightenment context is daunting. A lens is needed to clarify the issues and frame the discussion.

The hermeneutical thought of Hans Frei is such a lens. Frei's specific proposal for how Christians should read is important in its own right, but

[1] For an articulation of the claim that "[r]ight preaching is the interpretation of scripture," see David Lyon Bartlett, *Between the Bible and the Church: New Methods for Biblical Preaching* (Nashville: Abingdon, 1999), 11. For an interesting, but finally unconvincing, attempt to problematize this claim, see David Buttrick, *A Captive Voice: The Liberation of Preaching* (Louisville, Ky.: Westminster John Knox, 1994), 29–32.

it will also serve to structure the broader hermeneutical issues. Frei's project is helpful in this role for a number of reasons. In the first place, Frei self-consciously understood his work in relation to the reading practices of Karl Barth, which makes Frei's approach particularly suitable to the project of exploring a homiletical approach that is compatible with Barth's theology of the Word.[2] Furthermore, Frei was an exceptionally careful historian of ideas, and his diagnosis of the "wrong turn" in biblical hermeneutics since the Enlightenment has enjoyed broad influence, even among some who have not found his specific counterproposal persuasive. Another aspect of Frei's project that makes it instructive is the way his hermeneutics have been worked out over time in critical dialogue with first modern and then, in his more "cultural-linguistic" second phase, poststructuralist approaches to language and textuality.

Perhaps the most crucial feature of Frei's project for the purposes of the argument of this book is the way his thinking about biblical narrative provides a particularly compelling conversation partner for the hermeneutics of Paul Ricoeur. Frei and Ricoeur share much in common, but the inner workings of their respective approaches to narrative are quite distinct, if not divergent. Comparing and contrasting their positions will prove heuristically rich and lead to a well-rounded and nuanced engagement with the hermeneutical issues at the heart of this book.

Finally, Frei's hermeneutics are of special interest for this project because the homiletical implications of his thought have been worked out with great care by Charles Campbell.[3] The analysis that follows shows that Campbell's thorough appropriation of Frei's project in the domain of homiletical practice renders the strengths and weaknesses of Frei's approach all the more transparent and lays the groundwork for a Ricoeurian revision that builds on what is best and corrects what is least helpful in Frei's "postliberal" approach.

[2] "It seems to me that Barth's biblical exegesis is a model of the kind of narrative reading that can be done in the wake of the changes I describe in this book." Hans W. Frei, *The Eclipse of Biblical Narrative: A Study in Eighteenth and Nineteenth Century Hermeneutics* (New Haven: Yale University Press, 1974), vii. He then goes on to list several examples from the excursuses in the *Dogmatics*.

[3] See Charles L. Campbell, *Preaching Jesus: New Directions for Homiletics in Hans Frei's Postliberal Theology* (Grand Rapids: Eerdmans, 1997).

Hans Frei and *The Eclipse of Biblical Narrative*

Hans Frei was born in 1922 in Germany.[4] His family was of Jewish background and fled Germany after the Nazis came to power.[5] Frei was studying textiles on scholarship at North Carolina State University when a chance meeting with H. Richard Niebuhr led him to Yale for seminary and, after a brief stint in ministry, graduate school. In 1956 he completed his dissertation on Karl Barth's break with liberalism. His interest in a constructive proposal in the field of biblical hermeneutics grew out of his work on Barth. During the late 1950s and 1960s, working in relative obscurity and largely out of step with the fashion of the day, Frei engaged in a painstaking study of eighteenth- and nineteenth-century hermeneutics, formulating the thesis he later argued in his first and most influential monograph, *The Eclipse of Biblical Narrative*.

The Literal Sense

On one level, *Eclipse* is a descriptive historical analysis charting the collapse of a consensus about the primacy of the literal sense embodied in the sixteenth-century reformers,[6] especially Calvin. But on another level, Frei the theologian vigorously argues a thesis concerning what he perceives to be a fateful wrong turn in hermeneutics and theology—a misstep with roots in the period he discusses but with consequences that persist even to his present: "Were we to pursue our theme into the biblical hermeneutics of the twentieth century, I believe that we would find that . . . the story has remained much the same."[7] In this role of theologian, we see Frei in conversation with the

[4] The following brief biographical sketch draws from William C. Placher, "Hans Frei and the Meaning of Biblical Narrative," *Christian Century* 106, no. 18 (1989), 556–59. The most extensive biography available is by Michel Higton: http://people.exeter.ac.uk/mahigton/Frei.html#biog.

[5] Frei's holocaust testimony is on record with the Fortunoff Video Archive for Holocaust Testimonies, Yale University Library (HVT-170). The abstract of his interview reads, in part, "Professor F. pays particular attention to the insidious appeal and powerful organization of the Nazi program and asserts his belief in the necessity to bear witness."

[6] This claim needs to be qualified in a number of ways. Frei is talking about the way specific blocks of narrative material, especially the synoptic gospels with their "realistic" depiction of the unique and unsubstitutable identity of Jesus of Nazareth, were read according to an ascriptive logic. Frei states, "Other ways of reading portions of the Bible, e.g., in a spiritual or allegorical sense, were permissible, but they must not offend against a literal reading of those parts which seemed most obviously to demand it." Note also that the claim is not that the *sensus literalis* was always dominant, only that it "was never wholly lost in western Christendom," that it gained "new impetus" with the Renaissance, and that it finally emerged as the primary ecclesial hermeneutic by the time of the Reformation. Frei, *Eclipse of Biblical Narrative*, 1.

[7] Frei, *Eclipse of Biblical Narrative*, 16. "Much the same" implies exceptions, most notably Barth.

various heirs of the "Eclipse," a cast of thousands that includes everyone along a vast spectrum from the most reactionary fundamentalist, to the historical critic convinced of the historical improbability of most of the events depicted yet interested in the stories as evidence about the communities that produced them, to programs of demythologization—all, in his view, engaged in a futile attempt to read in the dark. Against these approaches, perhaps too neatly classified as attempts to find textual meaning as a function of reference either "behind" or "above" the text, Frei proposes to rehabilitate ecclesial hermeneutics by restoring attention to meaning "within" the text under the guidance of a *sensus literalis* that has been critically revised in the hope of restoring its viability in the wake of modernity.

Frei's position is built upon his understanding of the precritical *sensus literalis.* Rather than critiquing premodern reading practices from the perspective of the canons of post-Enlightenment hermeneutics, Frei attempted to approach them on their own terms, trusting that such a venerable tradition of serious and sustained engagement with the Bible likely enjoyed access to aspects of the text itself that have been occluded by the assumptions of modern readers. His description of the consensus approach to ecclesial hermeneutics before modernity highlights three interrelated features that build upon one another to limn a total picture of both the Bible and its ecclesial reader disposed in self-involving submission to the world it depicts. Each of these features will be considered in detail.

In the first place, to read the Bible literally was to take it as an account of actual occurrences. This seemingly straightforward claim needs to be distinguished carefully from the claim, made by contemporary conservative Christians, that the Bible is "historically accurate."

To frame the Bible's truth claims under the category "historical accuracy" is a distinctly early-modern (as opposed to premodern) project that embraces a set of assumptions quite foreign to the *sensus literalis* before modernity.[8] Frei argues that, since the Enlightenment, it has been broadly supposed that to read the Bible as a depiction of actual events is to take it as a reliable source of evidence in support of a particular historical reconstruction. In other words, the current intellectual milieu assumes that the historical accuracy of a document is always contested and so enforces the provision that even the most sympathetic reading of the Bible as literally true must authorize this claim to truth by construing the biblical text as an instance of the category "accurate

[8] For the dependence of contemporary conservative hermeneutics on early-modern as opposed to premodern thinkers, see George M. Marsden, *Understanding Fundamentalism and Evangelicalism* (Grand Rapids: Eerdmans, 1991), 117.

historical source." Such a source can achieve the status "true" by pointing behind itself toward history and then successfully navigating an adjudication process governed by criteria and standards external to the biblical text.[9]

The literal reading before modernity, on the other hand, operated according to very different assumptions. The Bible did not function as one source of information about the past to be measured carefully in relation to many other sources but was itself the metric of truth about the past, present, and future. It was not one contested account of reality but the field upon which all such contests were adjudicated. So understood, it becomes possible to imagine how the Bible could be construed as making the best sense when read literally (i.e., as predicating of its subjects) without situating this conviction under an epistemological scheme in which the appropriateness of the literal reading functions as a kind of evidence for the historical accuracy of the Bible's claims. The literal sense as a vehicle of meaning and the Bible's referential function vis-à-vis historical events were not tied together for the premodern reader in precisely the same way they have been for the modern.

The distinction is crucial for Frei because his project is to propose a way of reading that enjoys continuity with the *sensus literalis* without committing himself to the apologetic task of defending the Bible's historical accuracy at every turn. Frei is saying that although the consensus literal reading practices just before modernity took for granted that all that the Bible depicts as happening actually happened, the essential force of the story—its meaning and therefore its function within the church—was not necessarily (i.e., logically) entangled with that assumption. Thus, that same force is still available to postcritical ecclesial readers who wish to engage the literal sense of scripture as its meaning but do not share the same uncomplicated view of the Bible's relationship to past happenings.

A second and more essential feature of the precritical literal sense pertains to the question of the Bible's unity. Scripture was construed not as a haphazard collection of discreet and diverse fragments but as a single, continuous story depicting through the cumulative effect of its several narratives and other supporting genres a unified and complete temporal sequence

[9] Frei develops this argument in dialogue with the biblical hermeneutics of Anthony Collins but applies it broadly to subsequent historical critical approaches. The essential point for Frei is that Collins' "identification of literal and historical statements involved that he first break up their previous identity and then reintegrate them by subsuming literal meaning under the dominance of an independent criterion for deciding whether or not a statement is historical. A proposition is literal if it describes and refers to a state of affairs known or assumed on independent probable grounds to agree or disagree with the stated proposition." Frei, *Eclipse of Biblical Narrative*, 76.

corresponding to the one real world of natural and human history. The hermeneutical strategy for joining together the various smaller narrative units into this one sweeping story was typology. Typology, in Frei's view, was not an alternative to the literal sense but rather "literalism extended to the whole story or the unitary canon containing it."[10] Typological imagination was especially important in addressing the problem of reading the two testaments as a unified witness to a single grand narrative. Typological readings should not be mistaken for a strained argument about prophetic authorial intent but rather grew out of the conviction that the canon as a whole depicted the universal history of the one true world ordered and sustained under God's providence. The reader could venture bold interpretive juxtapositions of stories from different parts of the larger temporal sequence, confident in the conviction that without loss to their literal sense as depictions of persons and events, these stories were also mysteriously caught up and connected by a surplus of meaning at the level of the entire canon.

According to the *sensus literalis*, the Bible is a true, complete, and unified account of the "one and only real world" spanning all of natural and human history.[11] Therefore, third and finally, the Bible aspires, through the sheer audacity of its scope and claim, to gather up the life and world of every reader who submits to the logic of this literal sense.[12] The precritical *sensus literalis* was not simply a procedure for arriving at the meaning of the biblical text conceived as a discreet datum available for inspection by a disinterested autonomous knower. Frei's claim is that for the literal reader of the Bible before the Eclipse, to interpret the scriptural narrative was to find one's world

[10] Frei, *Eclipse of Biblical Narrative*, 7.

[11] Frei, *Eclipse of Biblical Narrative*, 3.

[12] Frei supported this claim about the extravagant claims of scripture by citing Erich Auerbach's distinction between the narrative ambitions of Homer and the Christian Bible: "The Bible's claim to truth is not only far more urgent than Homer's, it is tyrannical—it excludes all other claims. The world of the Scripture stories is not satisfied with claiming to be a historically true reality—it insists that it is the only real world. . . . All other scenes, issues, and ordinances have no right to appear independently of it, and it is promised that all of them, the history of all mankind, will be given their due place within its frame. . . . The Scripture stories do not, like Homer's, court our favor, they do not flatter us that they may please us and enchant us—they seek to subject us, and if we refuse to be subjected we are rebels. . . . Far from seeking, like Homer, merely to make us forget our own reality for a few hours, [the Bible] seeks to overcome our reality: we are to fit our own life into its world, feel ourselves to be elements in its structure of universal history. . . . Everything else that happens in the world can only be conceived as an element in this sequence; into it everything that is known about the world . . . must be fitted as an ingredient of the divine plan." Auerbach, *Mimesis: The Representation of Reality in Western Literature* (Princeton, N.J.: Princeton University Press, 1953), 14–15.

and one's self interpreted—caught up into the totality of the one available reality it depicted.

A short passage from Flannery O'Connor's *The Violent Bear It Away* can help clarify the cumulative effect of the three features of literal reading we have just discussed. Describing the education of young Francis Marion Tarwater in a shack situated in a remote clearing somewhere in the Georgia pine forest, O'Connor's narrator offers, "His uncle had taught him Figures, Reading, Writing, and History beginning with Adam expelled from the Garden and going on down through the presidents to Herbert Hoover and on in speculation toward the Second Coming and the Day of Judgment."[13] At first, biblical history seems to take its place obediently alongside the rest of the curriculum, but by the end of the sentence we are aware that a subversion has taken place. "Figures, Reading, Writing," "Herbert Hoover," and exactly everything else including Tarwater's own fledgling identity will be granted the status of real and significant only within the sweep of the one true story of the world, from creation to final consummation, offered by the Bible.

The "Great Reversal"

In tracing the history of the Eclipse of this kind of reading, Frei points to Johannes Cocceius (1603–1669) as a pivotal figure. The significance of Cocceius lies largely in the fact that (unlike Spinoza, for example) he had no intention of being an innovator. He made every attempt to remain true to the interpretive practices of the reformers. But in spite of himself, his reading of scripture reflected the growing rift between the world depicted by the literal sense and the "real" world of the new historical sensibility. The point is not that interpreters like Cocceius doubted the historical veracity of the Bible. Rather, their defense of the Bible's historical truth belied the appropriation of a new and modern assumption: the notion of human history as an autonomous reality against which the biblical narrative must be measured. The seventeenth-century project of situating biblical events within history stands in sharp contrast to Calvin's sense of the real as that world depicted in Scripture—a total world through which the reader is invited to make sense of her life and times. In Cocceius, Frei detects a certain insecurity about the capacity of the world depicted in the Bible to include and account for what now seemed to be the larger and more total account of reality offered by the new historical sensibility. Frei shows that it was precisely when those most

[13] Flannery O'Connor, *The Violent Bear It Away*, in *Collected Works*, Library of America 39 (New York: Library of America, 1988), 331.

committed to upholding traditional ways of reading started arranging their arguments within that new framework that true change was afoot.

If Cocceius was the canary in the mine providing the earliest hints that the interpretive atmosphere was changing, the transformation in hermeneutics commenced in earnest as the eighteenth century unfolded. As the logical split between the literal sense and historical "reality" grew larger in the minds of interpreters, a number of strategies for putting things back together emerged. The Bible's importance was unquestioned by most, and the agenda across the board was to find a way to salvage its relevance as a source of religious truth. While some attempted to put the pieces back together through ever more elaborate and at times tortured defenses of the historical veracity of the narratives,[14] other apologists let go of the historical project and began to look for the meaning of the stories in their capacity to refer to universal moral and religious truth.[15] In both cases, the meaning of the text was assumed to lie outside of its verbal sense in some secondary "subject matter" to which the words referred. The one thing almost everyone agreed on (Reimarus is one important exception) was that the stories were religiously true and meaningful. But across the theological spectrum from left to right, proliferating accounts of just how they could be so were being driven by criteria of religious truth and meaningfulness that were extrinsic to the stories themselves.

Frei referred to this hermeneutical sea change and its theological consequences as "the great reversal"—a fundamental shift from viewing the textually depicted world as the orienting ground of reality against which the reader's sense of self and world took shape to an autonomous sense of what counted as real, into which the Bible must be made to fit in one way or another as the bearer of significant religious meaning.[16] Along the way, the "realistic" character of the narratives got lost in the shuffle. Either their "history-likeness" was mistaken for "history-likeliness," or else the feature

[14] In Germany, these "Supernaturalists" included Christoph Matthäus Pfaff (1686–1760), Lorenz von Mosheim (1694–1755), and especially Sigmund Jakob Baumgarten (1706–1757), a professor at Halle. See Frei's section titled "Meaning as Historical or Ostensive Reference" in his *Eclipse of Biblical Narrative*, 86–95.

[15] A key figure in this connection is Johann Salomo Semler (1725–1791), who was Baumgarten's successor at Halle. On this trajectory, Frei gives special attention to Gotthold Ephraim Lessing and, of course, David Friedrich Strauss.

[16] "It is no exaggeration to say that all across the theological spectrum the great reversal had taken place; interpretation was a matter of fitting the biblical story into another world with another story rather than incorporating that world into the biblical story." Frei, *Eclipse of Biblical Narrative*, 130.

was disregarded altogether by one or another project to mine the text for its abstractable, universal truths.

One of Frei's most trenchant observations is that the salient feature of the biblical narratives that could have supplied the clue to their proper (narrative) interpretation—namely, their realistic character—was misconstrued or even ignored by interpreters even though it was often noted as a feature in the text. He argues that this fateful misstep came about through a kind of historical accident. In England, the cultural resources for appreciating realistic narrative were in place (as reflected in the prominence of the English novel), but the influence of the Deists had shifted the attention of religious scholars toward questions of factual external evidence and away from the Bible itself. In Germany, where attention was still tightly focused on a close reading of the text, the realistic character of the narratives had no cultural analogue in the realistic novel, and was therefore mistakenly assumed to indicate (reliably or unreliably reported) history that invites a historical critical method of inquiry.[17] In both cases, the single most prominent feature of biblical narrative, its "realism," slipped through the cracks in the history of ideas, leaving hermeneutics and theology to carry on their work in the gathering darkness of the Eclipse of this most essential feature of the Bible's stories.

"Realistic" Narrative

Frei was convinced that these three aspects of the *sensus literalis*—the sense that the events depicted were actual happenings, the program of reading the Bible as a unified account of reality, and the Bible's bid to situate the reader's reality within its scope—were in tune with something about the Bible itself, something that is absolutely essential to its proper interpretation even after modernity, and yet something that became increasingly difficult to see as modernity ran its course. Following Auerbach, Frei accounted for this quality of the text under the genre classification "realistic narrative."[18]

In order to explain the very particular sense in which Frei claims the quality of "realism" for biblical narrative, it will be helpful to scan briefly the hermeneutical positions against which Frei developed his proposal. It

[17] Frei, *Eclipse of Biblical Narrative*, 142.

[18] Obviously much of the Bible is not narrative, and Frei recognized that some of the narrative material in scripture—including parts of the Fourth Gospel—is far too stylized to fit easily within the genre as he described it. "But with all of this conceded, there is still general agreement that cumulative realistic narrative of a very serious rather than low, comical, or idyllic sort is characteristic of the Bible, especially if one compares it to other ancient literature of either sacred or profane character." Frei, *Eclipse of Biblical Narrative*, 16.

should be noted that almost without exception the practitioners of these reading strategies were engaged in good faith attempts to salvage the Bible's significance and centrality for Christian identity in the wake of modernity. These strategies can be broadly divided into two groups. On the one hand are those who have argued that the meaning of the Bible is to be found "behind" the text in the historical events to which it refers (historical, or ostensive reference). This group includes interpreters of remarkable diversity, including fundamentalists who hold that the Bible is a perfectly transparent and reliable historical account of events as they occurred; the so-called Biblical Theology Movement of the mid-twentieth century, which took the Bible's subject matter to be God's "mighty acts in history," a salvation history of interpreted events patient of historical investigation and referenced in the biblical accounts;[19] those in search of the historical Jesus; and a methodologically diverse array of historical critics who tend to equate the meaning of the biblical text with its ability to function as evidence for the reconstruction of the communities and thought world that gave it birth. On the other hand are those interpreters who hold that the meaning of the Bible is to be found "above" the text, and so strive to unleash its "religious significance" by either discerning the insights into authentic existence encoded within its mythological language (existential reference) or identifying and codifying its abstractable moral content (ideational reference).

What these two broad approaches share in common, and what causes them, in Frei's view, fundamentally to distort efforts to understand key biblical narratives, is that they insist on seeking the subject matter of the story outside of the story. The hermeneutical premise that biblical narratives be "religiously meaningful" smuggles in a finite set of possible meanings that can be assigned, and so tends to foreclose on meanings that might emerge out of a careful engagement with the stories on their own terms. Frei countered that when read on their own terms, scriptural stories do not point beyond themselves to some referent—whether historical-ostensive or existential-ideational—outside the story, but within the story itself. These stories predicate of their subjects, not other subjects. Frei simply equates verbal sense and reference: "For whatever the situation that may obtain in other types of texts, in

[19] The movement argued that historical events were recognized as God's acts only through interpretation, and the basic meaning-bearing unit under historical investigation was event-plus-theological-interpretation. Langdon Gilkey's famous and devastating critique points out the difficulty of the position: "[The Biblical Theology Movement maintains that] the Bible is a book of the acts Hebrews believed God might have done and the words he might have said had he done and said them—but of course we recognize that he did not." Gilkey, "Cosmology, Ontology, and the Travail of Biblical Language," *Journal of Religion* 41, no. 3 (1961): 197.

narrative of the sort in which character, verbal communications, and circumstances are each determinative of the other end [*sic*] hence of the theme itself, the text, the verbal sense, and not a profound, buried stratum underneath constitutes or determines the subject matter itself."[20]

The argument is that this way of meaning is determined by the formal qualities of the genre. No matter how well-intentioned, interpreters commit a kind of hermeneutical violence when they disregard these formal qualities and insist on seeking the meaning of a "realistic narrative" somewhere other than within the story and in terms of the story. By analogy, the meaning of a realistic novel cannot be accessed through judgments about the historicity of what is "reported." Nor can its meaning be reduced to an abstract moral—not, in any case, without loss and distortion. A realistic novel is "about" its characters and all that they do and suffer in relation to the circumstances in which they find themselves. In the same way, the realistic narratives of the Bible have a distinctive form that calls for a certain kind of interpretation:

> Realistic narrative is that kind in which subject and social setting belong together, and characters and external circumstances fitly render each other. Neither character nor circumstance separately, nor yet their interaction, is a shadow of something else more real or more significant.[21]

It may sound rather banal after all the elaborate distinctions that have brought the argument to this point, but Frei is essentially arguing that, in the first place, realistic biblical narratives are about precisely what they seem to be about. The modern turn in hermeneutics has obscured this otherwise obvious point. A gospel story about Jesus healing a paralytic, for example, is most appropriately interpreted as a story about Jesus. If we want to know what it means about Jesus, then we need to attend very carefully to the realistic interplay of character, circumstance, and action that renders his particular identity.

The least guarded statement of Frei's position on this matter came during informal, but I think illuminating, remarks that he made in response to Carl F. H. Henry's critique of his work, a short talk later published under the title "Response to 'Narrative Theology: An Evangelical Appraisal' ":

> When I wrote *The Eclipse of Biblical Narrative*, I had liberals much more than conservatives in mind. And what I had in mind was the fact that if something didn't seem to suit the world view of the day, then liberals quickly reinterpreted it, or as we say today, "revised" it. And my sense of the matter though I'm not antiliberal, was that you can revise the text to suit yourself only just so far. There really is an analogy

[20] Frei, *Eclipse of Biblical Narrative*, 280.
[21] Frei, *Eclipse of Biblical Narrative*, 13–14.

> between the Bible and a novel writer who says something like this: I mean what I say whether or not anything took place. I mean what I say. It's as simple as that: the text means what it says.[22]

The question of whether "anything took place" is thus separated from the question of the meaning of the text. Indeed, it is fair to say that Frei wants to bracket the question of truth in order to create space for textual meaning to flourish on its own terms. His concern is that talk of "truth" and "reference" inevitably invites systematic epistemological constraints that tend to foreclose on the meaning of the text by deciding ahead of time what kind of thing it is allowed to say. Frei wants to let the text's own formal qualities guide the reader and set the terms of signification. Of course, as will be seen below, questions about truth, and not least "the truth of what took place," cannot be suspended indefinitely.

Mark 2:1-12 as a Test Case

A test case will help clarify Frei's hermeneutical approach. Almost any synoptic pericope could illustrate the approach, but let Mark 2:1-12 serve as a case in point. Like most gospel stories, the narration is marked by restraint. One might even call the style minimalist. The depiction is riddled with lacunae, but the distinctive, sparse texture of biblical narrative that renders it so patient of expansive hermeneutical appropriation does not finally displace its fundamentally realistic character.

If we read that "some days" after the previously depicted episode Jesus returned to Capernaum, that a report went out that he was at home (v. 1), that as a result a crowd gathered such that the house and even the space outside the door were packed with people trying to hear his words (v. 2), it seems fair to conclude that this text is directing our attention toward the particular scene that it depicts. It is this depicted time and place,[23] not some never-time

[22] Hans W. Frei, "Response to 'Narrative Theology: An Evangelical Appraisal,'" in Hunsinger and Placher, *Theology and Narrative*, 208. Having defined his position against liberals, Frei attempts in the balance of the essay to distinguish his position from those of conservatives like Henry, whom he accuses of naïvely adopting a modern epistemological framework that distorts the very text they attempt to defend.

[23] To be perfectly clear, I mean a particular day and location within the framework of the setting the story itself creates through narration. By this qualification, I do not concede that the designation of events in "real" time (C.E. or A.D.) and space manage, as we sometimes pretend, to carve out un-narrated and thus disinterested positions from which to name reality, though I admit that such designations and the narrated positions they represent may "interact" with the extratextual world differently, more directly, and in some ways more usefully than designations such as Mark's "Capernaum" and "after some days."

and no-space of great mythological happenings,[24] nor a generic lecture hall thinly concealed beneath a narrative veneer and ready to echo with universal moral wisdom. Jesus is "speaking the word" to them (v. 2), but it is not a word that can be abstracted from the identity of the speaker. Even if the depiction expanded upon the moral content of "the word" (it does not), it matters that this depicted character Jesus is the one speaking it, for within the logic of the narrative they have come to hear him.

Quite apart from the fascinating historical question of whether Jesus really had a home in Capernaum, as readers of this story we are supposed to be thinking of a hole being dug in its roof (v. 4) as the friends of the paralyzed man make a way to Jesus by unconventional means that grow out of the tactical constraints of the particular circumstances the story describes. Both the tactic and our recognition of its unconventionality depend upon and at the same time contribute to the realism of the account.

Then there are the miracles. Extraordinary happenings are depicted in this story, and, though it may seem counterintuitive at first, the manner of their depiction is ingredient to the story's realism.[25] First, it is part of the character of this Jesus to "perceive in his spirit" what the scribes were thinking and privately discussing about the forgiveness he has offered the paralytic (v. 8).[26] All indications are that the meaning of this predication ("Jesus perceived") is a function of its position in the story as part of the realistic

[24] Concerning myth: "Myths are stories in which character and action are not irreducibly themselves. Instead they are representative of broader and not directly representable psychic or cosmic states, states in some sense 'transcending' the scene of finite, particular occurrences." Hans W. Frei, "Theological Reflections on the Accounts of Jesus' Death and Resurrection," in *The Identity of Jesus Christ: The Hermeneutical Bases of Dogmatic Theology* (Philadelphia: Fortress Press, 1975; repr., Eugene, Ore.: Wipf & Stock, 2000), 2. As we will see, the emphasis must be on "irreducibly themselves" and "finite, particular occurrences" and not on "not directly representable" since Frei himself took the gospel accounts as analogical narrative descriptions of realities not patient of direct, unstoried representation.

[25] "[I]n the biblical stories, of course, nonmiraculous and miraculous accounts and explanations are constantly intermingled. But in accordance with our definition, even the miraculous accounts are realistic or history-like (but not therefore historical and in that sense factually true) if they do not in effect symbolize something else instead of the action portrayed. That is to say, even such miraculous accounts are history-like or realistic if the depicted action is indispensable to the rendering of a particular character, divine or human, or a particular story. (And, in fact, biblical miracles are frequently and strikingly nonsymbolic.)" Frei, *Eclipse of Biblical Narrative*, 14.

[26] Strictly speaking, within the logic of the story this is actually the second of three extraordinary happenings, since the first is performed by the declaration of forgiveness (v. 5). However, even within the framework of the story the efficacy of the performative force of this utterance is contested.

interplay of character and circumstance. Jesus' perception of their disposition is not a shadow of some other reality behind or above this story; it fits within the scene as rendered. It might be more historically plausible within the worldview of certain readers if Jesus were said simply to have overheard their debate, but such a revision would not be more realistic in the particular sense we have in mind here. It is actually instructive that such a revision would have very little effect on the plot of the story. In other words, the miraculous perception functions within the logic of the plot in precisely the same way that a more "ordinary" (to our sensibility) apprehension of the scribes' disposition would; namely, it raises the conflict between Jesus and the scribes to an explicit verbal confrontation (vv. 8b-9) and calls for the healing as a rejoinder to their objections (vv. 10-12). There is a difference, of course, between having Jesus overhear and having him miraculously perceive, and it has to do with the way the central character's identity is being rendered. But the observation that these two ways of moving the story forward at this point are logically interchangeable in terms of the necessities of the plot highlights the "realistic" character of the miracle as we have it.

The healing of the paralytic (v. 12) introduces a layer of complexity to our account of the story's realism but should still be understood as a realistic feature. Strictly speaking, it is correct to say that the healing miracle points beyond itself, but the scope of its surplus of signification is dependent upon and contained within this narrated world itself and not outside it in another conceptual scheme supposed as its "real" referent. It is within the horizon of these depicted characters and events that the healing is a sign of a larger reality, namely "that the Son of Man has authority on earth to forgive sins" (v. 10).

This pronouncement itself is the feature that raises the most serious challenge to the claim that the pericope demonstrates the kind of realism Frei describes. If it can be shown that the interactions of setting, character, and circumstance amount merely to a memory prompt, or an elaborate mock-up staged in order to set up this "punch line," then at least in the case of this one story, form criticism may have the best of the argument.[27] In that case, the narrative would be exhaustively comprehendible as a *chreia*, a kind of dispensable vehicle for the delivery of a saying that is the exclusive locus of the story's meaning. But the story cannot be exhaustively accounted for in this way. Rather, the pronouncement feature shows us that there can be more than

[27] This pericope is included in Martin Dibelius' original list of eight "paradigms" that "represent the type in noteworthy purity." Dibelius, *From Tradition to Gospel*, Library of Theological Translations (Cambridge: James Clarke, 1971), 43.

one kind of signification going on in such a story.[28] The climactic saying does not negate the realistic quality of this narrative with its attending function but, by privilege of its rhetorically emphatic position, actually builds upon the realistic meaning in a way that allows for a kind of double address: Jesus speaks both (1) directly and "realistically" as a character addressing other characters in the story in a manner consistent with the narrative's overall verisimilitude, and (2) indirectly as the one who lives to God addressing the reading community as its Risen Lord. In other words, the structure of the story moving toward this pronouncement (without forfeiting its realistic character) invites the reader to "overhear" this final word as kerygma: "The Son of Man has authority on earth to forgive sins." The realistic features of the story are not occluded by but rather are logically necessary to this second mode of signification. It is because the pronouncement functions first realistically (i.e., as depicted upon the lips of the protagonist and effectively rendering his unique and unsubstitutable identity) that it is able to take on a second "nonrealistic" (not to say "nonreal") signification as an address from that same identity alive and present to the reader in the power of the Spirit.

The "nonrealistic" kerygmatic meaning of the pronouncement in verse 10 is finally consistent with Frei's central thesis: other ways of reading the Bible's realistic narratives are built upon and find their legitimate role in relation to the skeletal structure of the literal sense. If one wants to know what these stories are, in the first place, about, one has no recourse but to pay ever closer attention to the story as told, engaging what it says about the characters, events, and circumstances that unfold in relation to one another. This "saying" is not only indispensable to but also in fact synonymous with the meaning.

The Resurrection, Truth, Facts, and History

Frei's own attempt to develop a Christology grounded in this way of reading the gospels was published first as a series of essays in the Presbyterian adult education magazine *Crossroads* in 1967 under the title "Theological

[28] Although it is usually overlooked, Frei concedes multiple modes of signification: "The synoptic gospels (for example) are partly narrative in character. They may also be other things, such as *kerygma*, i.e. the proclamatory rather than didactic shape of the faith of the early Christian community or, to put the matter another way, written forms of self-committing statements which make sense by evoking similar dispositions on the part of the reader." This is an important concession because it admits that close attention to formal features of the gospels may point toward functions not exhausted by the category "realistic" narrative. Frei, *Eclipse of Biblical Narrative*, 12.

Reflections on the Accounts of Jesus' Death and Resurrection" and then later expanded into a monograph, *The Identity of Jesus Christ.*

The constructive mode of the argument of *Identity* helps to clarify Frei's theological position on a number of points, and it is a book full of striking insights, but the approach to the text itself is, in one crucial respect, peculiar. Although Frei championed a close reading strategy more akin to literary than historical or philosophical modes of analysis, his way of reading in *Identity* nevertheless tends toward a harmonizing of the gospel accounts that serves to obscure their distinctive literary features.[29] It is an open question whether Frei finally succeeded in following his own recommendation of a text-immanent approach that privileges the distinctive features of the stories themselves over any systematic methodological, epistemological, or ideological agenda. Or perhaps in Frei's tendency to harmonize the gospels into one account, we already see the tension between a literary approach focused on formal features of the text itself and the more "cultural-linguistic," ecclesial approach that will take center stage in Frei's later work.

Rather than a detailed recapitulation or critique of the argument of *Identity*, my purpose at this point is to explore one aspect of that work: Frei's response to the question of the truth of the gospel accounts—the very question he had insisted on suspending in *Eclipse*. Recall that for Frei, the text's meaning must be allowed to flourish apart from the philosophical constraints that tend to assert themselves when one wants to make truth claims. He essentially proposed that the biblical text be allowed the same privilege as a realistic novel that seems by its formal features to insist, "I mean what I say whether or not anything took place."

One may respond that it is all well and good to let novels go their own way without questioning them too sternly about their credentials as bearers of meaning about the real world outside their pages, but this will not do for gospel accounts of an incarnate Messiah who makes very real claims not just upon the literary sensibilities of ecclesial readers but also upon our flesh and blood in the physical and social space of everyday life. The biblical text may have once functioned to narrate univocally the primary world into which all contemporary experience must be fit, but now that we are able to imagine a

[29] David Tracy makes this critique in David Tracy, *Dialogue with the Other: The Inter-Religious Dialogue*, Louvain Theological and Pastoral Monographs 1 (Grand Rapids: Eerdmans, 1991), 110. For a discussion of Tracy's concern "that Frei's version of this narrative reading too easily harmonizes the different Gospels and pays insufficient attention to the multiple genres of Scripture," see M. A. Higton, "Hans Frei and David Tracy on the Ordinary and the Extraordinary in Christianity," *Journal of Religion* 79, no. 4 (1999): 568 n. 4.

past reality independent of its narration, there is no putting the genie back into the precritical bottle. We know how to ask these questions, and so we must. Christian claims about the identity rendered in the gospels must, to be perfectly frank, be claims about what is the case with the world both then and now, for we who would risk following this Jesus do not wish to be vindicated merely in the telling.

Frei addressed this concern in *Identity*, but he insisted on doing so in his own distinctive way. Only after the text is allowed to mean on its own terms may we begin to ask about the implications of that meaning for claims about the world outside the text. Even so, Frei remained very cautious about how the question of truth should be framed and never consented to the assumption that the concept of a "historical fact" was itself epistemologically innocuous and unburdened by potentially distorting values and assumptions.

In order to understand Frei's approach to these issues, we must begin by touching on his approach to identity. Following Gilbert Ryle, he rejected the modern notion of human identity as a private, invisible, disembodied, intending consciousness distinct from its derivative, public, outward, embodied, and enacted manifestation—the so-called "ghost in the machine." Frei thought that it was unnecessary to posit a separate realm of intention.[30] Actions do not reveal (or perhaps obscure) some authentic identity constituted by the invisible intentions that lie behind them.[31] It is more correct to say that enacted intentions constitute identity.

Enacted intentions as identity is a match for the kind of testimony Frei thought the realistic narratives of the canonical gospels supply. If there is a sense in which we simply are what we say, do, and suffer in relation to our

[30] "To perform intelligently is to do one thing and not two things." Gilbert Ryle, *The Concept of Mind*, Senior Series (London: Hutchinson's University Library, 1949), 40, quoted in Frei, *Eclipse of Biblical Narrative*, 281.

[31] Frei was not committed to any elaborate and thoroughgoing theory of identity that runs roughshod over ordinary language, preferring to make ad hoc use of Ryle's basic insight. E.g., while Ryle categorically denied the very possibility of a separate intention, Frei took the less theoretically ambitious Wittgensteinian approach of admitting that words like *intention* must have a useful function when we say, as we often do in everyday conversation, that we are aware of intentions within ourselves that are distinguishable from their fruition as action. But this does not commit him to endorsing the ontological autonomy of intention: "We try to follow at that point the path by which someone's particular intention develops into action. There is a real or hypothetical 'inside' description of that transition, of which all of us are aware but of which it is not easy to give an account. The intention is not an independent mental 'thing' having a spiritual life of its own in back of the act embodying it. Intention and action are one process. Yet it is obvious that there must be a distinction between them, for not all intentions are carried into action." Frei, *Identity of Jesus Christ*, 100.

physical and social circumstance, then a story that traffics in precisely those categories—a history-like story about what Jesus says, does, and suffers—may adequately render his identity.[32] The identity of Jesus, which the quests for the historical Jesus sought "behind" the biblical accounts, Frei sought within and in terms of those accounts.

In keeping with this logic, Frei's thesis in *Identity* develops in response to two questions about the gospel stories:

> The significantly unique identity of an individual, in this instance Jesus of Nazareth, is to be discerned by asking (1) where the bond between intention and action in this story is most clearly evident; and (2) where the direct bond between himself as individual subject and his outward self-manifestation is strongest and most clearly unitary in character.[33]

While any of the episodes in the gospels can function as anecdotes that help us understand what kind of person Jesus is, Frei held that there is one crucial, extended story arc in which his identity is definitively disclosed: "The answer to both questions is in the crucifixion-resurrection."[34]

It is here, on the unified narrative sequence that Frei called the "passion-resurrection," that the question of Jesus' identity turns, and so it is here that we are provoked to ask not just about the account's verisimilitude but about its verity. Frei understood that once the meaning of the gospels comes clear as a nonmythical identity description, the question of the truth of the resurrection accounts resurfaces with a vengeance: "The truth of myth is *religious* rather than historical or factual. In contrast, then, the resurrection account, by virtue of its exclusive reference to Jesus, and by virtue of its claim that here he was most truly manifested in his human particularity, allows and even

[32] Frei's Yale colleague David H. Kelsey put the matter lucidly and associated it explicitly with Karl Barth's way of reading the scriptural narratives: "There is another way in which biblical narratives may be used to authorize theological proposals. It consists in construing the narratives as 'identity descriptions.' Narrative can 'render' a character. A skillful storyteller can make a character 'come alive' simply by his narration of events, 'come alive' in a way that no number of straight-forward propositional descriptions of the same personality could accomplish. He can bring one to know the peculiar identity of the one unique person. Moreover, what one knows about the story's central agent is not known by 'inference' from the story. On the contrary, he is known quite directly in and with the story, and recedes from cognitive grasp the more he is abstracted from the story. . . . This way of construing scripture is widely used in Karl Barth's *Church Dogmatics*." Kelsey, *The Uses of Scripture in Recent Theology* (Philadelphia: Fortress, 1975), 39.

[33] Frei, *Identity of Jesus Christ*, 1.

[34] Frei, *Identity of Jesus Christ*, 1. And see the section "Jesus' Power and Powerlessness" for a more detailed explanation of this claim. Frei, *Identity of Jesus Christ*, 152–55.

forces us to ask the question, 'Did this actually take place?'"[35] Furthermore, in Frei's way of reading, absolutely everything is at stake in this question—not just the identity of Jesus Christ but also the coherence of both the Bible read Christianly and the world of experience the Bible makes possible for the Christian.[36]

But to admit that the question of actuality is now on the table is not the same as turning the matter over to the historical method and its particular set of analytical procedures. Partly, as has already been argued, the problem with this approach is that it is a kind of hermeneutical violence to force a text with these formal characteristics (i.e., "realistic narrative") into the role of historical source where its function is to supply evidence to a skeptical, autonomous, and supposedly disinterested subject seeking to adjudicate a dispute about occurrences in the past. But the difficulty of a purely historical approach is also and especially due to the nature of the case in question—resurrection is simply not patient of this kind of inquiry. The questioner in the critical historical mode wants to know, "But was Jesus really raised or not?"—as if there were some generally recognized and agreed upon thing called "being raised from the dead," and now we simply want to know if the purported resurrection of Jesus is really an instance of it. But, of course, nothing could be further from the case. It is impossible to make judgments about the probability (likelihood or unlikelihood) of the resurrection based on experience with ordinary events because—*if the resurrection happened*—it is a unique event. Resurrection is not a part of ordinary human experience and language, and so it is not possible to give an independent account of what kind of a thing it is, nor does it seem likely that there could even be a nonanalogical way of talking about it. It follows that, in the case that the resurrection happened, having access to its reality depends on a certain disposition vis-à-vis the gospel accounts: not the disposition of one seeking to be persuaded by the evidential function of these accounts that something terribly unlikely has happened,[37] but

[35] Frei, *Identity of Jesus Christ*, 175 (emphasis in original).

[36] William C. Placher explains this implication in his introduction to a collection of Frei's essays: "[I]f we read the Old and New Testaments as in some sense a unity, the identity of Jesus as the Resurrected One seems central not only to his own identity but to the storied world the text presents. If Jesus was not raised from the dead, then he was not who this story claims he is, and the narrative coherence of the story considered as a unity radically collapses. For Christians this story does not merely have a unity of its own; it sets the frame within which they understand the whole of their existence." Placher, "Introduction," in Hunsinger and Placher, *Theology and Narrative*, 14.

[37] Nor should we make the mistake of supposing that the resurrection takes center stage because it stands at the pinnacle of all the historically unlikely things the Bible claims—as if it,

one characterized by cooperation with their mode of depiction, and at least provisional openness to their claim to bear testimony to an impinging reality.

On the other hand, if the resurrection did not happen, the situation shifts radically, and we have then to do with a perfectly ordinary event patient of the typical historical analytical procedures. Thus, resurrection faith is not immune to historical critique: "[R]eliable historical evidence *against* the resurrection would be decisive. In other words, if the resurrection is true, it is unique, but if false, it is like any other purported fact that has been proved false: there is nothing unique about it in that case."[38] So, for example, if it were shown decisively that the empty tomb was a hoax, the demonstration would be germane. This is fitting, since, as Frei acknowledges, "if it were not so, in what genuine sense could Christian faith be said to be historical and to involve a historical risk?"[39] Evidence could yet emerge that would be devastating for resurrection faith.

In the meantime, the situation is split into two incommensurable epistemological scenarios. The question of the proper disposition of the inquirer to the claim depends upon the nature of the case, and the nature of the case depends upon the veracity of the claim. The only thing to do in this situation is precisely what Frei does: describe what belief in the resurrection entails for the one who disposes herself toward the gospels in faith.

Frei is clear that the gospel accounts are not evidential in the typical sense. Trying to stay close to the form of testimony the gospel authors give, Frei denies that these stories are in the mode of persuading us that the resurrection "belongs to a credible type of occurrence."[40] Rather, their persuasive power is a function of their capacity to render a particular and compelling identity, and the propositional claim they make is available only as a function of the logic of that unsubstitutable identity they narrate.

---

as the least likely of all, might serve as the "horse pill" that, once swallowed, makes every other purported wonder seem to go down more smoothly. (When it comes to that, floating axe heads are not inherently more likely than resurrected bodies.) Resurrection becomes the crux because of the literary judgment that identity is definitively disclosed here.

[38] Frei, *Identity of Jesus Christ*, 183 (emphasis in original).

[39] Frei, "Theological Reflections on the Accounts of Jesus' Death and Resurrection," 45.

[40] Frei, *Identity of Jesus Christ*, 183. This is most striking in the climactic episodes wherein Jesus' identity is most clearly at stake. Rather than trying to convince us that all the evidence is being presented objectively at this crucial juncture, the style of narration moves in the opposite direction, such as when the depiction grants access to the internal disposition of Jesus in Gethsemane, when all possible witnesses are absent and even asleep. "The narration is at once intensely serious and historical in intent and fictional in form." Frei, *Identity of Jesus Christ*, 178.

> What the accounts are saying, in effect, is that the being and identity of Jesus in the resurrection are such that his nonresurrection becomes inconceivable.[41]

Or again,

> To express the matter in a way totally uncongenial to the Synoptic writers, what they are saying is something like this: "Our argument is that to grasp what this identity, Jesus of Nazareth (which has been made directly accessible to us), is is to believe that he has been, in *fact*, raised from the dead."[42]

By putting the matter in this way, Frei is essentially making a "narratological argument" for the resurrection.[43] The only "argument" the gospels offer is that resurrection is what the logic of the story requires—what is entailed in the identity the story discloses.

Frei was extremely careful about how this descriptive unpacking of the claim implicit in the storied depiction of the identity of Jesus Christ should be distilled and formulated propositionally. Here is his specific wording: "[The believer] would have to affirm that the New Testament authors were right in insisting that it is more nearly correct to think of Jesus as factually raised, bodily if you will, than not to think of him in this manner."[44] The phrase "more nearly correct" is important because it resists epistemological reduction—we should not pretend that we know exactly what kind of thing the resurrection is. But if, in our cultural and epistemological context, we must think in terms of "facts" in order to think of something as both real and particular, then not only is the Bible's overall depiction of Jesus' identity "history-like," its claim about the resurrection is "fact-like."[45]

Frei's position on the historicity of the resurrection is subtle—too subtle for his conservative critics. In response to evangelical impatience with his coyness about the straightforward reference of the text, Frei expresses his own frustration: "The one thing I dislike about the term 'supernatural' is that it

[41] Frei, *Identity of Jesus Christ*, 179.

[42] Frei, *Identity of Jesus Christ* (emphasis in original).

[43] In the earlier form of this section, which appears in "Theological Reflections on the Accounts of Jesus' Death and Resurrection," Frei explicitly acknowledges the debt to Anselm's "ontological argument" by wondering aloud about the wisdom of making "Luke or John speak like a late eleventh-century theologian" (41).

[44] Frei, *Identity of Jesus Christ*, 182.

[45] "If I am asked to use the language of factuality, then I would say, yes, in those terms, I have to speak of an empty tomb. In those terms I have to speak of the literal resurrection. But I think those terms are not privileged, theory-neutral, trans-cultural, and ingredient in the structure of the mind and of reality always and everywhere." Frei, "Response to 'Narrative Theology,'" 211.

seems to be a gigantic, enormously portentous way of saying 'natural.' It is the same as referencing naturally except much more so."[46] In other words, when it comes to God's ways in the world, it is probably best to allow for the possibility that something even so seemingly fundamental as reference may be frustrated at the qualitative level. We should not pretend to clinical or even "clear and distinct" apprehension of things beyond our ken and kind. The better course is to stay within the limits of the depiction we have: "The truth to which we refer we cannot state apart from the biblical language which we employ to do so. And belief in the divine authority of Scripture is for me simply that we do not need more. The narrative description is adequate."[47]

Another Wrong Turn?

About a decade after *Eclipse* and *Identity*, Frei published an essay titled "The 'Literal Reading' of Biblical Narrative in the Christian Tradition: Does It Stretch or Will It Break?" in which he vigorously pressed a critique of two hermeneutical proposals that had risen to prominence among theologians in the years since his two influential monographs. In his view, both are guilty (though to different degrees) of the kind of theoretical overreaching he deplored. Frei was convinced that the more elaborate and systematic the theoretical apparatus employed, the greater its tendency to (1) obscure or usurp Christian theology's proper relation to the Bible and (2) expose theology's flank to critique by burdening it with unnecessary philosophical entanglements that are likely to become points of vulnerability once their epistemological underpinnings grow unfashionable.

On the one hand, he criticized the "phenomenological hermeneutics" of Paul Ricoeur.[48] On the other hand, he pointed out difficulties with a second position that, though "less high-powered" and so less "majestic and pretentious" than Ricoeur's approach, was nevertheless beset by "grave weaknesses."[49] This second project was his own proposal for grounding normative claims

[46] Frei, "Response to 'Narrative Theology,'" 209.

[47] Frei, "Response to 'Narrative Theology,'" 210. The quote continues, "'God was in Christ reconciling the world to himself' is an adequate statement for what we refer to, though we cannot say univocally how we refer to it." For the most systematic—and dare I say even "straightforward"—statement of Frei's understanding of the gospels as "adequate testimony to" but not "accurate report of" the resurrection, as well as his typology of other positions vis-à-vis the referentiality of the resurrection accounts, see Frei, "Of the Resurrection of Christ," in Hunsinger and Placher, *Theology and Narrative*, 200–206

[48] For a discussion of Frei's critique of Ricoeur's hermeneutics, see the section on "Reference, Truth, and Meaning" in chap. 4.

[49] Frei, "'Literal Reading' of Biblical Narrative," 64.

about biblical hermeneutics in observations about formal features of the Bible's narratives organized under the genre description "realistic narrative."

In "Literal Reading" Frei expresses misgivings about his alliance with New Criticism, which, by the 1980s, was certainly no longer a cutting-edge literary school. It had been a useful tool for pushing back against the reductionist tendencies of the modern hermeneutics he criticized in *Eclipse* but was itself now coming under attack from poststructuralism. Frei confesses his association with the movement, and dutifully offers a pro forma three-point critique of New Criticism.[50] But his heart is not really in it. Increasingly for Frei, the real problem with New Criticism is not that it is an especially bad theory but that it is a theory. He does become markedly more rhetorically animated when he turns from cataloging the shortcomings of New Criticism to critiquing what he now takes to be the methodological overreaching in his earlier work:

> There may or may not be a class called "realistic narrative," but to take it as a general category of which the synoptic Gospel narratives and their partial second-order redescription in the doctrine of the Incarnation are a dependent instance is first to put the cart before the horse and then cut the lines and claim that the vehicle is self-propelled.[51]

Frei now wants to speak less about the qualities of the text the church reads and more about the qualities, or better, "rules," of the church's reading praxis. He is convinced that it is the church that has taught itself to use these particular texts in this particular way, not literary criticism that has taught the church the true nature of its scripture.

There is some debate about the degree to which the argument in "Literal Reading" reflects a turning point in Frei's thought.[52] Some interpreters have

[50] His criticisms are as follows: First, New Critics arbitrarily insist on the self-referentiality of texts, but still wish to make truth claims, and so are lured into the theoretically ambitious and (for the otherwise philosophically disinclined) dubious project of delineating a "purely aesthetic kind of truth in literature." Second, New Criticism's denial of the contribution of the reader to the hermeneutical encounter "comes close to enthroning verbal repetition as the highest form of understanding." Third, New Criticism masks its dependence on a classic Christian doctrine, pretending to advocate a general principle of interpretation theory that is actually derived from a particular faith commitment: "Endowing the text with the stature of complete and authoritative embodiment of 'truth' in 'meaning,' so that it is purely and objectively self-referential, is a literary equivalent of the Christian dogma of Jesus Christ as incarnate Son of God, the divine Word that is one with the bodied person it assumes." Frei, "'Literal Reading' of Biblical Narrative," 64–66.

[51] Frei, "'Literal Reading' of Biblical Narrative," 66.

[52] Note that the argument in "Literal Reading" can be traced to Frei's earlier response to Paul

characterized it as a turn influenced by George Lindbeck's cultural-linguistic theory of religion,[53] while others have stressed the continuities with Frei's earlier work.[54]

The synergies between Frei's later work and Lindbeck seem clear enough, but what Frei appreciated most about the cultural-linguistic approach was not its sweeping explanatory power but its capacity to supply a theoretically sophisticated account of religious language and practice that effectively shields theology in its descriptive mode from critique. It is an open question whether Frei really thought he had ever gotten "the cart before the horse." His comments about New Criticism being a kind of crypto-theology suggest that he understood himself as right all along about the way of reading he described and advocated, but perhaps wrong to suppose that literary criticism had been instrumental in showing him this, except in a derivative and roundabout way.[55] The break with New Criticism demonstrates that Frei was becoming, if possible, even more bold about declaring the independence and sufficiency of the descriptive enterprise for theology.

The Frei of "Literal Reading" is less inclined to make even ad hoc use of explanatory models. If there is a trajectory in Frei's work, it is toward an ever more extreme and thoroughgoing descriptive methodology that distrusts all explanation as ultimately reductive. What began as an argument about how paying especially close attention to the formal features of biblical narratives

---

Ricoeur's work offered as a lecture at Haverford College in 1982, and later published as Hans W. Frei, "Theology and the Interpretation of Narrative: Some Hermeneutical Considerations," in Hunsinger and Placher, *Theology and Narrative*. 94–116.

[53] George A. Lindbeck, *The Nature of Doctrine: Religion and Theology in a Postliberal Age* (Philadelphia: Westminster, 1984). Charles Campbell argues for Lindbeck's work as the cause of a significant shift, and Campbell's sympathies are clearly with Frei's later, cultural-linguistic approach. Campbell, *Preaching Jesus*, 63–82. Also see George Hunsinger, "Afterword," in Hunsinger and Placher, *Theology and Narrative*, 258–59.

[54] One of his students, William Placher, has framed the matter as a shift in "emphasis" brought about because of a changed context. Placher, "Introduction," 16–17. Note that Placher explicitly states his preference for the earlier emphasis (24 n. 54). See also Mike Higton's attempt to frame Frei's later work as "commentary" on his earlier approach in *Christ, Providence, and History: Hans W. Frei's Public Theology* (London: T&T Clark, 2004), 178; and Jason Springs' assertion that Frei's career exhibits a "trajectory . . . that is consistently Wittgensteinian in sensibility, and indebted to . . . Karl Barth." Springs, "Between Barth and Wittgenstein: On the Availability of Hans Frei's Later Theology," *Modern Theology* 23, no. 3 (2007): 396. For the independent integrity of Frei's thought, along with an admission that his later work moved him (coincidentally?) closer to Lindbeck's position, see Paul J. DeHart, *The Trial of the Witnesses: The Rise and Decline of Postliberal Theology*, Challenges in Contemporary Theology (Malden, Mass.: Blackwell, 2006).

[55] Frei, "'Literal Reading' of Biblical Narrative," 64–65.

will help us see how to read them properly, finally morphs into the assertion that this is the way the church should read because this is the way that the church has read. The determination about whether this "plain" (i.e., received consensus) reading of the text is literal because of a kind of historical accident, or whether the literal sense distills a hard-won communal wisdom that has grown out of sustained close attention to the language of the text under the "vow of obedience," now seems to fall outside theology's purview. Frei assumes that theology's only pressing hermeneutical task is to discern and render explicit the rules implicit in the church's established reading practices.[56]

But a theologian in the purely descriptive mode exercises no critical leverage against the ecclesial tradition of reading. Frei's project began as an attempt to articulate the hermeneutical assumptions at work in Barth's use of scripture, but this notion of the Bible as the "church's book" would not have appealed to Barth. Barth understood the church to be positioned beneath the Bible—that is, accountable to its message, which the church neither creates nor controls.[57] The Barth of the Barmen Confession would not wish to be associated with any "cultural-linguistic" turn, but stands closer to Luther's maxim: "The church does not constitute the Word but is constituted by the Word."[58] Frei's later work is a significant departure from Barth in this respect.

The text-immanent emphasis of Frei's early work can be framed as a daring, constructive bid to submit to the text's own meaning in the trust that the Bible's meaning can become God's truth for those who embrace it in faith. But the later turn threatens to recast the entire project as a flight into fideism, first away from historical critique and into the house of language by means of New Critical literary theory, and then when deconstruction threatens the house of language itself, a retreat into the "safe room" of cultural-linguistic description. Cut off from all possible engagement with otherness (including the otherness of the text), all that remains for the theologian is to chronicle accurately the rules of the language game a community plays with its scripture. The later turn from close reading to cultural-linguistic description is itself another "wrong turn" that should not be allowed to "eclipse" Frei's earlier work on realistic narrative, which remains an engaging conversation partner for homiletics.

[56] See his version of the "Rule of Faith"; Frei, "'Literal Reading' of Biblical Narrative," 68–69.

[57] Willimon, *Conversations with Barth on Preaching*, 29.

[58] Martin Luther, *Luther's Works*, vol. 36, American ed., ed. Jaroslav Pelikan and Helmut T. Lehmann (St. Louis: Concordia, 1955), 145.

How to Preach during an Eclipse

A Postliberal Homiletic

Charles Campbell's carefully argued book *Preaching Jesus* provides a framework for appreciating the strengths and critiquing the weaknesses of Frei's project as a resource for homiletics. While I am most persuaded by Frei's earlier work focused on the form of biblical narrative as a clue to its proper interpretation, Campbell considers Frei's later "cultural-linguistic" turn to be his most important contribution.[59] Campbell critiques the notion that religious language generally—and therefore Christian preaching in particular—functions primarily to give outward expression to internal feelings and experiences of God that blossom spontaneously in experience. Instead, Campbell proposes that preaching functions paradigmatically for the church: rather than giving language to preexisting religious sentiments and experiences, it contributes to the formation that makes particularly Christian sentiments and experiences possible. This reversal of assumptions about the relationship between language and experience is the key that drives Campbell's critique and constructive proposal in *Preaching Jesus*.

Campbell takes aim at the "new" or "narrative" homiletic that has dominated homiletical theory and practice for a generation. He concedes that narrative homiletics has made important contributions, but after briefly summarizing some positive developments attributable to this generation of

[59] In keeping with his preference for this later turn in Frei's thought, Campbell's proposal for a postliberal homiletic makes extensive use of analytical categories outlined by Frei's Yale colleague George Lindbeck. Drawing on the work of anthropologist Clifford Geertz and sociologist Peter Berger, among others, Lindbeck proposes that at their core religions are not intricate systems of propositional claims to which people offer their intellectual assent (the "cognitive-propositional" understanding of most conservative theology), nor are they diverse expressions of some essential and universal experience of what matters most in life (the "experiential-expressive" assumption behind much liberal theology); rather, they are more like a culture or language (thus, a "cultural-linguistic" approach to religion proposed as a "third way" in theology). Therefore, Christianity "is not primarily an array of beliefs about the true and the good (though it may involve these), or a symbolism expressive of basic attitudes, feelings, or sentiments (though these will be generated). Rather, it is similar to an idiom that makes possible the description of realities, the formulation of beliefs, and the experiencing of inner attitudes, feelings, and sentiments. Like a culture or language, it is a communal phenomenon that shapes the subjectivities of individuals rather than being primarily a manifestation of those subjectivities." Lindbeck, *Nature of Doctrine*, 33.

homileticians,[60] Campbell proceeds with an extensive critique of some of the most prominent theorists in the field.[61]

Campbell charges that the "New Homiletic" is built upon experiential-expressive theological foundations. The result has been sermons that find their starting point in some presumably universal human need or experience and then correlate the gospel as the salve for that need, or the noblest expression of that experience. Campbell associates this homiletical approach with an unhealthy preoccupation with sermonic form. When the preacher assumes that Christian faith is organized around the expression of inner apprehensions of the transcendent, resources naturally flow toward discovering and refining forms capable of powerfully evoking these experiences. Campbell worries that such a form-driven homiletic neglects the distinctive Christian gospel, which is the proper content of proclamation.

Champions of a narrative homiletic have embraced the power of story to command the attention and sympathy of the hearer and celebrated the way stories invite the hearer into the meaning-making process. But Campbell doubts that it is really the power of story that Christians are called to preach. It may be true that everybody loves a good story, but Campbell argues that there is no reason to assume that the narrative genre is somehow mysteriously close to the heart of God. Against the claim that narrative qualities in a sermon automatically qualify it as a discourse in service of the gospel, Campbell urges that Christian proclamation should be interested in narrative only as a means to a distinctive end.[62] It is not stories in general that should interest the Christian preacher, but this particular Jesus whose identity is rendered by this particular narrative.

Campbell's central insight relates to the "ascriptive" language of preaching.[63] Frei convinced Campbell that gospel stories are essentially stories about

[60] Campbell mentions (1) a turn to scripture, (2) an enrichment of sermonic form, (3) an appreciation of the indicative character of the Christian gospel, (4) a recognition that the gospel appeals to the whole self and not just the intellect, and (5) a recovery of poetics and the importance of the religious imagination. Campbell, *Preaching Jesus*, 121.

[61] His detailed critiques are directed primarily at the work of Charles Rice, Fred Craddock, and Eugene Lowry. Campbell, *Preaching Jesus*, 117–45.

[62] "We are narrative preachers only to the extent that Jesus is what he does and undergoes. In a postliberal homiletic, narrative is important neither because it provides a 'homiletical plot' for sermons nor because preaching should consist of telling stories. Rather, narrative is important because it is the vehicle through which the gospels render the identity of Jesus of Nazareth, who has been raised from the dead and seeks today to form a people who follow his way." Campbell, *Preaching Jesus*, 189–90.

[63] Campbell does draw other homiletical conclusions from Frei's hermeneutical position,

Jesus—stories that render Jesus present to the reader by ascribing to him certain actions, words, and sufferings in proper relation to the circumstances they depict. The "ascriptive logic" of realistic narrative means that if a gospel story says that Jesus went somewhere, said something, did something, endured something—these are statements about the particular identity rendered in this telling, not a cipher for a shared religious sensibility hidden at the heart of all human experience. Frei called for interpretation that acknowledges Jesus as the subject matter of the gospel accounts. Campbell calls for sermons that do the same—sermons that "preach Jesus."

Campbell's strength is in urging preachers to stay close to the biblical text. He wants preaching that traffics unapologetically in the categories of the text, trusting the storied world of the Bible to bring us a word from beyond ourselves. Reading closely means attending to what is particular and distinctive in these stories and letting the stories themselves set the terms of the conversation the preacher negotiates between text and context.[64] Campbell has very helpfully reminded us that it is not the "old man with a wrinkled face who worked in Gibson's Hardware" that the church has gathered to encounter,[65] but the Jesus witnessed to in the gospels. In the midst of all the exuberance over poetics and the power of creative sermon form, Campbell appropriates Frei to remind us that Christian preaching, narrative or otherwise, can be tested according to a simple criterion: it must in the first place be about the Jesus rendered in the gospels.

Limited Options

But as Campbell leverages Frei's project to work out the details of his counterproposal, a number of problems emerge, and—not surprising for a

---

emphasizing, to name two examples, that preaching should direct its energies toward communal formation rather than individual appropriation and that the preacher should understand the act of preaching as "a form of discipleship shaped by the identity of Jesus Christ" and therefore as "an act of moral obedience." Campbell, *Preaching Jesus*, 216.

[64] This is good medicine for a generation of preachers who admire Craddock and share his passion for story but may lack an appreciation for the sometimes subtle ways he anchored his preaching in a richly informed close reading of the biblical text itself. Theologically and biblically, there is a vast gulf between a Barbara Brown Taylor masterpiece and one of the many "story sermons" on offer on any given Sunday in mainline pulpits, but pedagogically it has sometimes proven difficult to make that difference accessible and clear. See Fred B. Craddock, *The Cherry Log Sermons* (Louisville, Ky.: Westminster John Knox, 2001) and Barbara Brown Taylor, *The Preaching Life* (Cambridge, Mass.: Cowley, 1993), 89–174.

[65] This caricature of a folksy narrative sermon introduction typical of the New Homiletic is taken from the chapter "A Likely Story" in Thomas G. Long, *Preaching from Memory to Hope* (Louisville, Ky.: Westminster John Knox, 2009), 5.

hermeneutic that has denounced theory as necessarily reductive—the theoretical resources available to address them are limited. The first issue that emerges relates to the question of poetics. The approach in *Preaching Jesus* introduces an artificial division between plot and character in biblical narrative and in preaching. Campbell diagnoses the "obsession" with sermonic form prevalent in narrative homiletics as a symptom of the misguided focus on plot, in contrast to Frei's proper emphasis on character.[66] Campbell even goes so far as to suggest that once the character of Jesus has been rendered by story, narrative form becomes dispensable for the preacher. But this wedge between content and form, between character and plot, is at cross-purposes to the core of Frei's early work on realistic narrative. Frei insisted that character and plot always go together, that character, setting, and circumstance fitly render one another.[67] Jesus Christ is something available to the ecclesial reader in and in terms of this story. Attempting to distinguish the identity of Jesus Christ as the preachable subject matter—the kernel of true meaning to be extracted from the dispensable, formal husk of biblical narrative—reintroduces the very dynamic Frei found so troubling.

Campbell makes this move because he is concerned that the turn to poetics in preaching has displaced scripture's distinctive witness. When talk about the power of story becomes a focus for homiletics, Campbell worries that the text gets displaced as the controlling locus of meaning. He cites an example of a student substituting a children's story about a lost bird for the biblical story and then claiming that the gospel is proclaimed in its telling.[68] While acknowledging that no informed advocate of narrative homiletics would approve of such a thorough displacement of the Bible's particular story, he wonders whether it is really possible within the framework of the New Homiletic to explain why this is bad practice. But in his bid to restore scripture's role as an external authority, he ends up in a position that—contrary to one of the central tenets of Frei's hermeneutics—distinguishes sharply between content and form, and disparages the role of poetics in preaching. If it is agreed that poetics is essential to the meaning of a biblical text (Frei's early work on "realistic narrative"), it is strange for Campbell to claim that poetics is a matter of indifference for a sermon properly conformed to such a text. But

[66] Campbell, *Preaching Jesus*, 173.

[67] Frei was fond of quoting Henry James: "What is character, but the determination of incident? What is incident, but the illustration of character?" James, "The Art of Fiction," in *The Future of the Novel: Essays on the Art of Fiction* (New York: Vintage, 1956), 15, quoted (among other places) in Frei, *Eclipse of Biblical Narrative*, 14.

[68] Campbell, *Preaching Jesus*, 170.

without recourse to a general theory of poetics, including some framework for judging when the sermon's poetics are properly conformed to the text, Campbell is forced to make a distinction about what is essential in the biblical narrative, choose content (character) over form (plot), and urge homiletical allegiance to the former.

The second problem relates to the way context participates in textual meaning. Although Campbell's primary agenda is to secure the place of the biblical text as the controlling force behind the language of the sermon, he is also acutely aware that one can go too far down the path toward an autonomous text as the exclusive locus of a univocal meaning.[69] Taken alone and to its logical conclusion, Frei's early New Critical work suggests that biblical narrative, when approached within the proper literary analytical framework, consistently yields one meaning that is free of contextual contamination. The implications for a homiletic that fully embraces the notion of biblical narrative simply absorbing the world of the reader are clear: the single, unambiguous, and universally valid meaning of biblical narrative is available to the clever preacher who knows how to apply the proper literary analysis.[70] Such a homiletic essentially trades one (now discredited) modern bid for hermeneutical certitude through historical analysis for a new program of hermeneutical certitude through (New Critical) literary analysis.

Campbell knows that unnuanced claims about a radically autonomous biblical text that univocally dictates meaning to the reader without regard for context are unconvincing in light of the church's long conversation with scripture. Such claims also fly in the face of the experience of preachers who have to preach the same text in very different contexts and discover that such

[69] So while his main argument is with narrative homiletics on the left, he is also engaged in a rearguard action against a more conservative appropriation of Frei's work by Mark Ellingsen. In *The Integrity of Biblical Narrative*, Ellingsen frames the issue of biblical preaching as a struggle against "Kantian subjectivism": "The possibility of arriving at the meaning of the text without taking into account the interpreter's reactions to the text, their presuppositions or perspectives, has been largely rejected in our post-Enlightenment society. Since the Kantian era, philosophers and educators have tended to think of reality in terms of distinct points of view: 'you have your perspective; I have mine.' Normative meaning is an unintelligible concept on such grounds." Ellingsen, *The Integrity of Biblical Narrative: Story in Theology and Proclamation* (Minneapolis: Fortress, 1990), 34.

[70] Ellingsen pushes New Criticism to this unnuanced extreme: "[W]hen preaching becomes understood as the task of narrating the biblical account, Scripture effectively functions as its own interpreter. It interprets itself insofar as such preaching rejects the imposition of extraneous categories upon itself, and it allows its narratives to speak for themselves." Ellingsen, *Integrity of Biblical Narrative*, 19. And again, "[B]iblical accounts are not properly appreciated or understood when interpreted in light of foreign considerations, those that are not explicitly, literally present in the text." Ellingsen, *Integrity of Biblical Narrative*, 23.

texts do not really speak univocally. But again, without the resources of a general hermeneutical account of how context participates in the process of textual meaning, Campbell's options for addressing this problem are limited.[71] His answer is to appeal to the later, more cultural-linguistic Frei to say that the text can mean many things for the ecclesial community of interpretation, as long as they are all things that do not contradict the literal sense, and as long as the community has agreed that they are valid meanings. Yet even the provision about the primacy of the literal sense, which seems on the surface to concede some autonomy to the text, collapses upon further examination into the assertion that the "plain" (i.e., received) reading is a literal reading because this is the way the church has always read. Aside from the question of how it is even possible to speak simplistically of "the" ecclesial community (historical or contemporary) and its reading practices, the main problem with this response to New Critical overreaching is that, rather than wrestling with the dynamics of how textual meaning emerges out of the complex interplay of text and context in particular encounters between the Bible and Christian communities, it abruptly and unequivocally shifts the locus of meaning from the text all the way forward to the (idealized) reading community.

Third, and finally, there is the question of reference. There is an uneasiness in *Preaching Jesus* about Frei's refusal to address the question of how the biblical text accesses extratextual reality. This is especially on display in an extended section titled "Faith and History"[72] in which Campbell explores the question of biblical truth claims in Frei's work and arrives at conclusions similar to those I worked out under the heading "The Resurrection, Truth, Facts, and History," above. Frei himself, as he once admitted in response to an incredulous Carl F. H. Henry, wanted to speak of reference but found that he could not do so in good faith because it would entangle him in a number of potentially vulnerable and/or distorting philosophical commitments.[73] My own view is that Frei's wrestling with questions of history and reference is subtle, fascinating, and illuminating, but finally Frei's approach, as working preachers often lament, "will not preach." In other words, for all of its virtues, Frei's ideas about reference do not guide and shape the actual practice of preaching. However awkward it is to make three of the four evangelists "speak like a late eleventh-century theologian," it is even more awkward and indeed strains credibility to the breaking point to pretend that this has anything to

[71] For Campbell's response to Ellingsen, see Campbell, *Preaching Jesus*, 180–85.

[72] Campbell, *Preaching Jesus*, 16–28.

[73] "I did not mean to deny reference at all, as Dr. Henry worries I do, whether or not I intend it. I don't think any of us do want to." Frei, "Response to 'Narrative Theology,'" 210.

do with what the vast majority of Christians (in any age) mean when they confess "He is risen indeed!" Such disconnection from lived faith is simply not tenable for a practical theology, that is, one that takes seriously the theological implications of what the church does and understands itself to do. On some level Frei knew this, and he tried, especially in his response to Henry's pointed challenge, to say more.[74] What is needed, however risky, is a more or less straightforward account of how biblical language refers. With all due respect for Frei's warnings about the many, complex, and subtle issues that need to be appreciated, it is nevertheless necessary to endeavor, however provisionally, to give some account of how the Bible, and by extension Christian preaching conformed to it, is not only meaningful within the ecclesial community of interpretation but also, and simply, true.

These three problems in Campbell's postliberal homiletic based on Frei's hermeneutics show why Frei's later trend toward a cultural-linguistic understanding of religious language is an unfortunate turn that tends to take the focus off of a close reading of features of the biblical text itself, which was the great strength of his earlier work. In *Preaching Jesus* there is a tension between these two phases of Frei's work and, more troubling, a tendency to use the later cultural-linguistic turn as a hermeneutical panacea that too quickly resolves the complexity of the text-to-sermon process. The trump card of the ecclesial community as the arbiter of textual meaning dismisses, rather than responds to, hermeneutical problems that are central to the preacher's task. In the absence of a theory of how texts mean, Campbell's homiletic, following the later Frei, tends simply to assert how they have always meant to "us."

The next chapter introduces the hermeneutics of Paul Ricoeur. Ricoeur's approach to biblical narrative can help fund a homiletic that remains committed to a close reading of Christianity's unique story in scripture as a word to the human situation from beyond the human situation, while at the same time creatively engaging the three problems that emerge from Campbell's careful homiletic appropriation of Frei's project. Or, in terms that extend and clarify the thesis introduced in chapter 1, the hermeneutical theory of Paul Ricoeur offers a more suitable bridge between Barth's theology of the Word and a practicable homiletic, and it can be deployed to revise postliberal homiletics and fund a more adequate understanding of biblical preaching that accounts for (1) the role of poetics in proclamation, (2) the critical role of context in the appropriation of biblical meaning, and (3) the status of biblical and preached truth claims.

[74] So, e.g., "That does not mean that I don't believe that we refer *by means* of that story." Frei, "Response to 'Narrative Theology,'" 209 (emphasis in original).

Chapter Three

Paul Ricoeur and the World of the Text

Paul Ricoeur's philosophy of language and interpretation theory will be explored in depth. Though Ricoeur's hermeneutical thought has been explicated in connection to both Barth and Frei,[1] it has not been sufficiently appreciated in the field of homiletics.[2] The goal is to draw upon Ricoeur's approach to fund a homiletical proposal that responds to weaknesses that come clear through Campbell's homiletical appropriation of Frei.

Campbell deploys Frei's approach to biblical narrative in support of his argument that preaching should conform itself more closely to the particulars of the biblical text and its distinctive subject matter. He worries that the recent fascination with sermon form and a vague allegiance to the "power of story" have distracted attention away from the true calling of homiletics, which is to preach Jesus.

[1] See Mark I. Wallace, *The Second Naiveté: Barth, Ricoeur, and the New Yale Theology*, Studies in American Biblical Hermeneutics, 2nd ed. (Macon, Ga.: Mercer University Press, 1995).

[2] Though not developed extensively, two exceptions with respect to the application of Ricoeur's narrative theory to homiletics are Long, *Preaching from Memory to Hope*, 45–53, and Mary Catherine Hilkert, *Naming Grace: Preaching and the Sacramental Imagination* (New York: Continuum, 1996), 93–99. For a discussion of Ricoeur's general interpretation theory in relation to homiletics, see Nancy Lammers Gross, *If You Cannot Preach Like Paul . . .* (Grand Rapids: Eerdmans, 2002), 92–105.

But Frei, especially in his later cultural-linguistic turn favored by Campbell, offers a theory-averse theory that is not thick enough to fund a robust and pedagogically useful account of the text-to-sermon process. Frei assures us that the Bible is a book of stories that function within the ecclesial context to render the identity of Jesus, and Campbell builds on this assurance and urges that sermons be conformed in minute detail to biblical texts. But Campbell does not give an adequate account of *how* sermonic language makes the text's claim available in a new and different context than that of the original text, and therefore he has a hard time saying exactly what the sermon has to offer. The very existence of preaching as a practice is powerful testimony to the church's and the synagogue's long experience that even when it is properly conformed to the biblical text, preaching necessarily involves carefully negotiating the text's meaning in relation to a new situation (context) and bringing it to fresh and eventful language for a new hearing (poetics). A successful postliberal homiletic must honor this long history by giving a clear account of what is to be gained in preaching over merely repeating the biblical text.

Some who share this concern with Campbell's homiletic have attributed the problem to overreaching claims about the power of "realistic narrative" to render the presence of Jesus.[3] If the biblical genre itself is assumed to have the power to make Jesus present to the reading community, preaching is obviated. However, Campbell may not have as much at stake in the genre "realistic narrative" as may be supposed. Just as Frei pivoted away from claims about the autonomous text and toward the ecclesial community of interpretation in order to safeguard the meaningfulness of biblical language in the face of poststructural assaults, so Campbell turns to cultural-linguistic construals of religious language in order to address questions about the language of the sermon. For Campbell, the language of preaching is a special linguistic competence nurtured within a distinctive community—a kind of improvised variation on the themes established by the biblical text.[4] Campbell follows the later Frei in arguing that context is a nonfactor because the context of

[3] In an acerbic review of *Preaching Jesus*, James Kay presses this critique and attributes the problem to overreaching claims about "realistic narrative" when he wonders why, according to Campbell's theory, "anyone would bother to preach these narratives. Why not just read or recite them? Why muck things up with preaching . . . [?]" Kay, "Review of *Preaching Jesus: New Directions for Homiletics in Hans Frei's Postliberal Theology*," *Theology Today* 56, no. 3 (1999): 404.

[4] For an example of how Campbell attempts to leverage communal reading practices and the notion of a traditioned linguistic competence to address questions of context and poetics, see the section titled "Preaching as Linguistic Improvisation" in Campbell, *Preaching Jesus*, 231–41.

preaching is exclusively and hermetically the idealized reading community. Poetics, in turn, is simply a matter of competence in the community's established and distinctive way of speaking.

This is a pattern in *Preaching Jesus*. All roads lead eventually to the impenetrable authority of the ecclesial reading community. But Campbell's appeal to communal reading practices as the locus of textual meaning forecloses on the complexity of homiletical interpretation. It does not offer what a homiletic should, namely, guidance about how to shape sermonic language that is creative in its fidelity to the text and faithful in its engagement with a novel context.

Furthermore, the exclusive focus on the reading community as the arbiter of textual meaning not only fails to give a satisfactory account of context and poetics in preaching but also generates a third concern about the status of preached truth claims in a postliberal homiletic. Frei's refusal to engage the category of textual reference, and his tendency to seek shelter from critique in theories of religion that collapse explanation into description, makes it difficult for a homiletic so dependent on his thought to offer a compelling account of how biblical preaching bears truthful witness to what is the case about the world. The shift of emphasis from the autonomous text (early Frei) to the authoritative ecclesial reading community (late Frei) does nothing to answer the question about whether realistic narrative is truth bearing. It is a shift from "Here is a story that is self-evidently about a particular Jesus" to "Here is a story and we say it means this about Jesus." In neither case are we told why this story should be believed as true.[5]

Simply insisting that the question of truth be bracketed until communal formation makes all things clear is not a compelling position. Especially in a cultural context in which even those who take the Bible most seriously must negotiate identity at the intersection of many communities and many narratives, we must say more. If a homiletic is to honor what Christians believe to be at stake in Christian preaching, it must show how the Bible and sermons properly conformed to the Bible are not only meaningful to those who use its storied world to regulate communal identity but also true in their claims about the shared extratextual world of human experience.

[5] Gary Comstock has put the matter clearly: "I do not think that we can have it both ways; either we are making truth claims or we are not. If we are not, then we must be content to have others say about us: 'Oh, the Jesus narrative again; that's just their story about things.' If we are—if we think that in an important sense this story is a true story about things—then we must accept responsibility for showing not only *how* one ought to understand the claim, but *why* it should be affirmed." Comstock, "Truth or Meaning: Ricoeur versus Frei on Biblical Narrative," *Journal of Religion* 66, no. 2 (1986): 131 (emphasis in original).

So three problems grow out of Campbell's attempt to appropriate Frei in articulating a homiletic consistent with Barth's theology of the Word: inadequate sermonic poetics, inability to account for the new sermonic context, and a refusal to engage the critical question of how the Bible and the sermon properly conformed to the Bible are true. The hermeneutical theory of Paul Ricoeur offers resources to redress these problems.

Paul Ricoeur in Perspective

Paul Ricoeur (1913–2005) was born in Valence, France, just south of Lyon.[6] His mother died when he was an infant, and his father died soon after at the First Battle of the Marne. He was raised by his father's parents at Rennes. The Ricoeurs were devout Protestants in predominantly Catholic France, and he and his older sister were raised "in a strict atmosphere of reading, Bible study, and going to church."[7] Trained as a philosopher before his capture at the beginning of the Second World War, he was part of a group of university instructors who organized classes at their POW camp in Germany. (Remarkably, after the war the French government granted degrees to some of the prisoners who attended that makeshift school.)

Soon after the war ended, Ricoeur completed and published a French translation with commentary of Husserl that he had begun as a POW by writing in the margins of the copy he was granted by the Red Cross.[8] This was the beginning of his recognition as a leading phenomenologist. Ricoeur's career as a professor and public intellectual was distinguished, including tenures at the Sorbonne, the University of Paris at Nanterre, and finally the University of Chicago, with appointments in the Divinity School, the Department of Philosophy, and the Committee on Social Thought.[9]

Ricoeur and Frei: Different Lives

In 1982 Haverford College hosted a Symposium on Narrative Theology at which the two most prominent scholars in the field at that time, professors Frei and Ricoeur, were invited to present papers and respond to one another's

[6] For the following brief sketch, I am indebted to the biographical essay in Charles E. Reagan, *Paul Ricoeur: His Life and His Work* (Chicago: University of Chicago Press, 1996), 4–51.

[7] Reagan, *Paul Ricoeur*, 4.

[8] Edmund Husserl, *Idées directrices pour une phénoménologie*, trans. Paul Ricoeur (Paris: Éditions Gallimard, 1950).

[9] Mark I. Wallace, "Introduction," in Wallace, *Figuring the Sacred*, 6.

work.[10] This was, so far as is known, their only meeting, and one can scarcely imagine more divergent paths to a shared destination.

While Frei wrote slowly and published little, virtually all of it in the highly circumscribed field of hermeneutics, Ricoeur enjoyed a long, prolific, and very public career, with a record of scholarly production legendary for its quality, scope, and volume. His published intellectual odyssey is staggering, engaging every major figure in the philosophical tradition and including "detours" of remarkable depth and insight into fields as diverse as psychoanalysis, general and biblical hermeneutics, philosophy of language, historiography, and narrative theory. Frei called himself a theologian and a historian but had little regard for philosophy; Ricoeur described himself precisely as a philosopher, albeit one who was also "a listener to Christian preaching."[11] Frei understood himself as a Christian whose life's work was to give an account of how Christians have read and should read the Bible; Ricoeur's work in biblical hermeneutics is just one exercise among many in service of his larger project of exploring what it means to be human. Although he has been highly influential in biblical studies, a few years ago when Ricoeur passed away, many of the public eulogies celebrating his intellectual accomplishments and praising his irenic spirit betrayed no interest in or even awareness of his contributions to Christian theology and biblical hermeneutics. By contrast, though Frei's work commanded significant and growing interest among specialists in biblical studies and theology, his untimely death in 1988 went largely unnoticed in the wider academic world. So despite their shared passion for exploring the meaning of biblical narrative, Ricoeur and Frei come to the conversation from very different intellectual backgrounds.

Ricoeur and the "Long Route" through Hermeneutics

The single most important thing to understand about Ricoeur's body of work is his conviction that the quest to understand human existence must be mediated by language, symbol, and story.

This was a position he arrived at gradually after beginning with a very different methodological approach that ultimately proved unsatisfying in

[10] Ricoeur's presentation was later published as Paul Ricoeur, "Toward a Narrative Theology: Its Necessity, Its Resources, Its Difficulties," in Wallace, *Figuring the Sacred*, 236–48. Frei's paper was published as "Theology and the Interpretation of Narrative." Although Ricoeur was at that time still in the process of developing his full account of the workings of narrative, these two essays provide the most direct account of their engagement with one another's work as well as a perfect example of their contrasting intellectual styles.

[11] Ricoeur, "Naming God," 217.

his quest to understand the human condition. There are several accounts of Ricoeur's move toward a hermeneutical approach to truth,[12] but the clearest and most succinct explanation in his own words of Ricoeur's journey toward a linguistic and hermeneutical approach to existentialism took the form of a luncheon address to the University of Chicago Divinity School in the spring of 1971, which has been published as an appendix to *The Rule of Metaphor*.[13]

Ricoeur's earliest work reflected a debt to the phenomenology of Edmund Husserl and the existentialism of Karl Jaspers and Gabriel Marcel. Concerning his attempt to work out an account of human will, Ricoeur remarked,

> It was phenomenology . . . in the sense that it tried to extract from lived experience the essential meanings and structures of purpose, project, motive, wanting, trying and so on. . . . But if it was phenomenology, it was existential phenomenology in the sense that these essential structures implied the recognition of the central problem of embodiment.[14]

At this early point in his thinking, Ricoeur did not make a special problem of language because he assumed that ordinary language supplied a vocabulary ("purpose," "project," "motive") adequate to his task of describing reality as it presents itself to consciousness.[15]

The problem of language became acute for Ricoeur only when he explored the question of the distorted, or bad, will. When he turned from the question of the limits of the human will to the question of guilt, the problem of interpretation surfaced:

> Now the consideration of the problem of evil brought into the field of research new linguistic perplexities which did not occur earlier. . . . The fact is that we have direct language to say purpose, motive, and "I can," but we speak of evil by means of metaphors such as estrangement, errance, burden, and bondage. Moreover, these primary symbols do not occur unless they are embedded within intricate narratives of myth which tell the story of how evil began.[16]

[12] See especially the sections titled "Early Development" and "The Hermeneutical Turn" in Wallace, "Introduction," 2–10.

[13] "From Existentialism to the Philosophy of Language," in Ricoeur, *Rule of Metaphor*, 315–22.

[14] Ricoeur, *Rule of Metaphor*, 316.

[15] For Ricoeur's early phenomenological account of the will, see Paul Ricoeur, *Freedom and Nature: The Voluntary and Involuntary*, Northwestern University Studies in Phenomenology and Existential Philosophy (Evanston, Ill.: Northwestern University Press, 1966).

[16] Ricoeur, *Rule of Metaphor*, 316. For Ricoeur's early hermeneutical work in relation to the problem of the bad will, see Paul Ricoeur, *The Symbolism of Evil* (Boston: Beacon, 1969), and Ricoeur, *Freud and Philosophy*.

In wrestling with this discovery, Ricoeur became convinced that human consciousness cannot directly apprehend itself. Because humans always come to consciousness as "prior denizens of a world of symbols and myths,"[17] the path to self-understanding is necessarily the "long route" through hermeneutical engagement with the texts that shape and reflect what it means to be human: "It seemed, therefore, that direct reflection on oneself could not go very far without undertaking a roundabout way, the detour of a hermeneutic of these symbols. I had to introduce a hermeneutical dimension within the structure of reflective thought itself."[18]

The question of the meaning of human existence is posed in language, and Ricoeur became firmly convinced that it is through the mediation of language, especially mythopoetic discourse, that it must be explored. In other words, Ricoeur's existential phenomenology became hermeneutical.

Ricoeur on Language

The narrative Ricoeur supplies concerning this progression from existentialism to hermeneutics does not offer a clear explanation for why he has paid so much attention to, and showed so much sympathy for, biblical discourse in particular. In his remarks to the faculty of the divinity school, he transitions matter-of-factly to describing his recent "impulse" toward "studies devoted to the word of *God*."[19] At that time, he had not yet made his primary contributions to biblical interpretation and narrative theology, but the trajectory toward such matters is clear in his comments, even if the reasons for it are not.

Ricoeur consistently expressed disdain for what he called "cryptotheology," that is, theology disguised as philosophy. He wanted his philosophy to be "agnostic" even though he was clearly not.[20] Yet it can be argued that in all he did, his philosophy reflected an abiding concern for the possibility of a word addressed to the human situation from beyond the human situation.[21] Although he did not always name his motivations explicitly, his

[17] Wallace, "Introduction," 5.

[18] Ricoeur, *Rule of Metaphor*, 316.

[19] Ricoeur, *Rule of Metaphor*, 320 (emphasis in original).

[20] See, e.g., the discussion in the introduction to *Oneself as Another*. He speaks of his "concern to pursue, to the very last line, an autonomous, philosophical course," an "asceticism of argument" that he believes "marks all [his] philosophical work." Paul Ricoeur, *Oneself as Another* (Chicago: University of Chicago Press, 1992), 24.

[21] Even as he speaks of a "bracketing, conscious and resolute, of the convictions that bind me to biblical faith," he is not so naïve as to pretend "that at the deep level of motivations these convictions remain without any effect on the interest that I take in this or that problem." Ricoeur, *Oneself as Another*, 24.

philosophical hermeneutics can be understood as a long and patient project designed to work out an understanding of the conditions necessary, but not sufficient, for such a possibility.

Ricoeur's philosophy of language and the resulting concept of a textual "world" will be explored in that light. When Ricoeur pushes back against the reductions of structuralism, when he claims that as discourse language always seeks to say something to someone about something, and especially when he makes his case for the way poetic discourse in particular grants extraordinary access to the real, he is laying the groundwork for thinking more about what matters most:

> [A] religious faith may be identified through its language, or, to speak more accurately as a kind of discourse. This first contention does not say that language . . . is the only dimension of the religious phenomenon; nothing is said—either pro or con—concerning the controversial notion of religious experience. . . . What is said is only this: whatever ultimately may be the nature of the so-called religious experience, it comes to language, it is articulated in a language, and the most appropriate place to interpret it on its own terms is to inquire into its linguistic expression.[22]

Whatever else Christian faith may be, it "comes to language." Likewise, it comes to us as language. Because faith on some level simply *is* language, Ricoeur's linguistic turn is a fascination not just with language but with religious truth itself.

The hope and the wager for the Christian preacher is that this language that comes to us in the Bible mediates a word that is God's true word for us and for God's church.[23] It is the bold hope that, against all odds, we have been given something more to say than our own best human thoughts. In Ricoeur's approach to language, I seek resources for understanding this possibility better. The long route to understanding Ricoeur's insights into biblical discourse begins with an exploration of his ideas about metaphor and the nature of language itself.

Metaphor

Ricoeur's account of the inner workings of language begins with metaphor. His definitive treatment of the subject is found in *The Rule of Metaphor*,

[22] Paul Ricoeur, "Philosophy and Religious Language," in Wallace, *Figuring the Sacred*, 35.

[23] This is, of course, Ricoeur's hermeneutical wager transposed into the language of Christian theology and homiletics. For Ricoeur's original assertion that hermeneutical truth is a wager, see Ricoeur, *Symbolism of Evil*, 355. For Ricoeur's notion of "letting go" as a necessary risk of exploring Christian truth claims, see chap. 4.

which, as its subtitle indicates, argues that the proper exegesis of the concept of metaphor supplies no less than the key to understanding "the creation of meaning in language."[24]

Ricoeur's treatment of metaphor begins in conversation with classical rhetoric generally, and Aristotle in particular. In classical rhetoric, metaphor is classified as a "trope" ("turning"). In the numerous handbooks that codified the Aristotelian tradition, it was common to catalog such tropes extensively, and metaphor was taxonimized as a member of this class—one among many in a large repertoire of stylistic devices that each involved some variation on the theme of using an improper, or figurative, term in place of the proper, or literal, term. Ricoeur points out that this settled scholastic commonplace does not do full justice to the complexity of Aristotle's original discussion because for Aristotle the concept of metaphor, "far from designating just one figure of speech among others such as synecdoche and metonymy . . . , applies to every transposition of terms."[25] Ricoeur notes that there is some "equivocation" on this point for Aristotle: he sometimes uses the same term (*metaphor*) to refer to the genus ("a global reflection concerning *the figure as such*"), but sometimes to a particular species ("the *trope of resemblance*").[26] Aristotle's sometime practice of conceptualizing all figural speech under the term *metaphor* suggests that he discerned that the process at work in metaphor is more broad and significant than is suggested by classifying it as merely one among many forms of wordplay.

In this connection, Ricoeur is particularly fascinated with Aristotle's observation in the *Rhetoric* that metaphor at its best functions to "set something before the eyes."[27] This notion of rendering the subject concretely available to the hearer's "senses" (and what could this be but a metaphor for the way a striking metaphor plays in consciousness) points to the way Aristotle guessed that metaphor was more than mere wordplay—that it somehow participated generatively in the meaning effect of language. Another section in which Aristotle indicates that he understood metaphor to be productive semantically through a heuristic function comes a little further on (1412a), where he observes that metaphor involves "added surprise; for it becomes clearer [to the listener] that he learned something different from what he believed, and his mind seems to say, 'How true, and I was wrong.'"[28] And in

[24] Ricoeur, *Rule of Metaphor*.

[25] Ricoeur, *Rule of Metaphor*, 17.

[26] Ricoeur, *Rule of Metaphor*, 17 (emphasis in original).

[27] Ricoeur's translation of *Rhetoric*, 1410b33; Ricoeur, *Rule of Metaphor*, 193.

[28] Aristotle, *On Rhetoric: A Theory of Civic Discourse*, trans. George Alexander Kennedy, 2nd ed. (New York: Oxford University Press, 2007), 250.

his exposition of Aristotle's distinctive use of *epiphora* to describe the metaphorical transaction, Ricoeur speaks of the ancient philosopher's appreciation of the irreducibly creative dimension of metaphor:

> It is transposition, transference as such, that is, the unitive process, the sort of assimilation that occurs between alien ideas, ideas distant from one another. As such, this unitive process arises from an apperception—an insight—that belongs to the order of seeing. Aristotle was pointing to this apperception when he said: "To metaphorize well is to see—to contemplate, to have the right eye for—the similar." *Epiphora* is this glance and this genius-stroke, unteachable and impregnable.[29]

So there are intimations in Aristotle of metaphor as more than mere embellishment.

Nevertheless, Ricoeur argues that Aristotle conceptualized metaphor in a way that obscures its deeper significance. Aristotle understood metaphor to function at the level of the word and so defined it as an *epiphora* ("movement" or "displacement") of the *onoma* ("name" or "noun").[30] By adopting this definition first established in his *Poetics*, Aristotle's *Rhetoric* theorizes metaphor as a matter of diction, rather than as a feature of discourse at the level of the sentence. Ricoeur argues that this decision ultimately frustrated Aristotle's own instincts about the deeper meaning of metaphor and framed the matter in a way that would continue to impede the classical tradition's capacity to appreciate metaphor as semantically productive:

> What is the result, for a theory of metaphor, of this change of level [from sentence to word]? Essentially, it is that the term common to the enumeration of parts of speech and to the definition of metaphor is the *name* or *noun* (*onoma*). Thus the destiny of metaphor is sealed for centuries to come: henceforth it is connected to poetry and rhetoric, not at the level of discourse, but at the level of a segment of discourse, the name or noun.[31]

In the final analysis, Aristotle thought of metaphor as a kind of exceptional denomination.

Flowing from this approach is the long-standing view of metaphor as merely a stylistic twist, a case of unusual word choice. On this view, employing a metaphor is a matter of substituting a figurative term rather than the usual and expected term. The assumption behind this theory of metaphor is that the reader, who intuitively senses the resemblance between the figurative

[29] Ricoeur, *Rule of Metaphor*, 195.

[30] "Metaphor consists in giving the thing a name that belongs to something else." Ricoeur's translation of *Poetics*, 1457b6–9; Ricoeur, *Rule of Metaphor*, 13.

[31] Ricoeur, *Rule of Metaphor*, 14.

term and the usual one, simply reverses the process by mentally substituting the proper term for the improper: Empedocles speaks of "life's gloaming," and the competent reader immediately notes the displacement, recognizes the resemblance, supplies the proper term, and effectively reads "old age."[32] According to this understanding, the end result of the metaphorical encoding and interpretive decoding process is no different semantically than if Empedocles had simply spoken of "old age" to begin with—the difference being not a matter of substance but of "urbanity." So understood, metaphor, like any trope, is a ward against banality and serves to sustain interest and attention, keeping the reader pleasurably engaged in the task of following the argument. In summary, the decision to conceptualize metaphor at the level of the word has the effect of cementing its status as a form of verbal ornamentation.

When Ricoeur turns from ancient Greece to a contemporary interlocutor, namely structuralism, he finds that, for all its differences from the classical approach, it essentially shares the view of classical rhetoric that metaphor is best understood as an effect at the level of the word. Of course, *contra* classical theory, structuralism does not subscribe to the notion of a correlation between words and ideas. There is therefore no sense of the "proper" term, and so no sense of its displacement by an improper term. For structuralism, language is a synchronic, differential system—a code of signifiers and signs that derive their meaning in relation to each other and refer to each other in an endless lexical dance that can never point beyond itself. But for all its novelty, this radical break from a classical philosophy of language does not require or empower structuralism to rethink the notion of metaphor as a word effect. As a science of signs, structuralism is already given to semiotic reduction, and so has no resources for challenging the classical view of metaphor as a mere substitution, a kind of deviation in naming.[33]

Ricoeur is dissatisfied with this substitution theory of metaphor. To formulate an alternative, he draws on the work of English-language authors who have approached the problem from the side of propositional logic with its concern for the sentence, as opposed to structural linguistics with its focus

[32] I borrow this example from *Poetics* (1457b13). It appears among the "Supplemental Texts" supplied in Appendix I to Aristotle, *On Rhetoric*, 294.

[33] For a discussion of the relationship between classical philosophy of language and the "lexical preoccupations" of approaches dependent on Saussurean linguistics, see the section titled "Monism of the Sign and Primacy of the Word." Ricoeur, *Rule of Metaphor*, 101–4. Despite the "highly technical analyses" offered by structural theorists, "their fundamental hypothesis is exactly the same as that of classical rhetoric, namely that metaphor is a figure of one word only." Ricoeur, *Rule of Metaphor*, 101.

on the word-sign.[34] This semantic approach suggests that metaphor has to be appreciated not at the level of the word as a deviation in naming but at the level of the sentence as an unusual predication. Ricoeur defines metaphor as a "semantic impertinence," a "calculated error" of predication.[35]

In addition to grammatical rules (e.g., subject and verb must agree in number), there is a "law of pertinence" that demands that a predicate be semantically capable of fulfilling its role as predicate. With respect to its meaning, it must be the right *kind* of thing—the kind of thing that one can properly predicate of this kind of subject. Ricoeur supplies an expression from Mallarmé as a particularly "flagrant predicative impertinence": "The sky is dead."[36] This is, to borrow Gilbert Ryle's term, a category mistake since "is dead" is properly predicated only of members of the class "living beings." To speak of the sky being dead is a calculated error of predication, and its function is to precipitate a crisis for the reader.

Strictly speaking, metaphor is not the deviant predication itself but its rescue by the imagination of the reader.[37] The semantic impertinence of the predication causes a crisis for language *as discourse*. It is as an event of meaning that the category mistake offends and so must yield to the sense-making faculty. Metaphor is the process of this yielding of the lexical code for the sake of language's determination to be meaningful as discourse. "There is a sort of dominance of speech (*parole*) over language (*langue*), with the latter agreeing to change in order to give meaning to the former."[38] The rule of speech as discourse is that language must be meaningful, and this concern trumps, or refuses, the apparent meaninglessness of the unusual predication.[39] Frustrated at the literal level, the reader's imagination strikes out in search of the meaning that must be made in order to satisfy this mandate.

[34] Ricoeur follows the terminology of Émile Benveniste, who distinguished between "semiotic" and "semantic" approaches to language. "The sign is the unit of semiotics while the sentence is the unit of semantics. . . . To say with de Saussure that language is a system of signs is to characterize language in just one of its aspects and not in its total reality." Ricoeur, *Rule of Metaphor*, 69.

[35] Ricoeur, *Rule of Metaphor*, 151–52.

[36] Ricoeur, *Rule of Metaphor*, 152.

[37] "[M]etaphor is not deviation itself, but the reduction of deviation." Ricoeur, *Rule of Metaphor*, 152.

[38] Ricoeur, *Rule of Metaphor*, 152.

[39] This word, *unusual*, is chosen carefully. Ricoeur does not argue that the literal term is "proper" and the figural "improper" in the classical sense. "The literal sense is the one that is lexicalized." Ricoeur, *Rule of Metaphor*, 291.

Ricoeur takes an example from Baudelaire: "Nature is a temple where living columns. . . ."[40] The grammar works, but there is a crisis of meaning. According to the accepted lexical value of the signs, "temple" is not something that can be predicated of "nature" through a simple identity "is." The literal sense founders in this moment, but it is the nature of discourse to insist on meaning, so the effort is not simply abandoned. Instead, the reader ventures an attempt to salvage the meaningfulness of discourse by exploring how it might be possible to see nature *as* a temple. The rest of the poem, beginning with the words "where living columns," will help fund the imaginative process of redescribing nature in terms of a temple. The collapse of the literal sense is the necessary condition for the emergence of a new, figural sense—a semantic innovation occasioned by an impertinent predication, but now "focused" on the word. There is a net gain to the meaning of the word "temple," a new way of understanding this once-settled sign because and by means of its metaphorical juxtaposition with "nature" in the context of the poem. Then, in turn, there is a new insight into the meaning of "nature" through its identification with the now enhanced and extended "temple."

It is important to be clear that the meaning created through metaphor is not a function of simply capitulating to the novel pertinence, as if the reader were now to concede that nature really is, after all, a temple. This would simply be the classical substitution theory at a new level of sophistication. As long as the metaphor lives, it lives precisely in the tension between the figural and the literal sense. This is why Ricoeur speaks of the double meaning bound up within the metaphorical "is," which speaks at once both "is like" and "is not."[41] To understand Hopkins' absurd predication "O the mind, mind has mountains" is to apprehend both at once—to know to a certainty that the mind does not have any such thing, and then *at the same time* to begin to admit the way in which it can be seen to have both "mountains" and consequently "cliffs of fall."[42] Within this tension, the human mind is now seen as—in terms of—another domain, and there is a net gain to meaning.

At the same time, when a metaphor "dies," the tension breaks down and the once impertinent predication is finally endorsed as conventional. To say now that the table has a leg is not at all like saying that the mind has mountains—it is, in fact, not to metaphorize at all since the semantic gain for "leg" that came with its once unusual predication to "table" has now been

[40] Ricoeur, *Rule of Metaphor*, 247.

[41] Ricoeur, *Rule of Metaphor*, 248.

[42] Gerard Manley Hopkins, "No worst, there is none. Pitched past pitch of grief"; quoted in Ricoeur, *Rule of Metaphor*, 214.

codified as one of its definitions. Ricoeur insists, "The dictionary contains no . . . metaphors."[43] As a discourse event, metaphor is lively. But because its effect is "focused" in the word, the new meaning generated through metaphor is ultimately destined to crystallize in the language system as yet another differential lexical value. Dead metaphors decompose into the lexical code as polysemy.[44]

Understood in this tensional way, metaphor cannot be dismissed as ornamental. The crisis caused by the impertinent predication is a crisis of meaning, and it sets in motion a process that discloses new meaning. Metaphor yields a net gain of information. It is the metaphorical use of language that empowers discourse to say something new, something more than what is presupposed in the closed matter of the lexical code. Metaphor is not a cosmetic substitution but a semantic innovation occasioned through the tension between the impossibility of what is predicated and the new possibility that emerges through redescription.

Poetic Reference

Nothing is more characteristic of Ricoeur's philosophy of language than his decision to privilege language as discourse. For the semiotic approach of structural linguistics, reference is an illusion: sign plays against sign in a differential system that never reaches beyond itself to extralinguistic reality. But for Ricoeur, the synchronic language system (*langue*), for all its explanatory power, must finally be seen as an abstraction derived from language as it is actually used (*parole*). Language as discourse is grounded in the synthetic act of predication and always wants to say something *about* something. The discursive function of language is to refer.

But this immediately presents problems for poetic discourse.[45] The notion of a real referent for a metaphorical statement seems absurd. It is a commonplace to assert that poetic statements do not refer—that they intend

[43] Ricoeur, *Rule of Metaphor*, 346 n. 46.

[44] This is not to say that dead metaphors must stay dead. It is not too difficult to imagine a poem in which the table's having a "leg" is exhumed (defamiliarized) and resuscitated (restated) such that we are able to engage the impertinence of this predication and experience once again (or rather, for the first time) the surprise, delight, and semantic gain facilitated by this metaphor.

[45] Here I am following Ricoeur's use of the term *poetic* not to designate a particular genre of literature but to describe (1) a range of discourse, including poems and narratives of all kinds, and (2) a distinctive function of language that can break out in the midst of even the most prosaic discourse. Ricoeur, *Rule of Metaphor*, 222.

nothing beyond themselves.[46] Unlike an ordinary sentence that makes a claim about the world, a poetic predication is said to turn back on itself, drawing attention to its own verbal surface as an art object. Or, according to another view, poetic utterances exhaust themselves in a display of raw subjectivity—a kind of pure linguistic extract of emotion and connotation. So according to these views, Hopkins' impertinent predications about the treacherous terrain of the mind should not be taken as a real warning about real hazards. On the contrary, poetic discourse is seen from this perspective as a kind of idling of the language motor: no great surprise that it runs so impressively since it is completely unencumbered by the resistance that comes when language is enmeshed with reality through the gears of reference. But, of course, an idling motor can never do any real work. For those who deny poetic reference, Hopkins is not showing us something new, something we had not apprehended before about reality itself—rather the words of the poem are comparable to the artist's paint or clay, or at most reflect only the intensity of the poet's isolated feelings overflowing through the verbal faculty. Such sweeping critiques of the very possibility of poetic statements pointing beyond themselves to the realm of the real are grounded in a positivist epistemology that rigidly enforces the subject-object distinction and acknowledges only ostensive reference as real.

But Ricoeur is not satisfied with any epistemology that predecides the question of poetic reference. And although he does not state the matter explicitly, one of the primary reasons for his refusal to foreclose on the possibility of poetic reference seems to be his strong sense as a reader that one sometimes experiences metaphor as thoroughly engaged with and uniquely disclosive of what is most humanly real. Speaking of a particularly striking impertinent predication, Ricoeur suspects that something more than a merely semantic innovation has been achieved:

> When, for example, Shakespeare likens time to a beggar, he is faithful to the profoundly human reality of time. Therefore, we must reserve the possibility that metaphor is not limited to suspending natural reality, but that in opening meaning up on the imaginative side it also opens it toward a dimension of reality that does not coincide with what ordinary language envisages under the name of natural reality.[47]

Indeed, what is at stake in Ricoeur's proposal that poetic language refers is the very definition of what counts as real. As he introduces his case for metaphorical reference, Ricoeur warns us that he is challenging modern epistemology

[46] See the subsection "The Case Against Reference," in Ricoeur, *Rule of Metaphor*, 221–28.
[47] Ricoeur, *Rule of Metaphor*, 211.

at a fundamental level. He wonders "[w]hether or not, in the course of this process, our concepts of reality, of world, and of truth vacillate. . . . Do we actually know what 'reality,' 'world,' and 'truth' signify?"[48] This claim about the power of metaphor to disclose the real has profound implications for theology in general, and homiletics in particular.

With so much at stake in these claims, the contours of Ricoeur's argument for metaphorical reference will be engaged in detail. Ricoeur proposes that the previously established semantic gain that comes through metaphor corresponds symmetrically to a gain in referential power: "Just as the metaphorical statement captures its sense as metaphorical midst the ruins of the literal sense, it also achieves its reference upon the ruins of what might be called (in symmetrical fashion) its literal reference."[49] The suspension of normal reference provokes a discursive crisis comparable to the crisis of meaning provoked by unusual predication. If metaphorical statements founder semantically by predicating against the grain of accepted word meanings, how much more do they also founder referentially by boldly asserting against the grain of what the reader has previously imagined as possible. But Ricoeur's claim is that just as metaphorical meaning may be rescued as semantic innovation, so metaphorical reference may open the mind to new vistas of reality. What metaphor "invents" as a novel sense, it also "discovers" as a possible referent through its capacity to point toward what was previously beyond language's power to refer: "It would seem that the enigma of metaphorical discourse is that it 'invents' in both senses of the word: what it creates, it discovers; and what it finds, it invents."[50] Just as metaphor frustrates sense at the literal level and so clears a path to a surprising second-order sense, so also poetic discourse frustrates ordinary (ostensive) reference and so opens the way for a surprising second-order reference.

Beyond the symmetrical way in which metaphorical reference neatly supplies the missing term in the schema implied by his account of metaphorical sense, Ricoeur appeals to the notion of the scientific model in order to explain metaphorical access to the real: "The central argument is that, with respect to the relation to reality, metaphor is to poetic language what the model is to scientific language."[51]

[48] Ricoeur, *Rule of Metaphor*, 221.

[49] Ricoeur, *Rule of Metaphor*, 221.

[50] Ricoeur, *Rule of Metaphor*, 239. For the claim that poetic discourse "discovers" as it "invents," see also Paul Ricoeur, "The Function of Fiction in Shaping Reality," in *A Ricoeur Reader: Reflection and Imagination*, ed. Mario J. Valdés (Toronto: University of Toronto Press, 1991), 121.

[51] Ricoeur, *Rule of Metaphor*, 240.

Scientific models function on a number of different levels. At the most basic level, such models supply a representation that is faithful to the modeled phenomenon in some subset of features marked as relevant. Typically, such models accurately reproduce or imitate certain spatiotemporal features at a more convenient scale. Examples include the representation of spatial relationships by a map and an enlargement of the microscopic. Or a slow-motion video image might "scale" the temporal sequence of a high-speed impact in a way that serves descriptive discourse about the event.

As the phenomena modeled become more complex and remote from direct human observation, scientific models begin to rely on isomorphism, their functional or structural resemblance to what is modeled. At this level of abstraction, the feature marked as relevant for representation is not spatiotemporal but rather the intricate web of relationships between the elements of a complex system. Ricoeur cites Max Black's example of the way the workings of computer circuitry can be usefully modeled in terms of a hydraulic system.[52]

At the final level of abstraction, the *theoretical* model is not a construction proper, but rather "the important point is that the model's only properties are those assigned to it by language convention."[53] Just like the isomorphic models explained above, theoretical models describe the salient features of an unfamiliar structure in terms of a more familiar structure. But at this level of complexity and remoteness from direct observation, the familiar "structure" is not a "thing" at all but is purely a verbal description and is deployed just as a way of talking about the phenomenon being modeled. Ricoeur cites the example of James Clerk Maxwell's representation of an electrical field "in terms of the properties of an imaginary incompressible fluid." The "medium" of the model is imaginary, or rather linguistic in the sense that the "substance" behaves according to a set of rules that exist only as an agreement about how to talk about it.[54] And yet the deployment of this theoretical model has the remarkable effect of producing information beyond what is presupposed in the "construction" of the model itself. To the extent that such purely linguistic models allow the scientific imagination to engage dimensions of reality that are not otherwise accessible, they establish that linguistic innovation can be referentially heuristic. In such a model, language itself supplies a medium through which to try out mathematical relationships and perform rational operations that yield a net epistemological gain.

[52] Ricoeur, *Rule of Metaphor*.

[53] Ricoeur, *Rule of Metaphor*, 241.

[54] Ricoeur, *Rule of Metaphor*.

The heuristic power of purely linguistic scientific models provides a compelling analogue to Ricoeur's claim that metaphorical redescription (also a purely linguistic phenomenon) holds the power to disclose, to refer, to point toward what was not otherwise available. When language grants access to what is otherwise unavailable, there is a real sense in which the "seeing as" of the model's (or metaphor's) redescription is simply seeing what is. The invented way of talking is the only access to the reality described, and so it makes sense to say that what is "invented" as a way of talking points toward something newly "discovered." This is what Ricoeur means when he suggests that our very conception of reality is thrown into question by living metaphor. The semantic innovation (invention) has the surprising effect of expanding our world (discovery).

This remarkable claim raises a number of difficult questions about the domain of such linguistically mediated discoveries, and the nature of the referential capacity metaphorical statements realize by means of suspending their reference to the ordinary objects of experience. Ricoeur's most developed answers to these questions come into clearer view when he discusses how networks of metaphorical statements function together at the level of the larger "work" to display a "world." But at the level of discrete metaphorical statements—those irreducible units of discourse that function as the building blocks for the referential feat of the projected world—the sphere of reference is more difficult to name. Ricoeur's debt to Husserl and Heidegger is especially pronounced in his treatments of this question, and he tends to deploy their specialized vocabulary as shorthand rather than offering a full explication of the claim.

His clearest and most jargon-free discussion of the matter is found in the important essay "Naming God," which was first published in 1979, shortly after the English translation of *The Rule of Metaphor*. In "Naming God," Ricoeur lucidly summarizes his important findings from the extended monograph in the context of extending his general observations about poetic reference toward the question of religious, and specifically biblical, discourse.[55]

Two paragraphs from the essay will be closely examined in the form of a running commentary:

> If some have held the poetic function of discourse to exclude its referential function, this was because, at first, the poem (again understood in a wide sense that includes narrative fiction, lyricism, and the essay) suspends first-order referential function,

[55] The next chapter takes up Ricoeur's carefully nuanced claims about the Bible as poetic discourse. In this context, the focus is on a close reading of his exposition of poetic reference in that essay.

> whether it is a question of direct reference to familiar objects of perception or of indirect reference to physical entities that science reconstructs as underlying the former objects.[56]

This is a summary of the argument that metaphorical reference emerges as the rescue of a foundering literal reference, a process that mirrors figural sense as the rescue of a foundering literal sense. Also introduced here is the fundamental distinction between poetic reference and the referential function of descriptive discourse. The latter can be further distinguished as either (1) "direct" in relation to "familiar objects of perception" or (2) "indirect" with reference to "physical entities that science reconstructs as underlying the former objects." Direct reference is typical ostensive reference (e.g., "there is a table"), and indirect reference is the remarkable sort achieved by a theoretical model when it successfully (i.e., with predictive efficacy) redescribes certain relevant features of the underlying (i.e., not directly observable) structure of the domain of objects (e.g., "the behavior of electrical fields is to be understood as that of an imaginary incompressible fluid"). It will be remembered from our discussion above that it is this indirect mode of descriptive discourse—especially its surprising capacity to leverage a purely linguistic model (i.e., an agreed-upon way of talking) in a way that produces a net epistemological gain—that supplies a compelling analogy to the claimed heuristic function of poetic language.

Having delineated these two discursive modes for describing objects, Ricoeur continues with his account of nondescriptive reference:

> In this sense, it is true that poetry is a suspension of the descriptive function. It does not add to our knowledge of objects. But this suspension is the wholly negative condition for the liberation of a more originary referential function, which may be called second-order only because discourse that has a descriptive function has usurped the first rank in daily life, assisted, in this respect, by science.[57]

Ricoeur reluctantly concedes the nomenclature "first" order to descriptive reference, protesting that it is so privileged only because of the influence on the modern imagination of the regnant scientific worldview. But if, from within a situation still dominated by science, we must speak of descriptive (and usually ostensive) reference as "first," Ricoeur will also speak subversively of poetic discourse and reference as more "originary."

This more "originary" discursive function of language does not "add to our knowledge of objects," but it does add to our knowledge. Thus,

[56] Ricoeur, "Naming God," 222.
[57] Ricoeur, *Rule of Metaphor*, 222.

> Poetic discourse is also about the world, but not about the manipulable objects of our everyday environment. It refers to our many ways of belonging to the world before we oppose ourselves to things understood as "objects" that stand before a "subject."[58]

Now we see that "originary" corresponds to a way of relating to reality that is more original in the sense that it logically precedes the subject-object distinction. Ricoeur is trading on the fundamental Husserlian insight that there is no detached and disinterested consciousness; consciousness begins as and is always a consciousness *of* something. We come to being not as autonomous, remote perceivers, but as already invested in and belonging to the world. So there is a way of being in relation to reality that is more fundamental than the mode that constructs the self as a judging subject essentially separated from a world of objects under its gaze.

It is to this more originary way of being that poetic discourse refers. Poetic reference is counterintuitive for moderns because we have embraced an epistemology that keeps us closed off from the realities to which poetic discourse gives access.

> If we have become blind to these modalities of *rootedness* and *belonging-to* (*appartenance*) that precede the relation of a subject to objects, it is because we have, in an uncritical way, ratified a certain concept of truth, defined by adequation to real objects and submitted to a criterion of empirical verification and falsification. Poetic discourse precisely calls into question these uncritical concepts of adequation and falsification.[59]

Here some of the shorthand jargon emerges, but the point is clear. Poetic discourse makes it possible to give language to dimensions of reality that are inaccessible to scientific, descriptive modes of discourse.

Features of poetic discourse commonly dismissed as the "merely subjective" or "emotional" dimension of nondescriptive language are actually

> modalities of our relation to the world that are not exhausted in the description of objects. Basic emotions such as fear, anger, joy, and sadness express ways of belonging to things as much as ways in which we behave in relation to them; all the more reason why feelings, temperaments, moods, and *Stimmungen*, expressed, shaped, and instructed by poetic language, should throw us into the midst of things.[60]

Such realities are not "merely subjective" once we recognize that such a disparaging judgment uncritically presupposes the subject-object distinction as the

[58] Ricoeur, *Rule of Metaphor*, 222.
[59] Ricoeur, *Rule of Metaphor*, 222 (technical terms in original).
[60] Ricoeur, *Rule of Metaphor*, 222.

ground and arbiter of what counts as real. The claim is that just as the subject-object dichotomy of descriptive discourse privileges certain ways of being and gives access to certain kinds of knowledge, it also conceals and discredits other important dimensions of human existence that can be explored only through different forms of discourse that refer in fundamentally different ways. As we will discuss in the next section, poetic discourse has the potential to show us new ways of belonging in the world, new options for locating ourselves in the matrix of reality, new avenues for exploring our "ownmost possibilities" (Heidegger).

Ricoeur on Textual Discourse

Ricoeur's theory of metaphor argues that nondescriptive discourse can be both meaningful (sense) and true (reference). The implications of such a claim are profound, but the fascinating hermeneutical ramifications of his analysis come fully into view only when these insights are extended to units of discourse longer than the sentence. At the level of texts crafted as extended works, the same dynamics that make metaphor so lively take on an even more remarkable discursive power. Ricoeur's account of textual discourse lays the theoretical groundwork for a deeper understanding of how biblical language works and how sermonic language may be properly conformed to a biblical text.

The World of the Text

Soon after the original French publication of *The Rule of Metaphor* (*La métaphore vive*, 1975), Ricoeur published a short collection of essays (based on the Centennial Lectures at Texas Christian University) under the title *Interpretation Theory: Discourse and the Surplus of Meaning*. The argument in *Interpretation Theory* shares many features in common with the argument we traced in *The Rule of Metaphor*, but it extends the claims about semantic innovation and poetic reference at the level of the predicative statement (sentence) toward "understanding language at the level of such productions as poems, narratives, and essays. . . . In other words, the central problem at stake in these four essays is . . . that of language as a *work*."[61] Ricoeur argues that such extended works take on a surprising and robust new referential function, which he describes as the projection or display of a textual world.

[61] Paul Ricoeur, *Interpretation Theory: Discourse and the Surplus of Meaning* (Fort Worth: Texas Christian University Press, 1976), xi (emphasis in original).

The shift to understanding language at the level of the larger work puts Ricoeur in conversation with two primary interlocutors in *Interpretation Theory*: (1) structuralism with its notion of texts as nonpsychological objects with decipherable internal structures, but no significant connection to extratextual reality, and (2) the romantic hermeneutic tradition associated primarily with Schleiermacher and Dilthey that understands texts as the mediation of psychological experience. As is his custom, Ricoeur tries to learn from both of these divergent perspectives as he works out a position that successfully navigates between their seemingly intractable differences toward a new synthesis. From structuralism he borrows the notion of language's capacity to exist and be analyzed as an independent, externalized object. From romanticism he takes the conviction that language is actually used as discourse: an event in which someone says something to someone about something. Although Ricoeur has serious misgivings about some aspects of both these positions, he trusts that each has seen something essential about language that needs to be taken into account in a general hermeneutics.

With respect to romantic hermeneutics, Ricoeur challenges the core assumption that language seamlessly bridges conscious experiences from "genius to genius." Spoken language is the discourse situation best suited to showcase the romantic claim that understanding the author/speaker's psychological intention is the proper goal of hermeneutics. But according to Ricoeur, what is understood, even in the event of spoken language, is not a direct experience of another consciousness, but a meaning:

> My experience cannot directly become your experience. An event belonging to one stream of consciousness cannot be transferred as such into another stream of consciousness. Yet, nevertheless, something passes from me to you. . . . This something is not the experience as experienced, but its meaning. Here is the miracle. The experience as experienced, as lived, remains private, but its sense, its meaning, becomes public.[62]

This move toward objectification and externalization, which is present even in spoken language, Ricoeur summarizes with the following slogan: "If all discourse is actualized as an event, all discourse is understood as meaning."[63]

In the case of speech, this initial step toward objectification (from personal experience to public meaning) is difficult to appreciate for two reasons. First, spoken discourse enjoys the advantage of the shared situation of the dialogue partners. Speech creates the strong illusion of seamlessly bridging the gap between individual minds because referencing public objects in a

[62] Ricoeur, *Interpretation Theory*, 16.

[63] Ricoeur, *Interpretation Theory*, 12.

shared situation is literally a matter of demonstration: one can indicate what one is talking about. Second, in a dialogical situation any residual ambiguity can be resolved through feedback; misunderstandings in a conversation are reduced by a kind of intersubjective trial and error. One can ask, "Is this what you mean?" So the contextual and dialogical nature of spoken discourse functions as an effective filter for polysemy and significantly mitigates language's inherent ambiguity. Spoken discourse "partially succeeds in overcoming the non-communicability of experience."[64]

In fact, spoken language is so convincing that we must become analytical in order to isolate the underlying process that generates the strong illusion of the direct mediation of experience. Ricoeur argues that there is an intermediate step: in spoken discourse, the utterer's meaning (a private, psychological reality) becomes the utterance meaning (a public, linguistic reality) that is then appropriated by the hearer through interpretation. Ricoeur further clarifies that the meaning is externalized as *sense*. He speaks of "the ideal structure of the sense," an external, nonpsychological reality.[65] The speaker in a specific discourse situation uses this externalized sense to *refer* to something in the world.[66] Through spoken discourse a private experience comes to language. The referential event is transitory and contextual, but the "miracle" through which this referential feat is accomplished remains as an enduring, restatable, and even translatable public meaning.[67]

The motivation for pinpointing and highlighting the process whereby the speaker's private intention passes into the public realm as meaning is that this initial and subtle transformation anticipates the more remarkable transformation that occurs when discourse becomes fully realized and externalized as *text*. The difference between the speaker's intention and the meaning of the "said as such" which is present, but inchoate, in speech becomes much more

[64] Ricoeur, *Interpretation Theory*, 17. That the success is only partial can be confirmed by anyone who has experienced a genuine instance of the "failure to communicate." Sometimes conversations cannot be repaired because the participants are not aware that the conversation is broken.

[65] Ricoeur, *Interpretation Theory*, 20. This conceptualization of the sense as a nonpsychological reality is the contribution of structural theory.

[66] "To refer is what the sentence does in a certain situation and according to a certain use. It is also what the speaker does when he applies his words to reality." Ricoeur, *Interpretation Theory*, 20.

[67] "An act of discourse is not merely transitory and vanishing, however. It may be identified and reidentified as the same so that we may say it again or in other words. We may even say it in another language or translate it from one language into another. Through all these transformations it preserves an identity of its own which can be called the propositional content, the 'said as such.'" Ricoeur, *Interpretation Theory*, 9.

pronounced in the case of written discourse. As text, discourse becomes an enduring object with a destiny of meaning independent of its author's intentions. And as text, discourse takes on a new referential power qualitatively different from spoken discourse: the power to project a world. These claims will be explicated and developed in detail.

In the first place, while we may speak of the "objectification" of meaning in the event of spoken discourse, in the case of textual discourse meaning is literally objectified—borne by a physical object. Its physical manifestation perdures in history and so makes itself available across spans of time and space as the vehicle of a new meaning event. By the simple fact of its physicality, textual discourse transcends the contextual limits of the original discourse situation and makes its meaning available, at least potentially, to anyone who can read.[68]

When someone takes up a text and reads there is no dialogue partner, no assumed and pervasive shared situation of discourse. This can be clarified by considering that some genres function to *simulate* the shared situation of spoken discourse, adopting a mode of reference that feigns conversational ostensive reference "as if" the reader were alongside the author/speaker in a shared situation. Ricoeur lists several examples, among them letters, travel reports, geographical descriptions, and diaries.[69] Because this kind of text is so thoroughly integrated into our way of thinking, it may appear to *appeal to*, but rather should be recognized as actually *generating*, the idea that author and reader both belong to a shared spatiotemporal network greater than the particulars of a given situation. The reading contract implicit in such genres is this: "You are there and then as reader. I am here and now as author. But at least as regards certain relevant features of experience, let us agree that I can speak to you there and then, *as if* you were here and now because, let us say, we are both a part of one and the same larger world." It is precisely because author and reader do not share a situation that the useful "fiction" of a world becomes necessary and possible. This human capacity for living in an abstracted "world" and not just a series of concrete situations, Ricoeur attributes quite explicitly to textual power: "This first extension of the scope of reference beyond the narrow boundaries of the dialogical situation is of tremendous consequence. Thanks to writing, man and only man

[68] It is not piety, but a general theory of hermeneutics that motivates Ricoeur's insistence that "[t]he letters of Paul are no less addressed to me than to the Romans, the Galatians, the Corinthians, and the Ephesians." Ricoeur, *Interpretation Theory*, 93.

[69] Ricoeur, *Interpretation Theory*, 35.

has a world and not just a situation."[70] Note that, for the moment, we are analyzing only the expansion of referential power that corresponds to writing qua inscription, and for now only in the case of descriptive (i.e., nonpoetic) texts. The claim is that the experiential matrix of manipulable objects, states of affairs, and facts that spoken descriptive discourse gives us as "situation," written descriptive discourse expansively supplies to us as "world." This is an extraordinary transformation. It is all the more extraordinary because it achieves this referential augmentation through what is classically understood as a deficiency: the absence of the author. Ricoeur reverses the classical bias, which privileges speech as primary and relegates writing to derivative status. For Ricoeur, writing is discourse par excellence: "Only written language fully displays the criteria of discourse."[71]

But another transformation of discourse—another great leap in referential power—that comes through writing is not directly attributable to and assimilable with the brute fact of the text as marks on a page. This additional gain for written discourse corresponds not to inscription itself but to what writing as a medium of discourse robustly supports:

> [M]ost of the alterations of reference which will be considered are not to be ascribed to writing as such but to writing as the ordinary mediation of the modes of discourse which constitute literature. . . . Inscription, then, is only indirectly responsible for the new fate of reference.[72]

Inscribed language is the primary conduit in human culture for the development of language constructed as an extended "work" shaped according to the rules of genre.[73]

[70] Ricoeur, *Interpretation Theory*, 36. Though he does not employ Ricoeur's theory and categories, Jared Diamond provides a fascinating account of the difference between literate and preliterate civilizations, including the advantages that accrue to the former's ability to inhabit a world, rather than being limited to a situation. See "Collision at Cajamarca: Why the Inca Emperor Atahuallpa Did Not Capture King Charles I of Spain." Diamond, *Guns, Germs, and Steel: The Fates of Human Societies* (New York: Norton, 1997), 67–82.

[71] Ricoeur, *Interpretation Theory*, xi.

[72] Ricoeur, *Interpretation Theory*, 34.

[73] "Literary genres display some conditions which theoretically could be described without considering writing. The function of these generative devices is to produce new entities of language longer than the sentence, organic wholes irreducible to a mere addition of sentences. A poem, narrative, or essay relies on laws of composition which in principle are indifferent to the opposition between speaking and writing. They proceed from the application of dynamic forms to sets of sentences for which the difference between oral and written language is unessential. Instead, the specificity of these dynamic forms seems to proceed from another dichotomy than that of speaking and hearing, from the application to discourse of categories borrowed from another field, that of practice and work." Ricoeur, *Interpretation Theory*, 32.

Just as the laws of grammar supply a framework for constructing sentences, so literary genres supply a rule-based framework for crafting extended works. Ricoeur is highlighting a feature of literary production that is closely related to, but not coterminous with, writing as such: works of literature are not just *written*; they are *wrought*. That this "wrought-ness" is conceptually distinct from "written-ness" can be seen quite clearly by considering oral events that are produced in conformity to genre and share the essential features that Ricoeur is claiming for textual discourse:

> [W]e might even be tempted to say that even oral expressions of poetic or narrative composition rely on processes equivalent to writing. The memorization of epic poems, lyrical songs, parables and proverbs, and their ritual recitation tend to fix and even to freeze the form of the work in such a way that memory appears as the support of an inscription similar to that provided by external marks.[74]

So there is an important aspect of textual discourse that does not relate to writing as such but is closely associated with it because of the way inscription has robustly supported the production of discourse as a "work" of literature.

In exploring the implications of the poetic text as "work," it will be helpful briefly to revisit Ricoeur's theory of metaphor. We recall the discussion from *The Rule of Metaphor* about the semantic innovation and referential gain achieved by metaphor at the level of the sentence. For Ricoeur, language is always used as discourse, and discourse is unwavering in its determination to be *about* something. Or we may prefer to say that the pull of discourse in consciousness is toward reference. It is by suspending or frustrating ordinary sense and reference that metaphor provokes the resort to a "figurative" or second-order sense and reference. Metaphor refuses to signify and refer in the usual way, and so the resulting discursive crisis leads to (1) semantic innovation as new meaning emerges tensively through redescription and (2) a new and qualitatively different referential capacity as aspects of reality unavailable to normal descriptive discourse disclose themselves as they emerge to intercept discourse's determination to refer.

Ricoeur's insight in *Interpretation Theory* is that the process at work in metaphor that discovers new realities (reference) as it invents new meanings (sense) is "like an abridged version within a single sentence of the complex interplay of significations that characterize the literary work as a whole . . . [which] brings an explicit and an implicit meaning into relation."[75] The semantic logic of the literary text is analogous to that of metaphor. Whereas metaphorical

[74] Ricoeur, *Interpretation Theory*, 33.
[75] Ricoeur, *Interpretation Theory*, 46.

statements produce new meanings in the tension between the literal and the figurative sense of an impertinent predication, poetic texts are semantically productive in the tension between what a story (for example) explicitly says and the implicit significance it bears for a particular reader. Discreet metaphor creates new meaning through the tensive redescription of one thing in terms of another. Extended poetic texts create new meaning through the tensive redescription of the reader's possibilities in terms of the way of thinking made available in the text. Such is the analogy of sense.

Likewise, there is an analogy of reference. The mandate of discourse to refer is stated even more categorically when it is applied to lengthier literary works in *Interpretation Theory*: "My contention is that discourse cannot fail to be about something."[76] Because literary works, like metaphors, "cannot fail to be about something," and because, like metaphors, they refuse to be about something in the normal, descriptive way, something new must happen. The suspension of normal reference becomes the catalyst for opening up a new referential "space" in which the poetic text may carry out its referential agenda and so satisfy the discursive imperative.

The nature of this new "space" in which the poetic text achieves this referential feat is a function of both the poetic text qua inscribed object and the poetic text qua crafted work. The effect of the combination is synergistic, powerfully blending the ambiguity common to all reading with the bounty of new and customized meaning brought forth not just by the depth semantics of a single metaphorical statement but by the reader's complex interaction with an entire network of predications that function together according to the logic of metaphor. The result is that such texts display a world through which they may speak about the real in a fundamentally different way from descriptive discourse. "For me," says Ricoeur, "the world is the ensemble of references opened up by every kind of text . . . that I have read, understood and loved."[77] The reader who comes within the aura of this enlarged world embarks on a journey of discovery. "[W]hat we understand first in a discourse is . . . the outline of a new way of being in the world,"[78] or better, what the text offers should be "conceived in a dynamic way as the direction of thought opened up by the text."[79]

In summary, the remarkable referential feat achieved by the literary text is theorized in *Interpretation Theory* as an extension of the discursive function

[76] Ricoeur, *Interpretation Theory*, 36.
[77] Ricoeur, *Interpretation Theory*, 37.
[78] Ricoeur, *Interpretation Theory*, 37.
[79] Ricoeur, *Interpretation Theory*, 92.

of metaphor theorized in *The Rule of Metaphor*. It is a complex effect built upon two critical aspects of written discourse: (1) the physicality that allows it to transcend the dialogical situation and (2) its role as the conduit for the production of discourse as a work. Ricoeur seems to have something like the following schema in mind:

TABLE 3.1
Discursive Function of the Extended Poetic Text Compared to Metaphor

Discourse unit	Suspension of normal discursive function	Semantic innovation	Referential feat
Metaphorical statement	Bizarre predication suspends literal meaning and ordinary reference	New meaning emerges tensively through the redescription of one thing in terms of another	Grants linguistic access to dimensions of reality unavailable to ordinary descriptive discourse
Extended poetic text qua inscribed object	Decontextualization suspends access to speaker's intention as the arbiter of meaning and frustrates the ordinary reference suggested by belonging to a shared situation	Surplus of meaning emerges through the intensified ambiguity of the nondialogical event of reading	Organizes and extends linguistic access to dimension of reality unavailable to ordinary descriptive discourse through the display of a possible world and the proffer of a new way of being in the world
Extended poetic text qua crafted work	A network of predications with no obvious ostensive purchase on ordinary objects	Customized meaning produced through the tension between explicit sense of the text and its implicit significance for the reader	

Note that the second and third rows of the table are distinguished for the sake of theoretical clarity, but the total effect of poetic texts of all kinds when read cooperatively is to venture seamlessly all these semantic and referential achievements at a single stroke such that even in a schema that artificially atomizes a synthetic process, the referential feat of displaying an inhabitable world is best appreciated as a single outcome.

THE READER IN THE WORLD IN FRONT OF THE TEXT

The hermeneutical encounter that corresponds to reading, especially the reading of literary texts, is strikingly dissimilar to that which occurs in spoken discourse. Ricoeur describes the interpretation of a text as a dialectic in the reader between understanding and explanation. Generally, understanding is a way of orienting oneself toward what is humanly meaningful; we understand a motive, for example. Broadly speaking, explanation is a way of orienting oneself toward objects or natural events; we explain a lunar Eclipse. Texts, as we have seen, have both features, so they are properly engaged in both modes. But it is the discursive nature of the text that is finally decisive: hermeneutics begins and ends with understanding. Ricoeur speaks of a hermeneutical arc that flows from initial understanding, through explanatory procedures that refine this initial grasp of the whole by comparing it analytically to particular structural features of the text, toward a second, critically informed and refined understanding of the whole. Through the dialectic of understanding and explanation, the reader engages what is distant and appropriates it, makes it her own.

But the nature of the meaning that is understood and appropriated in this encounter is subtle and surprising. On the one hand, Ricoeur denies that the meaning of the text can be reduced to the circumstances of its original composition. Because he is so intently focused on offering an alternative to structuralism, historicism does not receive much consideration in Ricoeur's hermeneutics. Still, Ricoeur is aware that for certain historical critics, "[t]o explain a text . . . means primarily to consider it as the expression of certain socio-cultural needs and as a response to certain perplexities well localized in space and time."[80] Although he does not deny the historical interest of engaging texts in this way, he rejects the notion that textual meaning is somehow exhausted in terms of its "intelligibility from its connection to the social conditions of the community that produced it or to which it was destined."[81] For Ricoeur, historical critical considerations belong to a pre-hermeneutical phase—the philological procedures necessary initially to bring the text clearly into view. Historical expertise improves our competence as readers, but the understanding at stake in a hermeneutical encounter with a text from the past is not, primarily, an understanding about the past.

Neither, as we have seen, is it an author that the reader understands. As inscribed object, the text freely roams the world independent of its author's presence and supervision. The text is not a vessel for the storage and delivery of an author's psychological intentions but bears forward the objective meaning of the original discourse event, always ready to be activated in a new meaning event by any potential reader: "The sense of a text is not behind the

[80] Ricoeur, *Interpretation Theory*, 90.
[81] Ricoeur, *Interpretation Theory*, 90.

text, but in front of it. It is not something hidden, but something disclosed. What has to be understood is not the initial situation of discourse, but what points towards a possible world, thanks to the non-ostensive reference of the text."[82] The understanding at stake in reading is an understanding of the text, and not the author.

Finally and crucially, the understanding that emerges in the hermeneutical encounter is not simply an understanding of the reader, at least not in the sense of understanding better what she brings a priori to the text. For Ricoeur, texts have rights; there is an objective textual agenda that merits respect and cooperation. The cooperative reader acknowledges this textual itinerary of meaning when she agrees to "follow the 'arrow' of the sense" and "tries to think accordingly."[83]

This notion that the text pushes back with a reality of its own even as its meaning is appropriated subjectively is the crucial point in Ricoeur's interpretation theory.

> [By speaking of appropriation] are we not putting the meaning of the text under the power of the subject who interprets it? This objection may be removed if we keep in mind that what is "made one's own" is not something mental, not the intention of another subject, presumably hidden behind the text, but the project of a world, the pro-position of a mode of being in the world that the text opens up in front of itself by means of its non-ostensive references.[84]

It is not one's own meaning that is projected upon the text, but a new meaning projected by the text that is made one's own. "The reader . . . is enlarged in his capacity of self-projection by receiving a new mode of being from the text itself."[85] That new meaning is worked out in the space in front of the text. It is new because the text brings what the reader did not imagine as a possibility. It is one's own in the sense that it is the self that enters that space and interacts with the meaning made available there.

Ricoeur's account of the nonostensive referential power of metaphor, which he then develops into the generative notion of the textual world, shows how poetic texts have the potential to disclose aspects of reality that are beyond the reach of descriptive discourse, and yet do so without descending into sheer subjectivity. These claims have been examined in such detail because they provide a rich framework for thinking about how biblical discourse may fund the scandalous possibility of preaching as a word to the

[82] Ricoeur, *Interpretation Theory*, 87.
[83] Ricoeur, *Interpretation Theory*, 94.
[84] Ricoeur, *Interpretation Theory*, 94.
[85] Ricoeur, *Interpretation Theory*, 94.

human situation from beyond the human situation. Ricoeur supplies a general hermeneutical account that elucidates this possibility.

So, in summary, textual meaning is not the causal matrix that generated the text to begin with; it is not the psychological intention of the author; and it is not the latent meaning brought by the reader to be inscribed upon the text now demoted to mere pretext. Rather,

> [w]hat has to be appropriated is the meaning of the text itself, conceived in a dynamic way as the direction of thought opened up by the text. In other words, what has to be appropriated is nothing other than the power of disclosing a world that constitutes the reference of the text.[86]

To say that what the text offers is a "direction of thought" is to admit that, when fully appropriated, what such texts mean—what they are about—is in some sense the reader. Textual meaning is subjective in the sense that it is fully realized only in relation to a particular reading subject. But to claim that the text accomplishes this by "disclosing a world" is to insist that the new meanings the text invents and the new realities it thereby discovers have their own objective integrity, such that it is most accurate to speak of the text drawing the reader into the space it projects in front of itself. Read cooperatively, the destiny of the text is to offer to the reader an alternative world that is not of the reader. The reader enters the world in front of the text in order to encounter what is not yet the reader, but what the reader may yet become as the reader is made new in the light of that new world.

In the discussion of metaphor, we observed that abstract claims about the referential domain of discrete metaphorical statements are difficult to articulate apart from the appeal to specialized and highly abstracted existential philosophical categories. But when nonostensive poetic reference is carried out as a longer "work" arranged according to the conventions of genre, when it manifests its referential power as the display of a possible world, and when it is appropriated as a real and previously unavailable way of orienting the self toward reality, the phenomenology of reading implicit in Ricoeur's hermeneutical theory can be appreciated much more intuitively. To speak of a textual world is to name how immersive, immediate, and pervasive for the reader are the new options for being that open through an encounter with the language of the text.

Many readers who have seriously and sympathetically engaged a novel, to take a dramatic example, have an appreciation of Ricoeur's assertion that such a text makes a "world" available. The reader takes up the text and reads. The referential power of the sentences immediately stalls in relation to the

[86] Ricoeur, *Interpretation Theory*, 94.

ordinary spatiotemporal domain. The words on the page confidently assert that so-and-so does such and such, and yet the reader knows that nothing has changed: the same living room, the same reading lamp, the same glow from the neighbor's window, the same quiet of the night—all these features of experience continue to constitute the ostensive domain seemingly quite unperturbed by the bold predications of the text. And yet the ineluctable pull of discourse in consciousness is not only toward sense but also toward reference. The language of the story obviously has no purchase on the ostensive domain; another "space" must open up. As the reader follows the plot under the "vow of obedience," an alternative emerges. And now here is this undeniable insight, this palpable revulsion, this augmented awareness, this subtle subversion, this terror, awe, embarrassment, and fondness—a very real sense in which the reader is transported, shown something, enlarged, given access to a way of being that was not available or present apart from this encounter with this carefully crafted language. And having been shown this new world—Ricoeur has summarized its effect as "the shock of the possible"[87]—something is different. Even as the book closes and its projected world instantly gives sway in consciousness to the familiar ostensive domain, there is the powerful sense that something remains fundamentally changed for the reader—that she now enjoys new options in relation to the world of the reading lamp and the night sounds, and the neighbor across the street.

It is this phenomenology of reading that applies not only to narrative but also to any genre, literary or otherwise, which leads Ricoeur to assert, "For me, the world is the ensemble of references opened up by every kind of text, descriptive or poetic, that I have read, understood and loved."[88]

The narrative biblical hermeneutics of Hans Frei and the general hermeneutics of Paul Ricoeur are now in view. Already, it would be possible to venture some provisional responses to the problems of poetics, context, and reference that surfaced in Campbell's homiletical appropriation of Frei's work. But in order to bring Ricoeur's thought into more productive conversation with Frei for the ultimate purpose of revising postliberal homiletics, two more steps need to be taken. First, Ricoeur's general hermeneutics will be related to the special case of biblical discourse. Second, Ricoeur's approach to narrative texts in particular will be explored in detail. With these tasks accomplished, it will be possible to facilitate a more symmetrical conversation between these theorists and appreciate the benefits for homiletical theory.

[87] Paul Ricoeur, *Time and Narrative*, vol. 1, trans. Kathleen McLaughlin and David Pellauer (Chicago: University of Chicago Press, 1984), 79.

[88] Ricoeur, *Interpretation Theory*, 37.

Chapter Four

A Ricoeurian Revision of Postliberal Homiletics

Ricoeur's hermeneutical project is able to redress a number of problems that surface when Frei's approach is applied to preaching. Toward this end, Ricoeur's hermeneutics must first be developed in relation to both biblical discourse generally and narrative in particular.

Paul Ricoeur on Biblical Discourse

Ricoeur's account of the nature of the biblical text is subtle and rich. Of course, strictly speaking, the Bible is more than one text. A key feature of Ricoeur's approach to scripture is his insistence that the Bible's several genres be appreciated as diverse in both what they say and how they say it. Each mode of biblical discourse must be allowed to speak on its own terms. Nevertheless, it is important to understand how Ricoeur characterizes biblical discourse in general.

Biblical Discourse as Poetic Discourse

The previous chapter supplied a detailed account of the semantic and referential capacities of the broad class of discourse Ricoeur describes as "poetic." The qualifier "poetic" is not intended to designate a specific genre, nor does it necessarily correspond to stylistic features like rhyme or meter. For Ricoeur, to say that a discourse is poetic is to contrast it with descriptive discourse that refers to manipulable objects in the everyday world. In fact, poetic discourse is a use of language calculated to frustrate the ordinary discursive function of referring to and making claims about the objects of experience to which we oppose ourselves as subjects. This frustration or suspension of the ordinary discursive function is the precondition for opening discourse to another referential domain corresponding to a depth dimension of reality. Ricoeur's claim is that poetic discourse is a "more originary" use of language in the sense that it names qualities of our experience of reality that precede the subject-object distinction. Before we oppose ourselves to objects as a subject, we are rooted in the world and know it as one belonging to it. Poetic discourse gives voice to our experience of realities that slip through the filter of the assumptions that govern descriptive discourse—that is, discourse founded upon a presumptuous bid to "grasp" definitively all of reality as an object under the gaze and for the use of a sovereign subject.

According to Ricoeur, the Bible is poetry in this sense: "I do assume provisionally the assimilation of biblical texts to poetic texts."[1] With important provisos still to be stipulated, the Bible is a member of the class of "poetic" texts.

Ricoeur is even willing to speak of "revelation" as a *general* capacity of poetic texts. "[P]oetic discourse conceals a dimension of revelation in a nonreligious, nontheistic, nonbiblical sense of the word, yet a sense capable of furnishing a first approximation of what revelation in the biblical sense may signify."[2] At least as a "first approximation," the works of William Shakespeare or Alice Walker can be read as revelatory in the sense that these works powerfully tap into—both reveal and ratify—a depth dimension of human existence. According to Ricoeur, there is a fundamental kinship between what Christians mean by revelation with respect to the Bible, and the way all great works of literature open our eyes to an otherwise hidden drama, namely, that "in spite of the closed-off character of our ordinary experience, and across the ruins of the intrawordly objects of everyday reality and science, the modalities of our belonging to the world trace out their way."[3]

[1] Ricoeur, "Naming God," 221.

[2] Ricoeur, "Naming God," 222.

[3] Ricoeur, "Naming God," 223. Ricoeur's sympathy with poetic discourse generally and his sense of its struggle for validity in the wake of modernity are apparent in the wistfulness of this semipoetic phrasing. It is as if the fragile "tracings" of our depth dimension haunt like disembodied spirits the "ruins" of the closed, prosaic world delineated by our preoccupation with manipulable objects.

Ricoeur is treading dangerously close to the position that the Bible is reducible without remainder to great literature. If this is what he means, his hermeneutical project is transparently another case of what Barth disparaged as the futility of attempting to speak of God by speaking of humanity in a loud voice. Here again we come to the crux of the matter, the question of whether the call we hear in scripture is merely our own voice echoing back to us across the ruins of a deep and mysterious but godless world. Beneath all this talk of poetic disclosures and our rootedness in the world, is Ricoeur essentially saying that we are on our own to make the best sense we can of our lives? He is not.

Rather, as a philosopher who wishes to take Christian claims seriously about the Bible mediating a word from beyond the human situation, Ricoeur is searching for a way to *think more* about this idea of the Bible mediating revelation in the theistic sense. He finds a way to do so by noticing connections to certain extrabiblical uses of language that approximate this function of disclosing what is otherwise hidden from us. But exploring this connection does not necessarily commit Ricoeur to the position that the Christian idea of revelation can be explained (in the reductive sense of the word) by a theory of poetic discourse. Nor does Ricoeur insist that biblical hermeneutics should be understood simply as the regional application of a general theory of poetic discourse.[4] Nor does his approach assume (as Frei clearly feared that it did) that *what* biblical discourse refers to can be predecided in the abstract through appeal to a general theory apart from careful consideration of the Bible's particular message. Rather, in light of Ricoeur's willingness to position himself sympathetically and even obediently as a "listener" and so to take Christian claims about the Bible seriously, the assumptions and motivations behind his discussion of poetic discourse in relation to biblical discourse should be characterized in the following way: if biblical discourse really is revelatory in the theistic Christian sense of bearing an address to us from beyond ourselves and confronting us with ultimate realities that we cannot discover for ourselves, we should not be surprised to find in extrabiblical discourse analogical traces of this same capacity of language, and we should not be surprised if a hermeneutical theory that is illuminating in one of these cases should also prove illuminating for the other.

[4] I understand his method as a kind of oscillation that prioritizes first one and then the other, but he is clear that "[t]heological hermeneutics presents qualities so original that the relation progressively reverses itself, theological hermeneutics finally subordinating philosophical hermeneutics as its own *organon*." Paul Ricoeur, "Philosophical Hermeneutics and Biblical Hermeneutics," in *From Text to Action* (Evanston, Ill.: Northwestern University Press, 2007), 90.

In just this spirit, Ricoeur speaks of a "resonance" (rather than equivalence) between the way poetic discourse discloses hidden aspects of reality and the way biblical discourse reveals its subject matter.[5] Poetic discourse achieves a remarkable referential feat. At the intersection of the discursive augmentations corresponding to both inscription and the crafting of an extended work that functions according to the logic of metaphor, there is a surprising synergy that places before the cooperative reader the issue of the transcendent textual world. In this "space," a space liberated from both the tyranny of the subject-object distinction operative in the ostensive domain and the constraints of the author's and first readers' psychological agendas, the reader is invited to move and explore new possibilities—to encounter what is more than the self and to risk becoming a new self. Granting acceptance of a radical redefinition of what counts as real, we may say that poetic discourse has the capacity to disclose something more about the real world than we can see and know on our own.[6]

This capacity for disclosing new and previously unavailable dimensions of reality is the feature of poetic discourse that "resonates" with and even offers a "first approximation" to what Christians claim about revelation and the Bible. For Ricoeur, it is no accident that the Christian tradition looks to a text to mediate extraordinary disclosures about God. For it is precisely as text, and as a poetic text in particular, that discourse establishes the necessary, but not sufficient, conditions for accomplishing what Christians claim the Bible does. By saying this, Ricoeur does not reductively assert that the Bible refers to the same thing other poetic texts point toward. Indeed, it is in light of what he rightly calls the Bible's "eccentric" subject matter that Ricoeur's discussion of biblical discourse begins to detour significantly from his general treatment of poetic texts.[7] But this initial recognition of a kinship is very important because it supplies an approximation of how the Bible refers. One particularly significant implication is the insight that biblical truth is not propositional: "Revelation, if the expression is meaningful, is a trait of the biblical *world*."[8]

[5] Paul Ricoeur, "Toward a Hermeneutic of the Idea of Revelation," in *Essays on Biblical Interpretation*, ed. Lewis Seymour Mudge (Philadelphia: Fortress, 1980), 102.

[6] Ricoeur is challenging the regnant modern epistemology that limits truth claims to propositions that can be verified in the sense of corresponding adequately to objects. To this way of knowing by "verification" he opposes the possibility for a knowing through "manifestation," through "letting what shows itself be." Ricoeur, "Toward a Hermeneutic of the Idea of Revelation."

[7] "But religious language is not simply poetic. Or, if one prefers, it is so in a specific manner that makes the particular case a unique one, an eccentric one. What differentiates it is precisely the naming of God." Ricoeur, "Naming God," 232.

[8] Ricoeur, "Philosophy and Religious Language," 44 (emphasis in original).

The Bible does not reveal by means of a series of verifiably true statements about objects in our given world. It is the inhabitable world displayed by the total effect of the biblical text as an extended work that mediates revelation. Therein lies the resonance between the Bible and poetic discourse generally.

On the other hand, biblical discourse is distinctive, and the difference begins with its audacious bid to speak about God. The several biblical genres (narrative, prophecy, wisdom, hymn, parable) are like the intermeshing gears of a machine—each contributing uniquely to a combined motion of thought that attempts to "name God."[9] This is Ricoeur's somewhat awkward attempt to coin an alternative to the traditional language of biblical "inspiration." He argues convincingly that the traditionally dominant notion of revelation as the divine voice behind the biblical author's voice is a distortion that allows one biblical mode (prophecy) to set the terms for all thinking about how biblical discourse is revelatory. "Naming God" may seem to privilege human agency, but it will be recalled that for Ricoeur it is a text that speaks to a reader, not an author. Ricoeur acknowledges the diverse and mysterious ways in which "God is designated . . . as the one who communicates through the multiple modalities of discourse."[10]

Of course, in an important sense, no discourse can really presume definitively to name God. Ricoeur points to the story of Moses' encounter with God in the burning bush (Exodus 3) as a narration of the limits of narrative in this regard. God, even when depicted as a character in a narrative, cannot be definitively located and named. Or rather, "[T]his name [YHWH] is precisely unnameable. To the extent that to know a god's name was to have power over that god, the name confided to Moses is certainly that of a being whom humanity cannot really name, that is, hold at the mercy of our language."[11] God is not grasped or made available for our inspection and use by the Bible. Even biblical narrative with its bold bid to trace God's movements amid the contingencies of human history acknowledges this limit: God is disclosed through story as hidden and untamable. In these texts we are encountered by the One we cannot name, summon, or control.

For even if God is, broadly speaking, the referent of biblical discourse, as a form of poetic discourse the Bible does not achieve its discursive goals by making true statements about objects, least of all a supernatural object called "God." And this feature of poetic discourse is theologically fitting, for

[9] Ricoeur, "Naming God," 228. For the image of biblical discourse's several genres as a network of intermeshed gears, see Wallace, *Second Naiveté,* 36.

[10] Ricoeur, "Naming God," 228.

[11] Ricoeur, "Naming God," 228.

the living God is not another manipulable object in the world.[12] The idea of poetic discourse as revelation in a theistic sense means that God, a beckoning but uncontrollable presence lingering just beyond the horizon of all the Bible's significations, encounters and transforms us through the world scripture displays—a world that Ricoeur has not hesitated to identify as "the Kingdom of God."[13]

History, Testimony, and "Letting Go"

But if there is a basic fit between Ricoeur's account of poetic discourse and the Bible's bid to speak of God in God's transcendence and mystery, there is also something about Christianity and the Bible itself that stands in tension with a hermeneutic that speaks only of a "textual world." An interpretation theory that collapses concern to a textual world alone (i.e., to the categorical exclusion of any concern for what happened "behind" the text) does not really engage the nature of scripture itself and the long history of its reception. Ricoeur's textual hermeneutics may insist that textual meaning and reference break completely free of the context that generated the text, but Christians claim that scripture witnesses to the truth that the transcendent and hidden God who is no object in the world has nevertheless encountered us within history. This God is revealed within history as the God of Abraham, Isaac, and Jacob. Indeed, this God has come near to us in the person of Jesus. An explicitly incarnational theology cannot entrust itself to an account of biblical discourse that builds its poetic meanings and referents exclusively upon the ruins of ordinary meaning and reference.

Ricoeur, too, senses the disparity. He understands what Christianity has at stake in its claim to encounter the absolute in "individual events and particular texts that report them."[14] When it comes to the Bible, to speak only of

[12] This is comparable to Frei's misgivings about talk of the supernatural being a "gigantic, enormously portentous way of saying 'natural.'" God is not an object, not even a "super"-object in relation to which we may oppose ourselves as gazing subjects.

[13] With this assertion, Ricoeur gestures toward the scandal of particularity precipitated by a serious engagement with Christian claims about the Bible. He concedes that no theory of poetic discourse can claim to decide the matter of what the Bible is "about" in the abstract. The mode of the Bible's significations may be elucidated by a theory of poetic reference, but the true issue of the biblical text—the world it proposes and the new options it proffers to its cooperative readers—are as distinctive and particular as this phrase from its narrative tradition. Finally only the Bible can show us what it is about, namely, "the realities unfolded before the text, which are certainly for us, but which begin from the text." Ricoeur, "Philosophy and Religious Language," 44.

[14] Ricoeur, "Naming God," 217.

symbols and metaphors, to speak only of poetic reference achieved through the subversion of reference to the world of everyday experience, to speak, in other words, exclusively of a *textual* world that is poetically rendered is to forfeit the "historic density" of what the Bible claims and what Christians believe.[15] No doubt the Bible is a kind of poem, but it is a poem that places itself under the constraint of a debt to an encounter with the absolute that has taken place in the midst of the contingencies of a particular place, time, and people. It is poetry that speaks not in perfect creative freedom about what is possible but rather under an obligation to a particular vision of the possible it has received in history. The world displayed by this text is forged under and by means of an obligation to a reality that precedes it. This is why so much of the Bible's poetry takes the form of a narrative art: "God's imprint is in history before being in speech."[16]

This is a scandal. Few notions are more compelling for the philosopher than the intuitive conviction that absolute truth must not depend upon what is contingent. Ricoeur quotes Jean Nabert (*L'Essai sur le mal*): "Does one have the right to invest with an absolute character a moment in history?"[17] For this reason, the temptation is very great to assume that insofar as the Bible discloses truth, it does so only by appeal and in relation to what is most universal and abstract in human experience. Whatever the community claims about the Bible's origins and warrants, the philosopher suspects that any essential truth it discloses could not truly depend upon anything so accidental as a wandering Aramean or a Nazarean with no place to lay his head. It is clear that Ricoeur himself feels the influence of this deeply ingrained philosophical predilection.[18]

He is, nevertheless, determined to resist the temptation. He wants to draw near to the Bible and its peculiar claims so that he may think more about it. And he insists that such a project is not a *sacrificium intellectus*, for it is precisely the philosopher in Ricoeur that seeks to do what is necessary in order that it may really be the Bible and its claims that he is thinking about. Partly because of the nature of texts in general, but also and especially because of the extraordinary claims of this particular text, this calls for listening. And

[15] Ricoeur, "Toward a Hermeneutic of the Idea of Revelation," 122.

[16] Ricoeur, "Naming God," 225.

[17] Quoted in Paul Ricoeur, "The Hermeneutics of Testimony," in Mudge, *Essays on Biblical Interpretation*, 122.

[18] For Ricoeur the existentialist, the pull toward what is most universal and encompassing takes a predictable form. Of all the possibilities for wrangling the Bible and its message to the more respectable side of Lessing's ditch, Ricoeur admits that "the amalgamation of being and God is the most subtle seduction." Ricoeur, "Naming God," 223.

this listening comes at a shocking cost: "[F]or the philosopher, to listen to Christian preaching is first of all to let go (*se dépouiller*)."[19]

The first thing that must be relinquished is the feigned sovereignty of the self as an autonomous, rational, unsituated knower—master of all that falls under its dispassionate gaze. But Ricoeur's "letting go" is a more radical self-divestment even than the one philosophy has already attempted by its own resources and on its own terms. Kant perfectly understood and exposed the limits of autonomous reason and the self-deception of the speculative bid to grasp God as an object. But "if a first hubris is knocked down, that of metaphysical knowledge, a second one replaces it. . . . This knowledge does not stand on the side of objects to be known but on the side of the conditions of possibility of knowing."[20] The Kantian turn to preoccupation with the transcendental categories of the human mind shatters the foundationalism of objects only to then make the self-positing subject "the foundation that founds itself, in relation to which every rule of validity is derived."[21]

By contrast, what Ricoeur undertakes in order to think more about the Bible is an even more radical self-divestment, for his is a double renunciation: a letting go of both the absolute object and the absolute subject. To listen is to admit that truth may come to the self from beyond both the self's grasping after objects and the false humility of the self's sophisticated project of delineating the limits of what it can know. The philosopher risks listening in the hope of thinking more. But true listening always begins as an act of selflessness: "*Listening excludes founding oneself.* The movement toward listening requires . . . giving up (*dessaisissement*) the human self in its will to mastery, sufficiency, and autonomy."[22] Because the Bible speaks about that which, if true, cannot be grasped by human striving alone, the only path is to let go and trust "contingent signs of the absolute which the absolute in its generosity allows to appear."[23]

The category Ricoeur deploys to capture what is at stake in this "letting go" to the possibility that the absolute has disclosed itself in the textual tradition of a particular community is *testimony*. The Bible's claim to reveal God must be approached as "extraordinarily fragile testimony."[24] The testimony

[19] Ricoeur, "Naming God," 223.

[20] Ricoeur, "Naming God," 223–24.

[21] Ricoeur, "Naming God," 224.

[22] Ricoeur, "Naming God," 224 (emphasis in original).

[23] Ricoeur, "Toward a Hermeneutic of the Idea of Revelation," 111.

[24] Paul Ricoeur, Charles E. Reagan, and David Stewart, "The Critique of Religion," in *The Philosophy of Paul Ricoeur: An Anthology of His Work* (Boston: Beacon, 1978), 219. The quote continues, "There is no proof which can support either the experience or the rationale. In this sense, the Cross *remains* a folly for the intelligent, a scandal for the wise."

is fragile because it attests to so much of such consequence. It is "extraordinarily" fragile because of the devastating possibility of "a lie in the heart of the witness," whether in the form of an explicit betrayal or, given the nature of the case, the very real possibility of the self-deception of idolatry.[25] This is Ricoeur's philosophical wager: not that the philosopher must stop thinking or unconditionally trust all that is said, but that in order to think about this matter, in order to test it, the philosopher must begin by thinking along with what is attested, but unproven. Ricoeur's willingness to "let go" and take seriously the Bible's claim to offer *testimony* to a scandal of particularity transforms his biblical hermeneutics. By this leap he honors the "historic density" of the Bible—that feature that so vigorously resists a hermeneutic that stops at the shores of a merely textual world.

On the other hand, it is vital to qualify this appeal to testimony carefully so as to locate it convincingly within Ricoeur's hermeneutical project. In the first place, it is significant that even in its original actualization as an event of discourse, testimony does not supply raw sense data: "What is a true witness, a faithful witness? Everyone understands that this is something other than an exact, even scrupulous narrator."[26] Even before the transition to inscription, testimony is more than the lending of one's eyes through language. From the very beginning it is at a remove from past happenings in the sense that it is the attestation to a judgment. What is given in testimony is not the thing itself, not even someone's experience of the thing, but a construal of an experience. So there is already a trajectory toward externalization in the sense of interpretation and "making sense" even prior to the passage from spoken to written testimony. Testimony is hermeneutical even before it is textual.

Second, if this testimony was already on a path toward externalization as an interpretation even in its first articulation, as textual witness it is now completely transformed into an objective meaning both wrought and inscribed. Quite apart from the testifier, this testimony now enjoys its own independent career as a text. What began in speech as a constructed interpretation passes on that same trajectory into a textual object that can be reactualized in a new context. Like all discourse, testimony is "actualized as event" but "understood as meaning." Talk of biblical discourse as testimony is not a return to authorial intention as the safeguard of textual meaning. It is still precisely as a text that this testimony is given, and it is still a textual world that bears this testimony forward in the act of reading.

[25] Ricoeur, "Hermeneutics of Testimony," 128.

[26] Ricoeur, "Hermeneutics of Testimony," 129.

With these two qualities of biblical testimony in mind, we can say that without losing its essential character as a meaning forged under a debt to extratextual reality, the original attestation is shaped into language under the constraints and potencies of genre and so passes from the situation of the original testifier into the realm of all possible readers. Testimony becomes a testament.

So it remains true that, even as testimony, the Bible, like any text, offers only a textual world. And it remains true that the Bible's diverse genres are closer to poetic than scientific or descriptive discourse. But, thought through the category of testimony, the Bible's poetry, the world it imagines and displays, is best understood as a testament to an encounter with the real that precedes it. "Testimony, each time singular, confers the sanction of reality on ideas, ideals, and modes of being that the symbol depicts and discovers for us only as our most personal possibilities."[27]

As poetic testimony, biblical discourse must be understood dialectically. The testimony the Bible gives is poetic because it attempts to bear witness to a profoundly elusive and mysterious referent—a referent that is not merely an object that can be thought like other objects. But the Bible's poetic discourse is a testament because it attests that this elusive referent that stands just beyond the horizon of all the Bible's significations has graciously given signs of itself in history. In this way, testimony "introduces the dimension of historical contingency which is lacking in the concept of the world of the text," a world that is otherwise "deliberately nonhistorical or transhistorical."[28] At this intersection between the power of poetry to name what cannot be grasped as an object, and testimony with its debt to the real, the Bible stands in its notoriously complex relation to our categories of fiction and history.

Ricoeur on Narrative

The last feature of Ricoeur's hermeneutics that needs to be in view in order to negotiate a symmetrical conversation between his project and that of Hans Frei is his theory of narrative. In one sense, this transition pulls us back from the special case of biblical discourse and returns us to Ricoeur's general hermeneutics: *Time and Narrative*, Ricoeur's influential three-volume treatment of the subject, is not explicitly oriented toward biblical interpretation. But his theory of narrative is of paramount interest for Ricoeur's biblical hermeneutics because of the genre's centrality in scripture: "The whole of contemporary

[27] Ricoeur, "Hermeneutics of Testimony," 122.

[28] Ricoeur, "Toward a Hermeneutic of the Idea of Revelation," 109.

exegesis has made us attentive to the primacy of the narrative structure in the biblical writings." For while "God's imprint is in history before being in speech" so that "[s]peech comes second inasmuch as it confesses the trace of God in the event,"[29] it is nevertheless true that in scripture the realities that precede speech come to language as story. It is primarily through narrative that the Bible makes its "extraordinarily fragile testimony." And it is Ricoeur's narrative theory that will prove most generative in terms of a homiletical proposal indebted to his hermeneutics. In his treatment of narrative, we get a glimpse at the inner workings of biblical discourse, a way to think with some precision about how poetic testimony does its work on the preacher who reads the Bible in the hope of hearing a call that authorizes her to speak and gives her something to say.

For Ricoeur, the Aristotelian concept of *mimesis* (not slavish "imitation," but rather the representation of human action in time through emplotment) is the universal poetic activity through which humans struggle to make sense of their temporal existence. Or, as he says repeatedly in *Time and Narrative*, time becomes "human time" (as opposed to phenomenological time, or cosmological time) to the extent that it is narrated; conversely, narrative is meaningful only insofar as it portrays or gives shape to temporal human experience.[30]

Ricoeur begins with an analysis of Augustine's ruminations in book 11 of the *Confessions*, wherein he seeks to make sense of the riddle of time.[31] Aporias blossom as the elusive concept is pondered. Time becomes a problem precisely for reflection. Augustine admits in astonishment that he seems to know all about it until he begins to try to think about it with precision.[32] When we stop using the concept of time in ordinary speech and reflect upon it directly, we come quickly to a surprising impasse: time seems to have no ontological status. The past no longer exists; the future is not yet; the present, upon reflection, collapses to a vanishing point. On the razor-thin, even dimensionless ledge of the present, all direct human experience of the world is perilously perched.

But through a series of ingenious reflections on ordinary language and temporal experience, Augustine proposes that time does exist after all—it

[29] Ricoeur, "Naming God," 224–25.

[30] Ricoeur, *Time and Narrative*, 1:3.

[31] The following discussion corresponds to chapter 1, "The Aporias of the Experience of Time: Book 11 of *Augustine's Confessions*." Ricoeur, *Time and Narrative*, 5–30.

[32] "What then is time? I know well enough what it is, provided that nobody asks me; but if I am asked what it is and try to explain, I am baffled." Ricoeur's translation, quoted in Ricoeur, *Time and Narrative*, xi.

exists as a stretching of the mind (*distentio animi*). Within the human soul the duration of one sound can be retained as an imprint in memory and so compared to a subsequent sound. The mind anticipates a verse before reciting it and then progressively relegates its lines to the past as they pass through the performed attention of the present. In short, Augustine locates time phenomenologically. It is within the human mind's capacity to anticipate, attend, and remember in the present moment of consciousness that Augustine situates the being and extension of time.

But this speculative "solution" highlights an existential paradox. The soul finds that even as it actively attempts to orient and center itself in relation to temporal existence, it can do so only by dividing itself between future and past. Indeed, in contrast to God's eternal present, the soul in time is not only stretched, but stretched thin—at turns "torn asunder" and distracted, burdened by worries for an uncertain future and memories of a chaotic past.[33] Through his exegesis of Augustine, Ricoeur depicts temporal existence apart from an organizing narrative as a kind of mute terror and inarticulate lamentation.[34] Upon reflection, one aporia transforms into a deeper and more troubling aporia.

It is to this "aporetics of time" that Ricoeur correlates Aristotle's *mimesis* as the "poetic solution."[35] *Mimesis* is the operation through which the poet gathers up the discordance of temporal experience into the concordance of a plot (*muthos*). A plot is the careful selection and configuration of events into a meaningful whole. Through mimetic activity, the raw material of brute

[33] "*Distentio animi* no longer provides just the 'solution' to the aporia of the measurement of time. It now expresses the way in which the soul, deprived of the stillness of the eternal present, is torn asunder: [quoting *Conf.* 29:39] 'But to win your favor is dearer than life itself. I see now that my life has been wasted in distractions [*distentio est vita mea*].'" Ricoeur, *Time and Narrative*, 27.

[34] As Ricoeur's argument is unfolded, it will become clear why we rarely experience our own being in time as profoundly disorienting. In short, our time is already at least tentatively structured by story. The terror of mute temporal existence apart from story belongs to a prearticulate primeval past. "[W]e are not born into a world of children, but . . . as unspeaking children, we come into a world already full of all our predecessors' narratives." Paul Ricoeur, "Narrative Identity," in *On Paul Ricoeur: Narrative and Interpretation*, ed. David Wood (London: Routledge, 1991), 182. Perhaps only in moments when our story of ourselves is most profoundly called into question by discordant experience do we catch a hint of the vertigo of radically unstoried temporality. Speculatively, this may be what we mean when we speak of having an acute memory of where we were and what we were doing in the moment of receiving world-altering news—such moments may be phenomenologically intense because they throw us suddenly into a situation that has not yet been convincingly narrated.

[35] This discussion corresponds to chapter 2, "Emplotment: A Reading of Aristotle's *Poetics*." Ricoeur, *Time and Narrative*, 31–51.

sequential experience is fashioned into a followable arrangement that moves from a designated beginning, through a middle, and toward a definite and significant ending.

Through *mimesis*, episodic succession gives way to causal configuration. In this way, the poet achieves the representation of human action in the medium of language. In the *Poetics*, Aristotle develops the theory of *mimesis* as emplotment in relation to tragic poetry specifically, but Ricoeur appropriates the *mimesis/muthos* pair as the universal, transcultural narrative rejoinder to the aporias of temporal existence.[36] A soul torn asunder, driven to distraction and confusion by the divided attention of temporality, finds reprieve in narrative's capacity to present a confusing array of experience under the relatively orderly and graspable sense-making unity of a plot.

Threefold Mimesis

In order to develop and extend this Aristotelian notion, Ricoeur divides mimetic activity into three parts or moments, which he designates mimesis_1, mimesis_2, and mimesis_3. Each of these aspects of the representation of human existence in time needs to be considered in detail.

Mimesis_1 points to the way all narrative is built upon pervasive assumptions that make narration possible. We are always already thrown into the midst of shared conceptual strategies for imagining human action (e.g.,

[36] Galen Strawson has published a widely read critique of narrative identity in which he vigorously objects to this kind of sweeping claim about narrative sensibility as a fundamental structure of all existence identifiable as human. Strawson argues that narrative is not a feature of his own self-understanding, nor that of many others like him whom he identifies as "episodics." He asserts that he has no self-consistent "I" to author and narrate such a story, no diachronic "I" to be its protagonist. He has instead an episodic "I*," a pronoun he has coined to designate his sense of self in the immediacy of each new present. Strawson disputes what he terms the "Psychological Narrativity Thesis" (the descriptive assertion that story is in fact how humans make sense of themselves in time) but saves his most scathing and polemical critique for the "Ethical Narrativity Thesis" (the prescriptive assertion that self-narrated identity is a good thing), which he specifically associates with religion and which he disparages as encouraging a tendency toward revisionist remembering and an exaggerated sense of the significance of one's own life. Strawson, "Against Narrativity," *Ratio* 17, no. 4 (2004): 428–52. In addition to Ricoeur, Strawson has a broad array of narrative theorists in view with this critique. See, among others, Johann Baptist Metz, "A Short Apology of Narrative," in *Why Narrative? Readings in Narrative Theology*, ed. Stanley Hauerwas and L. Gregory Jones (Grand Rapids: Eerdmans, 1989), 251–62; Alasdair C. MacIntyre, *After Virtue: A Study in Moral Theory* (Notre Dame, Ind.: University of Notre Dame Press, 1981); and Stephen Crites, "The Narrative Quality of Experience," in Hauerwas and Jones, *Why Narrative?*. The most concise explication of Ricoeur's views on narrative identity can be found in an essay titled "Personal Identity and Narrative Identity" in Ricoeur, *Oneself as Another*, 113–68.

"agent," "motive," "goal"), including its symbolic representation and standards for its ethical evaluation.[37] In other words, mimesis_1 names a basic assumed competence in the categories of practice, an ability to recognize and navigate the practical field, which can be imagined as a network of interrelated answers to questions of "what," "why," "who," "how," "with whom," "against whom," and so on.[38] This is the conceptual apparatus that permits us to distinguish human action from mere movement. The poetic representation of human action begins with, works within, and builds upon such given cultural codes for recognizing, organizing, and evaluating human action. Mimesis_1 is Ricoeur's acknowledgment that every experience worthy of the designation "human" has already and necessarily been *prefigured* within a framework that renders it patient of narration.[39]

Homiletician Thomas Long elaborates this Ricoeurian notion, describing our sense of our everyday lives as fragmented but suggestive almost-stories:

> But even though life at the level of *mimesis*$_1$ is a cluster of shards and fragments, nevertheless all of the ingredients for a narrative are in place. . . . There are actors, there is action, and there are motives, partial and fragmented though they may be. This is *mimesis*$_1$—a narrative lurking beneath the rippled surface, a narrative ready to happen.[40]

Mimesis_1 means that we come to every narrative with a readiness to see our own lives as a story, indeed with some vague sense of our lives as already an inchoate narrative.[41] We are searching for the plot.

Mimesis_2 is the domain of the poetic work proper; it designates the characteristics of a narrative text as a composition.[42] Mimesis_2 is explicitly

[37] "[T]he practical understanding authors share with their audiences necessarily involves an evaluation of the characters and their actions in terms of good and bad. There is no action that does not give rise to approbation or reprobation, to however small a degree, as a function of a hierarchy of values for which goodness and wickedness are the poles." Ricoeur, *Time and Narrative*, 59.

[38] Ricoeur, *Time and Narrative*, 55.

[39] This is very close to what Stephen Crites has called "the narrative quality of experience." Crites, "Narrative Quality of Experience," 65.

[40] Long, *Preaching from Memory to Hope*, 46.

[41] For Ricoeur's discussion of "the prenarrative quality of experience," and for our lives as "(as yet) untold" stories that "need and merit being narrated," see Ricoeur, *Time and Narrative*, 74–75.

[42] Ricoeur refuses to assimilate mimesis_2 to the term *fiction*. While he does acknowledge the difference between the truth claims of "history" and those made by "fiction," he wants to problematize an overly simple opposition between these two ways of categorizing texts. For Ricoeur, historiography is also a mimetic activity that achieves its effects through emplotment.

an operation. It is not simply the mimicking of human action but the creative reworking of incidents into an intelligible whole in accordance with the logic of a rule-governed imagination. Drawing on the Kantian notion of a productive imagination that "grasps together" a broad manifold of stimuli ("intuitions") under the unity of a concept, Ricoeur speaks of emplotment as an activity that brings an array of sequential incidents under the unity of a plot.[43] The "one thing after another" of a raw episodic sequence becomes a plot through a number of devices including (1) the selection of events, (2) their arrangement and discursive expansion so as to achieve the more or less subtle attribution of cause and effect relationships between various features of the sequence, and especially (3) the demarcation of a beginning, middle, and ending, thereby supplying the governing framework within which all of the plot's incidents must be appreciated as belonging to an intelligible whole.[44]

Even the discordance of chance and unintended consequence can be named—its threat accounted for and perhaps even purged—within the larger arc of the plot's concordance. There is a kind of tribute paid by the plot to the discordance brought about when raw experience refuses to yield easily to our desire to make sense of our temporal existence. This leads Ricoeur to characterize the constructed plot as a "discordant concordance." That which resists assimilation is acknowledged, and, precisely by means of that acknowledgment, drawn into the sweep of the plot's concordance.

Ricoeur's explication of the inner workings of metaphor has been explored in relation to extended poetic works generally. Mimesis$_2$ is Ricoeur's way of designating how the logic of metaphor (the basic building block of all poetic discourse) works itself out in the specific case of narrative discourse. Metaphor grasps together two different things through an impertinent predication and sets in motion a "semantic innovation" by means of redescribing one thing tensively in terms of another. Narrative grasps together heterogeneous incidents under the sign of a plot and invites the reader to redescribe the temporal field in a novel way in light of this configuring activity.[45] (The

---

"History" is therefore patient of analysis by appeal to the same theoretical categories applied to other narratives.

[43] Ricoeur, *Time and Narrative*, 66.

[44] "[L]iterary works depict reality by *augmenting* it with meanings that themselves depend upon the virtues of abbreviation, saturation, and culmination, so strikingly illustrated by emplotment." Ricoeur, *Time and Narrative*, 80.

[45] For the relationship between *The Rule of Metaphor* and *Time and Narrative* concerning "semantic innovation," see Ricoeur, *Time and Narrative*, ix–xi.

corresponding referential dimension of this discursive operation belongs to the third mimetic moment of narrative, below.)

In addition to drawing on the general symbolic resources for describing human action outlined in our discussion of mimesis$_1$, mimesis$_2$ is also constrained and empowered by cultural paradigms at the discursive level. Mimetic activity recapitulates and gradually extends the distinctive forms (e.g., plot as discordant concordance), genres (e.g., novel, gospel, diary), and types (e.g., the gospel of Mark) that constitute the "sedimented" achievements of the productive imagination within a narrative tradition. Just as our vast repertoire of sentences is funded by the generative limits of grammar, so

> [t]hese paradigms, themselves issuing from a previous innovation, furnish the rules for a subsequent experimentation within the narrative field. . . . In the same way as the grammar of a language governs the production of well-formed sentences, whose number and content are unforeseeable, a work of art—a poem, play, novel [biblical text, sermon]—is an original production, a new existence in the linguistic [*langagier*] kingdom.[46]

Mimesis$_2$ names what we ordinarily call the plot of a story, but it also recognizes that such plots always stand upon the shoulders of prior achievements in humanity's long and diverse bid to respond to the aporetics of time.

Finally, mimesis$_3$ designates the dimension of mimetic activity related to reading and corresponds to Ricoeur's general account of hermeneutical appropriation of poetic discourse understood as the exploration of a textual world. In the case of narrative discourse in particular, appropriation means that the reader's own temporality is *reconfigured* in light of the configuration (mimesis$_2$) encountered in the text. As we have seen, Ricoeur does not hesitate to claim a reference for poetic discourse; like all discourse, it intends a world. Because they are normally told in the past tense, narratives create the surface impression of "referring back" to something behind them, but they actually "refer forward" in the sense that only in the act of reading is a narrative world unfolded and its discursive destiny fulfilled. Mimesis$_3$ points to that site between the text and the reader where the world projected by the text intersects with the world of the reader and, through what Gadamer has called a "fusion of horizons," engenders new possibilities for being in time. In other words, mimesis$_3$ names the way the reader's own life narrative interacts with and is transformed by the encounter with the narrative text: "I shall say that mimesis$_3$ marks the intersection of the world of the text and the world of the hearer or reader; the intersection, therefore, of the world configured by

[46] Ricoeur, *Time and Narrative*, 69.

the poem and the world wherein real action occurs and unfolds its specific temporality."[47]

The third mimetic moment is of great consequence for Ricoeur's approach to narrative and thus for a homiletic indebted to it. The refiguration of the reader's practical field occasioned by the encounter with the text can have implications for all levels of activity from the most private and idiosyncratic to the global. It runs the gamut from reinforcement of the conventional to radical subversion of the social order through what Ricoeur felicitously terms "the shock of the possible."[48] To follow the plot and cooperatively enter the world of the text is to embark on an adventure in the sense that something unplanned and unanticipated may happen. To appropriate a narrative truly is not just to understand it at arm's length but to understand oneself and one's relation to reality anew before it, and thus to put it to work in the world of action.

A Depiction of Threefold Mimesis: The Telling of the "Good Samaritan" Parable

The biblical story of the telling of the parable traditionally known as the "Good Samaritan" can help clarify the workings of the mimetic process. This is a story about the telling of a story—a story which, within the narrative world it displays, recounts and enacts the entire mimetic process.[49]

A remarkable feature of the biblical literature is the recurring theme of stories about telling stories. Because the faith community has so much at stake in the way narrative shapes faith, the Bible incorporates into its storied world numerous depictions of the narrative hermeneutical process itself (see, among many others, Exod 12:26-27; Deut 6:20-25, 26:4-10; Josh 4:6-7;

[47] Ricoeur, *Time and Narrative*, 71.

[48] Ricoeur, *Time and Narrative*, 79. John Dominic Crossan has supplied a helpful taxonomy of the way narratives reconfigure the practical field. He describes a spectrum of five types of stories ranging from "myth," which "establishes" a world for the reader, all the way to "parable," which "subverts" the reader's world. Crossan, *The Dark Interval: Towards a Theology of Story* (Niles, Ill.: Argus, 1975).

[49] The decision to show how stories work generally by "entering the world" of one particular story may appear unnecessarily confusing—why entangle the "what" of the analysis with the methodological "how"? I am aware that it is impossible to separate my own mimetic engagement with the story in Luke from the depiction of the lawyer's engagement with the parable. In fact, any attempt to exemplify or analyze threefold mimesis by explicating the workings of a particular story is, either consciously or unconsciously, to enter the mimetic cycle at some point as a participant and not a dispassionate observer. The hope is that by explicitly acknowledging this and "performing" my own mimesis$_3$ encounter with this story about storytelling, certain aspects of threefold *mimesis* will be clarified.

2 Sam 12:1-15).[50] The narrative-parable (i.e., a parable spoken by a character and so embedded within the larger narrative) so common to the Synoptics is a particularly compelling case. These mimetic depictions of the mimetic process simultaneously throw the reader into (1) an engagement with the micro universe of the parable itself and (2) reflection upon stories and their meaning effects. In other words, by depicting the telling and reception of parables, the Gospels model the way one story can serve as an extended "metaphorical process" that is able to redescribe another story or situation productively. This has caused Ricoeur to celebrate the narrative-parable as "the most complete illustration of the biblical form of imagination," one that is "implicitly at work everywhere else."[51]

The story of the telling of the parable of the Good Samaritan (Luke 10:25-36) will be read through the lens of Ricoeur's account of the mimetic cycle as a depiction of how stories do their work upon the religious imagination of the hearer/reader. This reading takes the biblical story of the telling of the parable as a portrayal of how a mimetically depicted hearer/reader (the character of the lawyer) has his prefigured narrative self-understanding refigured through an encounter with a narrative "text" (the parable) that is told and elaborated upon (we might even say "preached") by the character of Jesus.

In the world of the story about the telling of the parable, the lawyer's $mimesis_1$ (prefiguration) is disclosed through a dialogical exchange between the lawyer and Jesus (vv. 25-28) and a single question the lawyer poses in the context of a discussion about neighbor love (v. 29). This brief dialogue and short question economically render a surprisingly robust view of a practical field that has been organized according to a particular set of relational assumptions, a distinctive way of orienting self to world. It is a testimony to the power of narrative that it is difficult, if not impossible, to parse everything exhaustively we are shown about the lawyer's prefigured world through this brief exchange.

His prefigured world is depicted with particular force and clarity through the question by which he seeks to "justify himself": "And who is my neighbor?" The question evokes a world in which love is guarded as a scarce resource and dispensed only reluctantly. Perhaps it would be fair to characterize the

[50] There are many other texts that, upon reflection, can be shown to be patient of such a reading. E.g., in a brief exposition of Ricoeur's narrative theory and its implications for preaching, Mary Catherine Hilkert takes the resurrected Jesus' encounter with the disciples on the road to Emmaus (Luke 24:13-35) as a narrative depiction of the mimetic process at work in the preaching of Jesus. See Hilkert, *Naming Grace*, 92–95.

[51] Paul Ricoeur, "The Bible and the Imagination," in Wallace, *Figuring the Sacred*, 147.

lawyer's prefigured world even as one in which love has been imagined as a commodity that must be managed according to the logic of a zero-sum game. In such a world, one must be careful to love the right people because there is only so much love to go around. Furthermore, there is the suggestion that it is the lawyer who has privileged access to this precious commodity and needs guidance in its wise deployment. The lawyer's question belongs to a prefigured world in which he presumes his own moral agency as the principal consideration. He is not in doubt about, or at least not focused upon, the problem of his own worthiness to receive love, but rather assumes the privilege and responsibility of carefully discerning those upon whom he should bestow the love that God's law commands.

Jesus does not answer the question directly. To answer the question on its own terms is to enter its frame, consent to its prefigured construal of experience, and thereby become complicit in a lesser moral world than the one Jesus is determined to announce. The break between the lawyer's question (v. 29) and Jesus' response (v. 30) is absolute—a passage between worlds. Without transition or explanation, Jesus simply begins to narrate (mimesis$_2$): "A man was going down from Jerusalem to Jericho. . . ." In a stroke, the world evoked by the lawyer's question is set aside. Instead, we (both lawyer and reader) find ourselves on a road. As we follow the plot, a new world comes into view—one marked by a movement from brutality, caution, and indifference to serendipity, grace, and extravagant self-sacrifice (vv. 30-35). It is significant that in Jesus' subversive configuration of events, the Samaritan is not narrated as the contested object of neighbor love, but its surprising agent. It is this surprising reversal of the social reality prefigured in the lawyer's question that most effectively exposes both the lawyer's question and its prefigured world as obscene. But now we are already on our way toward refiguration.

In Luke's neat frame, the move to mimesis$_3$ is marked when the lawyer who began by asking a question now consents to answer one: "Which of these three, do you think, was a neighbor . . . ?" (v. 36). Unlike the lawyer's prefigured question, this one is framed in terms of the surprising new world configured by Jesus' plot. (As readers of the whole gospel, we recognize this world immediately as the kingdom of God.) Simply by following the way of thinking offered by the plot and identifying its protagonist as "the one who showed mercy," the lawyer finds himself already implicated in a world refigured by the parable even before Luke has Jesus make the move to mimesis$_3$ explicit: "Go and do likewise" (v. 37).

There are a number of complex meaning effects here, many of which grow out of the reader's "privileged" position of watching a character travel the mimetic circuit even as the reader walks the same path at one level of remove.[52] Ricoeur's narrative theory funds a particularly satisfying account of what happens for the character of the lawyer. Threefold *mimesis* and the notion of the textual world provide a useful and subtle set of tools for thinking about the parable's impact on the practical field. The parable does not set an example or give a caution about how to go on living a bit differently in the same world the lawyer already inhabits. If difference has been introduced, it is because the parable has *shown* a different possibility for inhabiting a world. This showing has the force of a total vision, not a suggestion for different conduct. While the story does its work, from horizon to horizon things are quite different and the hearer has leisure and "space" to imagine himself in the midst of it all. *Life could be like this.* There is an implicit invitation to something better, something more vital, winsome, and satisfying than life as it was. The eventfulness of experiencing this parable's plot is best captured by the notion of entering its world and "having a look around," rather than in terms of the communication of abstract moral propositions, or talk of examples and warnings.

When the lawyer emerges from the world displayed by the parable and reenters the world of action, everything will be just as it was before he asked his question and received a story for an answer. No object will have been altered or even directly described by all this impertinent predication. Everything will be just as it was, save one thing. The lawyer himself will now be different for what he has experienced in the world displayed in front of the parable. But the point of this analysis is not to make claims about the lawyer.[53]

[52] E.g., we are not told how the lawyer responds to the new world he has been shown in the parable. Speaking for myself, this lacuna intensifies my own identification with the lawyer; this is how the parable becomes most transparently a parable for me. The story's abrupt ending means that if this mimetic encounter is to become productive, if it is to bear fruit in the domain of action, it will have to do so in my own refigured world. Likewise, the satisfying symmetry of the lawyer first asking and then answering a question and the shocking juxtaposition of the assumed world of the lawyer's question and the serendipitous world that opens up through the window of the parable are meaning effects for the reader of the larger story, not the lawyer. But like the depicted effect of the parable on the lawyer, what these things "mean" is best understood in terms of what they "do" to our thinking and feeling when we follow them, and enjoy them, and allow them to show what they show.

[53] And, of course, it is not finally decidable whether I have got the lawyer's prefigured world "right" or not—whether I have "correctly" judged the impact of the parable in refiguring his world. He is a character in a story, and I am one of its readers—one who brings a concern for the inner workings of story. If this analysis is revealing about a "person," that person is surely me. But this depiction of someone encountering a story does help me explicate what I understand threefold *mimesis* to entail.

This story about storytelling facilitates the explication of how the prefigured practical field (mimesis$_1$) may be refigured (mimesis$_3$) through the mediation of the poetic configuration of a plot (mimesis$_2$).

The Mimetic Cycle: Progressive or Vicious?

Threefold *mimesis* is a cyclical process. We are always moving out of a *pre*figured temporality, through an encounter with a *con*figured temporality in the form of a "text," and then back into the world of experience, but now possessed of a new and *re*figured temporality. But, of course, we encounter new stories all the time, and the cycle repeats. The *re*figured temporality negotiated in our last encounter with a story points toward a new *pre*figuration that defines our baseline for encountering the next story.

Recognizing this circularity, one must then confront the objection that the mimetic cycle might be, to use Ricoeur's term, "vicious": "[T]he end point seems to lead back to the starting point or, worse, the end point seems anticipated in the starting point. If such were the case, the hermeneutical circle of mimesis and temporality would resolve into the vicious circle of mimesis alone."[54] *Mimesis* qualifies as a meaningful poetic "solution" to the aporetics of temporality only if it can be shown that our repeated encounters with story are progressive in their interaction with extratextual reality. The worry is that our encounter with story might not genuinely move us along in our understanding of ourselves in unstoried time—that encounters with narrative distract for a moment but finally leave us just as we were. Rather, Ricoeur wishes to show how the text throws us back into the flow of time with new resources for making sense of our existence in the real world in which we must act and suffer. No doubt the process of threefold *mimesis* is circular, but not necessarily a closed circuit: "I would rather speak of an endless spiral [spring coil] that would carry the meditation past the same point a number of times, but at different altitudes."[55] By imagining the mimetic cycle as following the path of a spiral, Ricoeur is arguing that the process is progressive in relation to temporal experience. When we encounter a new story (or even if we encounter the same story again), we begin at a new and different "altitude."

Broadly speaking, there are two bids to "compress the spring" and flatten the supposed progression of the spiral of threefold *mimesis* into an endless repetition. Or rather, there are two bids to expose its depth dimension as an illusion and demonstrate that those who travel its circuit make no real

[54] Ricoeur, *Time and Narrative*, 71–72.

[55] Ricoeur, *Time and Narrative*, 72.

progress but are consigned to an endless repetition on the hermetically sealed plane of fabricated emplotment.

The first challenge grows out of the suspicion that the configuring activity of mimesis$_2$ is a lie about temporality—not a lie in the sense that the events in a given short story, for example, did not "really happen" (for the short story, of course, makes no such claim), but a lie in the sense that the very intelligibility of temporality implicitly claimed and explicitly modeled in the short story's plot is utterly unsupportable within the "raw" temporal existence in which we must act and suffer. The charge is that the configured plot of mimesis$_2$ offers only a brief reprieve that "consoles us in the face of death."[56] On this view, the momentary escape into the delusional realm of story does not move us along in our engagement with the real because emplotment has no purchase on real temporality. The ordering of the plot is fleeting, deceptive, and escapist, for life itself is at root a discordant chaos.

Ricoeur accepts that the struggle between concordance and discordance is essential to our narrative wrestling with temporality, but he protests that we are wrong to identify discordance simplistically with our actual temporal experience and concordance with the world of the configured story. Narratives are themselves worked out in the tension between concordance and discordance.[57] And raw experience itself is not purely discordant.

There is a kind of "proof" for this claim in our encounter with certain types of narratives. There are instances of mimesis$_2$ that are striking because the temporality they portray is markedly more discordant than our raw experience of temporality. Consider the following short narrative:

A Common Confusion

> A common experience, resulting in a common confusion. A has to transact important business with B in H. He goes to H for a preliminary interview, accomplishes the journey there in ten minutes, and the journey back in the same time, and on returning boasts to his family of his expedition. Next day he goes again to H, this time to settle his business finally. As that by all appearances will require several hours, A leaves very early in the morning. But although all the surrounding circumstances, at least in A's estimation, are exactly the same as the day before, this time it takes him ten hours to reach H. When he arrives there quite exhausted in the evening he is informed that B, annoyed at his absence, had left half an hour before to go to A's village, and that they must have passed each other on the road. A is advised to wait. But in his anxiety about his business he sets off at once and hurries home.

[56] Ricoeur, *Time and Narrative*.

[57] Occasionally one does hear a sermon that speaks only concordance, but those who persevere in following such a ponderous discourse all the way to its conclusion are unlikely to describe it as possessing narrative qualities.

> This time he covers the distance, without paying any particular attention to the fact, practically in an instant. At home he learns that B had arrived quite early, immediately after A's departure, indeed that he had met A on the threshold and reminded him of his business; but A had replied that he had no time to spare, he must go at once.
>
> In spite of this incomprehensible behavior of A, however, B had stayed on to wait for A's return. It is true, he had asked several times whether A was not back yet, but he was still sitting up in A's room. Overjoyed at the opportunity of seeing B at once and explaining everything to him, A rushes upstairs. He is almost at the top, when he stumbles, twists a sinew, and almost fainting with the pain, incapable even of uttering a cry, only able to moan faintly in the darkness, he hears B—impossible to tell whether at a great distance or quite near him—stamping down the stairs in a violent rage and vanishing for good.[58]

Within the peculiar configuration of this plot, the reader is shown a world more discordant than expected. The surprise is not just that a story should be so fractured but that the story shows us the possibility of a being in time that is more chaotic than our actual experience of being in time. In this case, the "shock of the possible" (and the irony of the title) is that life could make a good deal less sense than it normally does. There is a strong impulse to make some sense of this incoherence in relation to our actual experience of temporality: perhaps the consciousness depicted here is altered; or perhaps the protagonist is suffering from a dissociative disorder; or maybe this is a depiction of a nightmare. In any case, the point is that this plot is a configuration of temporal experience that is *more* discordant than most raw, unstoried temporality. Emplotment may do hermeneutical violence to prefigured temporality, but it is simply not true that it must do so, nor that it always does so in the direction of concordance. For example, Ricoeur suggests that the modern fascination with discordance as exemplified in the antinovel is just as suspect in its relentless entropic drive as certain traditional narratives can be in their too-easy triumphs of order and harmony. Lived experience is both discordant and concordant. Stories are both concordant and discordant. The mimetic cycle is a theoretical account of the productive interaction between lived experience and stories.

The second challenge to Ricoeur's claim that the mimetic cycle progressively mediates our experience of being in time at different "altitudes" is the charge of "redundancy."[59] If refigured temporality (mimesis$_3$) is simply and directly equated with the prefiguration (mimesis$_1$) that awaits the next

[58] Franz Kafka, *The Great Wall of China: Stories and Reflections*, trans. Willa Muir and Edwin Muir (New York: Schocken, 1946), 119. Used by permission of Random House.

[59] Ricoeur, *Time and Narrative*, 73.

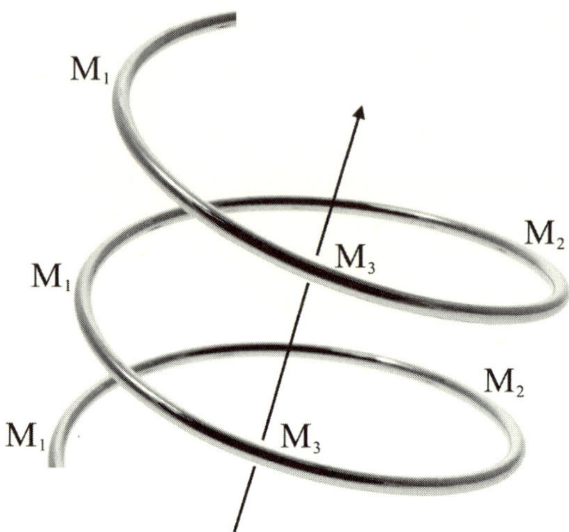

FIGURE 4.1
Threefold *Mimesis* as a Progressive Spiral, or Spring Coil

configuring "text" (mimesis$_2$), then the cycle is exposed as vicious.[60] In this case, *mimesis* does not mediate our experience of temporality because actual experience in time is excluded from the hermeneutical circle. The progress of the cycle is stalled as story acts upon story in an endless loop, unperturbed by incidents in the real world of action.

Ricoeur's response to this charge is to provide several examples of what he takes to be the "prenarrative" quality of raw experience. Ricoeur asserts that "[w]e tell stories because in the last analysis human lives need and merit being narrated."[61] It is very difficult to adjudicate such a claim, but it does seem clear that if we grant that our life is a question that justly begs narration, then our cyclical engagement with the stories we tell is not vicious but progressive. Thus, in the graphical representation of threefold *mimesis* above (see figure 4.1), the arrow of force that stretches the circle of the mimetic process into a third dimension is the density and integrity (not to say complete autonomy) of our experiences in the world of action. We do not pass immediately from text to text, story to story. The world outside the text intervenes and pushes back against our attempts to narrate our lives. Our

[60] Ricoeur puts it this way: "This [redundancy] would be the case if mimesis$_1$ were itself a meaning effect of mimesis$_3$." Ricoeur, *Time and Narrative*, 73–74.

[61] Ricoeur, *Time and Narrative*, 75.

cyclical encounter with stories achieves "new altitude" because these encounters always point us back toward and so are interwoven with the world of events, actions, and sufferings. Such extratextual incidents are in and of themselves sufficiently story-like to mingle creatively with our last negotiated mimesis_3 and so beget a new mimesis_1 that is not simply anticipated or dictated by our previous encounter with a configured plot. Departing from Ricoeur's own terminology, but not from his account of *mimesis* in *Time and Narrative*, the encounter that takes place in the world projected between the narrative text and the reader needs to be understood as an *interaction*.[62] Narrative succeeds in moving along the conversation about what it means to be human in time because it neither unilaterally constructs, nor completely absorbs, nor slavishly reflects, nor irresponsibly escapes the real world of our doing and suffering; it interacts with it.

Ricoeur and Frei in Conversation

With both Frei's and Ricoeur's hermeneutical projects now in view, a comparison and contrast of their approaches can be ventured with special attention to the implications for homiletics. Problems with Frei's approach that came clear in Charles Campbell's homiletical appropriation of his work will frame the following discussion, which will show how Ricoeur's insights into the workings of poetic discourse generally and narrative in particular fund a significant revision of postliberal homiletics with respect to the issues of reference, context, and poetics.

Common Ground

Significant differences between the intellectual lives of Ricoeur and Frei have already been noted. Yet despite their contrasting intellectual backgrounds and orientations, in the field they share, the interpretation of biblical narrative, the similarity of their approaches is striking. The primary focus in this section will be to distinguish their work, but any differences between Frei and Ricoeur are best understood against the background of their shared convictions—a common ground that makes the tensions between their approaches all the more salient and generative.

[62] For this notion of "interaction," I am indebted to Robert E. Scholes' discussion in *Textual Power* in which he argues that "we neither capture nor create the world with our texts, but interact with it." Scholes, *Textual Power: Literary Theory and the Teaching of English* (New Haven: Yale University Press, 1985), 111–12.

A number of common features have emerged in the discussion of these two theorists. First, and perhaps most important, both agree that the post-Enlightenment search for the meaning of the Bible (and so the essence of Christianity) "behind," "above," or otherwise apart from the biblical stories themselves is misguided. Ricoeur's work presumes that religious language is meaningful in its own right, and he privileges its ancient forms, speaking of the need to "get as close as possible to the most *originary* expressions of a community of faith."[63] When Ricoeur thinks of getting to the heart of the matter, he thinks not of the history or experience concealed behind the text, or abstract religious truths floating above the text, but of a return to the language of the text itself.

This turn to language means that Ricoeur, like Frei, vigorously rejects the assumption that the genre of narrative—the form of the biblical witness—is a dispensable vehicle for the transport of some abstractable religious freight that can and should now be borne with greater precision by categories less taxing to the credibility structure of the post-Enlightenment sensibility. They agree, in other words, that narrative is integral to the Christian understanding of God, and that it is *in* and *in terms of* the biblical stories that such understanding is properly sought.

Following from this shared interest in paying close attention to the language of the biblical witness is their agreement that the language of the text signifies by making available an alternative "world." Both of these theorists want to speak of a textual world in order to communicate how immersive, immediate, and pervasive for the reader are the new options that open through an encounter with the language of the text. For both thinkers, to speak of a textual world is an attempt to name the way a text mediates access to "something more" than one is able to achieve independently through reflection on experience. The textual world is not primarily a window into other times, places, and events, but a present alternative to the reader's prior settled construal of life and its possibilities.

Ricoeur is more explicit and precise in elaborating this notion of a textual world as a general hermeneutical claim about written discourse. And for Ricoeur, the world of the text is a site of interaction with, not domination of, the reader's pre-self-understanding. Frei makes no general claims about texts as world making but asserts that the church, through long practice, has come to understand the function of this particular collection of "realistic narratives" as establishing the world in terms of which the ecclesial reader comes to understand her life. Frei emphasizes that for most of its history, the

[63] Ricoeur, "Philosophy and Religious Language," 37 (emphasis in original).

Christian church understood the Bible to offer a seamless account of the real world from its created beginning to its anticipated consummation—a depiction that functioned to incorporate and provide the context for making sense of the reader's present everydayness. It was Frei's Yale colleague and close ally George Lindbeck who put the matter most memorably: "It is the text, so to speak, which absorbs the world, rather than the world the text."[64] In a postcritical context, this claim must exchange descriptive for prescriptive force: now that even the ecclesial reader is aware of other compelling ways of construing the world, the Bible's proffer of an inhabitable world of meaning that may transform human subjectivity depends upon the reader's cooperation.

This leads to a third feature of biblical hermeneutics broadly shared by these theorists: the conviction that full access to the world of meaning made available by the biblical text is necessarily a function of one's cooperative disposition toward the text. Again, for Ricoeur this is a general hermeneutical principle applicable to all texts. And Ricoeur maintains that this sympathy with the textual itinerary of meaning is always held in tension with the need for critical distance. The move toward appropriation can be described as reading under a "vow of obedience," which is in turn balanced by distanciation under a "vow of rigor."[65] Ricoeur employs a number of metaphors for this disposition of cooperation with the textual agenda, ranging from the more passive notion of allowing oneself to be drawn into the "aura" of the text,[66] to a more determined and intentional willingness to "follow the arrow of the sense."[67] Ricoeur understands that the biblical text in particular makes exceptional demands upon the disposition of the reader that correspond to the extraordinary nature of its subject matter and its claim to "name God," but the idea that textual meaning is a function of cooperative reading is universal for Ricoeur. For Frei on the other hand, the disposition of the believer toward the Bible is not a regional instance of a general hermeneutical principle.

[64] Lindbeck, *Nature of Doctrine*, 118. Recent work by Paul DeHart has problematized the easy conflation of the positions of Lindbeck and Frei, but in my judgment Lindbeck's postliberal slogan is fair to Frei's understanding of the "tyrannical" (Auerbach) quality of realistic narrative. DeHart, *Trial of the Witnesses*; Auerbach, *Mimesis*.

[65] "Hermeneutics seems to me to be animated by this double motivation: willingness to suspect, willingness to listen; vow of rigor, vow of obedience." Ricoeur, *Freud and Philosophy*, 27.

[66] "But then I must quit the position, or better, the exile, of the remote and disinterested spectator. . . . No interpreter in fact will ever come close to what his text says if he does not live in the aura of the meaning that is sought." Paul Ricoeur, *The Conflict of Interpretations: Essays in Hermeneutics*, Northwestern University Studies in Phenomenology and Existential Philosophy (Evanston, Ill.: Northwestern University Press, 1974), 294.

[67] Ricoeur, *Interpretation Theory*, 94.

Rather, this particular text has a special relationship with ecclesial readers. It is only within the context of the church with its distinctive practices and commitments that the text can be properly followed. Christian community is the concrete situation, the particular form of life from within which the unique and unsubstitutable identity disclosed in the New Testament can be recognized and embraced as the risen Lord. As is so often the case, Ricoeur and Frei follow very different routes to similar judgments.

Reference, Truth, and Meaning

For all this shared perspective on biblical narrative, there are crucial differences between Frei and Ricoeur, and they begin with the important question of textual reference. Frei could be a bit contrarian about how to classify his own work, but he was perfectly clear in all cases that he was not a philosopher.[68] What this disavowal meant to him was that he was not engaged in the project of showing how the Bible is true according to some external canon of truth. As a believer, Frei was surely committed to the truth of the biblical story, but as a thoroughgoing nonfoundationalist, he saw no advantage to arguing the case publicly. Shunning talk of truth and reference, Frei was satisfied with the more modest project of explaining how the Bible is meaningful for its ecclesial readers.

Ricoeur's project was more ambitious. As a Christian, Ricoeur shared key features of Frei's basic orientation toward biblical narrative; but as a philosopher, he wanted to make claims about the truth of the Bible that could be argued publicly. Doing so involved him in the complicated philosophical project of challenging the modern epistemological assumption that all real knowledge is verifiable knowledge about objects that is available to an autonomous and objective knower. For Ricoeur, the Bible does make (potentially falsifiable) claims about what is the case, but it makes them in a domain more akin to poetic than scientific or descriptive discourse. In the face of the same complexities and complications that led Frei to reject the categories of truth and reference altogether, Ricoeur argued for a new understanding of truth and reference—one more adequate to the mode of biblical discourse.

Frei was suspicious of attempts, including Ricoeur's, to discern an extralinguistic referent for the Bible's stories. His own reticence to employ this

[68] "In the company of historians I always insist that I am a theologian but when thrown with theologians I identify myself as a historian. I deny that this is either evasive or confused because under all circumstances I am clear about one fact: I am *not* a philosopher." Letter to Jane, February 15, 1977, Collections (Yale Divinity School Library, 1-4), quoted in Higton, *Christ, Providence, and History*, 253.

category reflected his conviction that sophisticated talk of what the Bible is "really" about reduces quickly to a bid to co-opt Christianity's distinctive narrative in service of one or another supposedly more fundamental and universal philosophical project. Such efforts may be well-intentioned, he argued, but they are ultimately misguided and symptomatic of the "Eclipse" he so carefully documented. When philosophy is allowed to frame the very possibility of biblical truth, the Bible's odd stories tend to be read in a way that ratifies a prior agenda. For Frei, grounded as he was in a particular reading of Wittgenstein's approach to language, there is great risk but no reward in trying to frame the Bible's claims in terms of a general plausibility structure. Those who would know more about the reality made available by these stories should join the community committed to being shaped by them. Only those conformed to the church's distinctive form of life can make sense of the language-game that corresponds to and functions within that life.

Frei held that the genre "realistic narrative" invites a reading like that appropriate to a novel. It makes no sense to ask what a novel is "about," unless one is requesting a plot summary. And in that case, the most adequate response is to recount the entire story. Realistic narrative is characterized by verisimilitude; it is "history-like." And its logic is ascriptive; it predicates of its subjects. If the gospel narrative says that Jesus did or said something, the meaning of that sentence is a meaning about the character Jesus. What the gospels are about is the Jesus whose story they tell. As the plot unfolds, the identity it renders is disclosed through the fit (i.e., "realistic") interplay of character and incident. The story has always functioned, and for the postcritical ecclesial reader can still function, primarily to render an identity: Jesus of Nazareth who is identical with the risen Lord recognized as present to the reader in the power of the Spirit. In this sense, it is more proper to speak of the *function* of the biblical text as forming a people capable of recognizing this presence than to speak of its reference. Frei wanted to speak of reference but worried that to do so was to overreach and to invite devastating critique. When pressed about the question of reference, Frei could speak of the ecclesial community referring "by means of the story," but not of the text's own independent reference. For Frei, biblical narrative has a truth "use," but not a truth reference.[69]

[69] Recall Frei's exchange with Carl F. Henry in this connection. From a very different perspective, Gary Comstock, a student of Ricoeur, wrote two influential essays that pushed Frei's intramural approach to "realistic narrative" to its logical nonrealist conclusion. See Comstock, "Truth or Meaning"; and Comstock, "Two Types of Narrative Theology," *Journal of the American Academy of Religion* 55, no. 4 (1987): 687–717. In a personal letter to Comstock, Frei complained of being misrepresented: "If I suggest that, philosophically, 'meaning' and 'truth' . . . should be sharply distinguished in a hermeneutics of realistic New Testament narrative, and hermeneutics

Frei suspects that Ricoeur, in trying to show how the Bible makes general truth claims in its own poetic mode, succeeds only in showing how to use biblical narrative to illustrate general and independently derived ideas about religion and human experience. Frei quotes David Tracy—a theologian whose New Testament hermeneutics he takes as a "close reading and precise regional application of Ricoeur's general hermeneutics"—to support this claim:

> One may formulate the principal meaning referred to by the historically reconstructed re-presentative words, deeds, and destiny of Jesus the Christ as follows: the principal referent disclosed by this limit-language is the disclosure of a certain limit-mode-of-being-in-the-world; the disclosure of a new, and [*sic*] agapic, a self-sacrificing righteousness willing to risk living at that limit where one seems in the presence of the righteous, loving, gracious God re-presented in Jesus the Christ.[70]

Noting the telling solecism ("the principal referent disclosed . . . is . . . the disclosure"), Frei charges that Ricoeur's hermeneutics have here funded a claim about the meaning and reference of the gospels that has very little, if anything, to do with the particular and unsubstitutable identity of Jesus. Jesus becomes merely an illustrative archetype, a "temporary personal thickening" of the supposed textual referent which is a certain "dispositional attitude."[71] Jesus, Tracy seems to be assuring us, is an exemplary religious person, and reading stories about him can help us to become one also. Frei is convinced that this is exactly backward from the church's traditional literal reading, in which Jesus' identity is constitutive of any proper understanding of what the Christian religion is about: "The archetype is identified by the virtues, not they by him through his self-enactment in significant temporal sequence."[72]

Turning from the student to the teacher, Frei finds in the exegetical practice of Ricoeur himself further evidence to fuel these fears. And, in fact, in his early work on the parables, Ricoeur does seem to justify Frei's concern when he declares,

---

confined to the level of meaning, I'm supposed to be implying that Christians don't make truth claims for their beliefs. But of course I'm saying nothing of the sort." Letter to Gary Comstock, November 5, Collections (Yale Divinity School Library, 12-184) (see http://people.exeter.ac.uk/mahigton/frei/transcripts/YDS12-184.html). Frei did not want to be read in a nonrealist way, but he had a hard time explaining why he should not be.

[70] David Tracy, *Blessed Rage for Order: The New Pluralism in Theology* (New York: Seabury Press, 1975), 221, quoted in Frei, "'Literal Reading' of Biblical Narrative," 47. See also Frei's discussion of Tracy in Hans W. Frei, George Hunsinger, and William C. Placher, *Types of Christian Theology* (New Haven: Yale University Press, 1992), 30–34.

[71] Frei, "'Literal Reading' of Biblical Narrative," 48.

[72] Frei, "'Literal Reading' of Biblical Narrative," 48.

> In this sense we must say that the ultimate referent of the parables, proverbs, and eschatological sayings is not the Kingdom of God, but human reality in its wholeness. . . . Religious language discloses the religious dimension of *common* human experience.[73]

This *Semeia* essay may be the basis for George Lindbeck's bald assertion that Ricoeur is an experiential-expressivist.[74] It is difficult to dispute that in his earlier biblical hermeneutics Ricoeur's enthusiasm for forcefully explicating his approach to hermeneutical appropriation can sometimes obscure the basic point that the Gospels are, in the first place, about Jesus from Nazareth and the God of Abraham, Isaac, and Jacob, not universal human experience, even at its most profound limits.[75] Ricoeur himself came to regard this early work on the parables as insufficiently nuanced on this point:

> I must admit that the [distinctive use of the parables by the particular character of Jesus] completely escaped me in my earlier work on the parables published in *Semeia*. I got trapped there by the question, "What makes us interpret the narrative as a parable?" I did not see the resources for responding to this question offered by the too easily overlooked trait that the narrative-parables are narratives within a narrative, more precisely narratives recounted by the principal personage of an encompassing narrative.[76]

Though in my judgment Ricoeur's hermeneutics are not finally guilty of the charge of displacing the Bible's distinctive subject matter, Frei's concerns should be heeded. This is the principal danger that must be guarded against in appropriating Ricoeur's hermeneutical project.

Despite some concerning passages in Ricoeur, he should not be dismissed as an experiential-expressivist. Frei and most of his Yale allies are suspicious of Ricoeur because he simply does not fit neatly into any of the analytical categories they deploy in organizing and promoting their understanding of theological hermeneutics.[77] But as the argument above demonstrates, Ricoeur's

[73] Paul Ricoeur, "Biblical Hermeneutics," *Semeia* 4 (1975): 127–28 (emphasis in original).

[74] Lindbeck, *Nature of Doctrine*, 136 n. 5.

[75] This propensity surfaces intermittently in Ricoeur's thought, but it is most pronounced in his students. Gary Comstock, e.g., formulates the reference of biblical narrative in an utterly nontheological way: "[R]eligious stories can and do make truth claims. What are these claims about? They are about the nature—at once mundane and extraordinary—of living in time. . . . The truth claims of the biblical stories are claims about the innovative capacities and persistent characteristics of our species. Those stories purport to tell us about the outer borders and central heartlands—the ultimate limits and daily rhythms—of specifically human existence." Comstock, "Truth or Meaning," 135.

[76] Ricoeur, "Bible and the Imagination," 149.

[77] The notable exception is William C. Placher, who reads Ricoeur carefully and is therefore

approach respects and remains open to the otherness of the particular realities to which the biblical narratives bear witness.

What the postliberals fail to appreciate is that in Ricoeur's account we do not have to choose between objective meaning and subjective appropriation. These are simply two moments in the same seamless event of reading. For Ricoeur, the projected world that is the referent of biblical narrative must be understood from both angles simultaneously.[78] The concept of a textual world always involves a kind of split reference. The referent of the text is at once both objective (in the sense that the text intends a particular world that the reader has not imagined apart from the text) and subjective (in the sense that this textual agenda comes to fruition as a new possibility in relation to a particular reader). The adventure of the reader in the world projected in front of the text is about the possibility of the reader being made new in light of that new world.

When the hermeneutical encounter involves a narrative, this same conclusion can also be stated in terms of threefold *mimesis*. In the case of biblical narrative, the split reference should be understood as both God (in the second mimetic moment) and our lives transformed before the reality of God (in the third). In other words, from the perspective of mimesis$_2$, the biblical text refers to "the arc of divine action."[79] The biblical plot that "names God" organizes and re-presents to us what we cannot grasp apart from this particular telling: the ways of God in our midst. But from the perspective of mimesis$_3$, the referent is a new possibility for the reader that emerges through her interaction with the issue of the text: the reader's world and her way of being in it reconfigured in light of the reality of God. The secondary referent (a new way of being made available to the reader) does not replace but is built upon the primary referent. Ricoeur's is a thoroughly theological hermeneutical disposition that waits and listens expectantly for the possibility of a transforming

---

perfectly clear that, whatever his differences from the postliberal position, Ricoeur must not be dismissed with Lindbeck's sweeping byword: "Such a modest philosophy, willing to listen, willing to remain silent, seems to pose no necessary challenge to postliberal theology. . . . I hope I have shown that Ricoeur is not an 'experiential-expressivist.' He seems open to hear the questions posed by the biblical texts, to enter into their world." Placher, "Paul Ricoeur and Postliberal Theology: A Conflict of Interpretations?," *Modern Theology* 4, no. 1 (1987): 41.

[78] Mark Wallace states the distinction clearly: "[T]he object-referent of the Bible (God and the New Being) always proceeds from the Bible in order to redescribe imaginatively the subject-referent of these texts (human experience). My sense concerning the bulk of Ricoeur's work on biblical hermeneutics indicates that he wants to preserve both the subject-side and the object-side of the biblical world, his problematic comment in the *Semeia* article notwithstanding." Wallace, *Second Naiveté*, 100.

[79] Long, *Preaching from Memory to Hope*, 50.

voice not its own. It is difficult to imagine how a postcritical hermeneutical position could take Christian claims about the distinctive subject matter of the Bible more seriously.

Ricoeur and Frei think and speak differently about biblical narrative. It is possible to press these distinctions and conclude that their hermeneutical positions are finally divergent. With a little simplification, Frei can be seen as a champion of the preaching *about* Jesus, and Ricoeur the preaching *of* Jesus. Frei can be aligned with those who read the gospels as passion narratives with extended introductions and celebrate the scandal of particularity communicated in that distinctive story about a unique and unsubstitutable identity. Ricoeur can be associated with those who focus on the parables as a clue to Jesus' participation in and exemplification of some essential human religiousness and celebrate the universal scope of the Father's inclusive kingdom. But the matter need not be framed in this way.

There is more to be gained from holding their approaches together as complementary. Ricoeur's work can be read as an attempt to give a convincing account of how biblical narrative could do what Frei claimed that it does. Ricoeur is offering a rigorous, fascinating, and truly seminal understanding of what happens when someone reads the Bible as Christians do. By exploring such a phenomenology of reading, Ricoeur seeks to establish the conditions for biblical narrative to be taken seriously by thinking persons as a place where truth is disclosed and lives transformed. So Ricoeur need not be read as trying to make an argument about what the Bible is *really* about (i.e., temporal existence, limit experience). It would be better to understand him as attempting to show how the distinctive referent of biblical narrative (God, Christ) can be mediated through a narrative text and so transform a reader who is, after all, a being who exists in time. Frei gives an important caution to careless talk about humanity as the primary referent of biblical discourse and (at least in his early work on realistic narrative) reminds us that close attention to the form of the biblical witness tends to highlight the particularity of its subject matter. Ricoeur urges us toward a more stimulating and homiletically useful account of what happens when we read, and makes a case for how this could all be true.

But if Ricoeur dares to give an account of how biblical narrative is true while Frei limits himself to an account of its meaning, in the final analysis neither Ricoeur nor Frei is able to untangle the notoriously difficult knot of how to explicate the notion of an "act of God in history" in a way that is accessible to most Christians. If Frei's "narratological argument" for the truth of the resurrection bears almost no resemblance to what most Christian's mean when they confess "He is risen!" it is equally unlikely that Ricoeur's way of making the case would resonate with those who join their voices to the Easter proclamation, at least among the many who are not philosophically inclined.[80] For both thinkers, "something happened." But if the world behind the biblical text is the site of a crucially important happening, it is nevertheless a happening that is cloaked in mystery and comes to us only as a fragile testimony in narrative form. Frei wrote (but Ricoeur could well have written),

> God's work is mysteriously, abidingly mysteriously, coexistent with the contingency of events. The history of his providence is one that must be narrated. There is no scientific rule to describe it and eliminate the need for narration. Nor is there any historicist perspective or universal claim that can eliminate history's narrative form.[81]

Frei and Ricoeur agree: in the Bible we have adequate testimony, not accurate report. And the adequacy of this testimony is because—not in spite—of the written narrative form in which we receive it.

Nevertheless, Ricoeur's approach to this issue of reference is more suitable for homiletics. Though the intricacies of Ricoeur's account of how the Bible makes truth claims are not accessible to the many, the existential implications of his account correspond closely to what most Christians have at stake in their faith. Working from either hermeneutical perspective, the preacher would be obligated and authorized to read closely and shape the sermon in conformity to the particulars of biblical narrative, trusting that the storied world of scripture is the indispensible mediation of the realities in question. But only the Ricoeurian would have a theoretical foundation for understanding the stakes of such a bold endeavor in much the same way as the hearers because only the Ricoeurian would be making public claims about what is the case. Only the Ricoeurian would be taking the scandalous risk of getting it all wrong—not wrong in the sense of failing to participate competently in an intramural language-game but wrong in the sense of propagating a public lie about the reality of God and the blessed life conformed to God's will. And only the Ricoeurian would be speaking in a way that can be taken up into a meaningful public dialogue with a plurality of other distinctive religious claims—a dialogue that grows more urgent with each passing year. As mentioned above, Frei did not wish to be read in a nonrealist way, and I do not suggest that Frei the theologian had any doubts about the stakes of Christian preaching. The point is that Frei's approach to biblical narrative does not

[80] Frei makes this precise point in his letter to Comstock: "And would you really want to tell me that [Ricoeur's account of biblical reference] is how Christians intend to refer when they greet each other on Easter morning?"

[81] Frei, *Identity of Jesus Christ*, 193.

supply adequate warrants for the claim that sermonic language properly conformed to the biblical text is not only meaningful, but true.

Context

The conversation between Frei and Ricoeur concerning the role of context in the hermeneutical encounter will be brief, and for two reasons.

In the first place, Ricoeur's account of how context participates in the meaning of a biblical text has already been anticipated in our discussion of reference. For Ricoeur, meaning and reference are entangled and given together at the intersection of text and context.[82] The meaning of a biblical narrative is always a negotiation between the text's own itinerary of meaning and the contextual agenda brought by the self that reads,

> [T]he meaning of a narrative . . . occurs at the intersection between the world of the text and the world of the readers. It is mainly in the *reception* of the text by an audience that the capacity of the plot to transfigure experience is actualized. By the world of the text I mean the world displayed by the text in front of itself, so to speak, as the horizon of possible experience in which the work displaces its readers. By the world of the reader I mean the actual world.[83]

The reader who reads along with the grain of the text imaginatively enters the world of the text and comes into contact with the direction of thought opened up by the text.[84] This meaningful encounter is negotiated as a transaction between all that the reader carries with her into the dialogue and the text's own power to disclose a new way of looking at things. Through a Gadamerian "fusion of horizons," the text and the reader work together in an imaginative synergy that makes available to the reader a new self-understanding, a new form of life, a new way of being in the world. There is no textual meaning

[82] The meaning, reference, and application (better, *appropriation*) are given together as a function of the reader's adventure in the world the text projects. For this reason, Nancy Lammers Gross has rightly discerned that Ricoeur's hermeneutical thought points away from the two step hermeneutical process in which one first understands the original meaning of the text, and then moves toward application. Gross, *If You Cannot Preach Like Paul . . .*, 71–105. For the classic explication of the two-step process of discerning first what the text originally meant and then what it means in a given context, see Krister Stendahl, "Biblical Theology, Contemporary," in *The Interpreter's Dictionary of the Bible*, vol. 1, ed. George Arthur Buttrick et al. (Nashville: Abingdon, 1962), 418–31.

[83] Ricoeur, "Toward a Narrative Theology," 240 (emphasis in original).

[84] "To read a narrative is to redo with the text a certain 'line' or 'course' (*parcourse*) of meaning" which "incites the reader . . . to understand . . . herself in the face of the text and to develop, in imagination and sympathy, the *self* capable of inhabiting this world." Ricoeur, "Bible and the Imagination," 150; and Ricoeur, "Naming God," 232.

apart from the contextual meaning; textual meaning is always occasioned by actual instances of reading.

The second reason for the simplicity of comparing these two figures with respect to context is that Frei does not offer an account of how context participates in textual meaning. The early Frei, in an attempt to defend the distinctive Christian message from other agendas, promotes an autonomous text as the sole locus of textual meaning. The later Frei, in an attempt to defend the distinctive Christian message from the poststructuralist assault on the possibility of textual meaning, turns to the ecclesial community of interpretation as the sole locus of textual meaning. In neither case does the reader's context factor, except as the site of a textual coup. Frei's reader is either a passive candidate for total "absorption" by the supposed tyrannical power of the biblical world or a proxy for the community's settled construal of the text.

There is no dialectic to be established between Ricoeur and Frei concerning context: Ricoeur's account is compelling, and Frei denies the relevance of the category. Ricoeur succeeds in articulating the way a text enjoys its own integrity, which does not dominate but rather interacts creatively with the context of the reader. The task in the following chapter will be to show how the preacher fits into this equation as a mediator of the hermeneutical encounter between text and context.

Poetics

Finally, there is the question of poetics, that is, how the language of the sermon should be shaped. Here, the conversation is complicated by the two phases of Frei's thought. Not that Frei had any published position on sermonic language, but rather if we follow the early Frei we will reach different conclusions about the importance of poetics than if we do as Campbell has and pursue the homiletical implications of the later Frei.

Campbell, perhaps polarized by his strong sense that the field of homiletics was too focused for too long on sermon form, appealed to the later (cultural-linguistic) Frei to argue that what truly matters for preaching is not how the sermon is shaped linguistically but that it be singularly focused on the particular identity of Jesus. This split between form and content makes very little sense when read against the hermeneutics of the early Frei, who made a compelling case that the reader who would see the Jesus depicted in the New Testament has no recourse but to pay ever more careful attention to the particular language in which that identity is depicted. Campbell's wedge between character and plot and his privileging of the former over the latter in homiletics is an almost perfect inversion of Frei's explication of how realistic narrative mediates the unsubstitutable identity of Jesus. It is striking that a homiletical project indebted to Frei could so emphatically contradict this feature of his work on realistic narrative, which has important implications for how the language of the sermon should be shaped.

Frei was at his most persuasive when he was arguing that the form of biblical narrative is the best clue to its proper interpretation. The homiletical implications of that early work are clear. If Frei is right when he insists that theological language must be closely conformed to the linguistic shape of the biblical narrative,[85] this must be true of sermonic language as well. The difficulty is that if we follow Frei's approach strictly it is hard to show how sermonic language could differ *at all* from biblical language. In this sense, Frei's refusal to engage the category of context in his account of textual meaning becomes a problem for any attempt to pursue his insights into poetics.

In an early essay on truth, Ricoeur argued that Christian preaching is always perched perilously between the "two mortal poles of anachronistic repetition and hazardous adaptation of the Word to the present needs of the community of the faithful. The truth of preaching," he argued, "is therefore always in search of a fidelity that would be creative."[86] This is the basic hermeneutical insight that Frei's project does not convincingly address. But if Frei had appreciated that the preacher is searching for a message both faithful in its novelty and fresh in its fidelity, he certainly would have insisted that such a message be influenced stylistically and formally by the qualities of biblical narrative he organized under the genre description "realistic narrative." Frei's careful demonstration that the form of the biblical witness is integral to the realities it mediates locates his early hermeneutics on a trajectory toward a homiletic that cares deeply about poetics.

Ricoeur can help us become much clearer about why poetics matters to preaching and what is actually involved in conforming the sermon to biblical narrative. By clarifying that the truth of the Bible is a function of the world it displays, and that the world it displays is a function of its poetic mode of discourse, Ricoeur shows us why sermonic language must be "poetic" in the Ricoeurian sense of the term. His approach helps preachers get clear about the nature of the text they are commissioned to interpret and proclaim. The Bible is not a deposit of revealed propositional truth. Its revelatory character abides in its ability to redescribe reality by displaying a world. Biblical discourse labors to bring forth something beyond the ken of ordinary descriptive

[85] "The truth to which we refer we cannot state apart from the biblical language which we employ to do so." Frei, "Response to 'Narrative Theology,'" 211.

[86] Paul Ricoeur, "Truth and Falsehood," in *History and Truth* (Evanston, Ill.: Northwestern University Press, 1965), 177.

discourse, and so must preaching properly conformed to it. To preach these texts is to join the preacher's own voice to the text's work of displaying a particular world.

In terms of threefold *mimesis*, the sermon is an instance of mimesis_2 that is deliberately conformed with great care to the mimesis_2 of the biblical text. Homiletician Thomas Long has named this relationship precisely:

> [T]he text is treated as a form of *mimetic_2* action that exerts configuring power over the potentialities of the sermon, which consequently exerts *mimetic_2* force upon the event of proclamation. In short, preaching enters into the world of the text seeking to discover the expression of the action of God there and then creatively imitates, describes, narrates, and proclaims that action in the sermon.[87]

We have already noted that a spoken event can function as poetic discourse in the same way that a text may. The key is that the oral event be constructed or "wrought" in conformity to the generative grammar of genre. Here, again, is the relevant passage from *Interpretation Theory*:

> Literary genres display some conditions which theoretically could be described without considering writing. The function of these generative devices is to produce new entities of language longer than the sentence, organic wholes irreducible to a mere addition of sentences. A poem, narrative, or essay relies on laws of composition which in principle are indifferent to the opposition between speaking and writing. They proceed from the application of dynamic forms to sets of sentences for which the difference between oral and written language is unessential. Instead, the specificity of these dynamic forms seems to proceed from another dichotomy than that of speaking and hearing, from the application to discourse of categories borrowed from another field, that of practice and work.[88]

Though spoken rather than inscribed, the sermon is just as capable of functioning as an instance of mimesis_2 as a biblical text.

Furthermore, as we discussed above, every instance of mimesis_2 is already dependent on prior instances of mimesis_2 in a mimetic tradition. Ricoeur speaks of the "sedimentation" of a narrative tradition: layer upon layer of constructed plots that constitute a culture's repertoire for configuring temporal experience in meaningful ways. Every new instance of mimesis_2 is dependent upon the paradigm established by prior instances at a number of discursive levels from broad forms, to genres, to particular works that function as exemplary types.

[87] Long, *Preaching from Memory to Hope*, 50.
[88] Ricoeur, *Interpretation Theory*, 32.

Preaching is a deliberate intensification of this dependence. Whereas every new plot is casually and generally indebted to the narrative sedimentation upon which it stands, the sermon constructed under the auspices of the commission to preach the authoritative biblical text is a special case: here is a form of $mimesis_2$ that is self-consciously conformed to a particular prior instance of $mimesis_2$.

The broad contours of a Ricoeurian homiletic are now in view. Having identified three weaknesses in postliberal homiletics, and having supplied a provisional sketch of how Ricoeur's hermeneutics redresses these shortcomings, the final task is to flesh out a constructive proposal for preaching as threefold *mimesis*. The final chapter will show how each of the three mimetic moments contributes to our understanding of the text-to-sermon process. Then it will conclude with an analysis of two sermons, demonstrating that this proposal for a homiletic grounded in Ricoeur's approach to interpretation theory offers helpful resources for naming the ways sermonic discourse more or less convincingly participates in the display of the Bible's "strange new world."

Chapter Five

Preaching as Threefold *Mimesis*

Hermeneutics and Homiletics

Ricoeur's approach to interpretation supplies resources for a more compelling account of the text-to-sermon process than is currently available in the homiletical literature. In particular, his understanding of the hermeneutical encounter with narrative texts as threefold *mimesis* is enlightening at two distinct points in the text-to-sermon process. First, it describes and enhances our understanding of the preacher's encounter with the biblical text as she prepares to preach. Second, it clarifies our understanding of the congregation's encounter with the sermon as text-like oral event. Some preliminary remarks about these two interpretive situations will clarify the task of the working preacher and facilitate the homiletical appropriation of Ricoeur's hermeneutics.

Text and Preacher

Looking first at the preacher's encounter with the biblical text, there are a number of features of this particular hermeneutical transaction that distinguish it from the generic reading situation Ricoeur theorizes. First, the biblical text is exceptional in the sense that the preacher understands herself to be under the authority of this text. Read cooperatively, all narrative exercises the power to project a world, but biblical narrative enjoys exceptional textual power corresponding to the exceptional cooperation of ecclesial readers. When the biblical text is read by a preacher preparing a sermon, the world it projects is engaged with extraordinary seriousness and deference. While it may not be correct to say that the Bible is a book with which the preacher is obliged to agree, and while the authority of the biblical text is understood in diverse ways in different ecclesial contexts, we can risk the generality that the preacher does not go to this text as just another narrative. Rather she goes to it in the hope of being met by a Word that will place her under a special obligation, namely to listen with exceptional care and respect, and to consider well.

This special obligation of the preacher with respect to the biblical text is related to a second exceptional feature of this hermeneutical encounter: the preacher is sent to this particular text by and on behalf of a community whose identity is constituted in part by a pledge to submit to the authority of this text. On the one hand this deepens our appreciation of the preacher's obligation to read under the vow of obedience. On the other, it shows us that the preacher preparing a sermon reads the biblical text as the congregation's surrogate. This suggests that the preacher's encounter with the biblical text is marked by an unusual self-awareness about the hermeneutical process. The preacher is more intentional about interpretation because she is aware of mediating the hermeneutical process on behalf of others for whom she is responsible and to whom she is accountable.

Finally, and again closely related to the preceding point, the preacher reads as one who is chosen. Without exploring the question of the person of the preacher in great detail, it should be acknowledged that the preacher is an exceptional reader. By gift, ecclesial formation, and in some contexts formal education and ordination, the preacher is commissioned to interpret and mediate the text for the community. In most ecclesial contexts, the community chooses one person and grants her leisure and permission to read closely on behalf of the many. It is the word of God the congregation gathers to hear, but it is the preacher the congregation trusts to proclaim rightly that Word by carefully and faithfully engaging the biblical witness.

Sermon and Congregation

Strictly speaking, the preached sermon, like the biblical text it interprets, is a mimesis$_2$ event. Though the event of preaching is oral, it is a carefully shaped discourse that shares with textual discourse the essential quality of "wroughtness" in conformity to the empowering "grammatical" constraints of genre. Therefore, sermons, like texts, display inhabitable worlds in which communal and personal possibilities may be explored. But the sermon is atypical insofar as it is a "text" that is directly tied to the biblical text it interprets. In most ecclesial contexts, the congregation will listen together to a reading of the biblical text (an encounter with an instance of $mimesis_2$), and then they will listen to the language of a sermon (an encounter with a second instance of $mimesis_2$) that conforms itself to and expands upon the lection. As model reading and performed interpretation, the sermon recapitulates the biblical text and explicitly wrestles with its displayed world, bringing its implications sharply into focus for the ecclesial gathering.

The sermon makes biblical interpretation communal. Again, Ricoeur's account assumes an individual reader engaged in a private hermeneutical encounter with a narrative text. But reading the lection aloud in the ecclesial assembly points toward a shared interpretation. One function of the sermon is to take up the vector that begins with a communal reading and extend it toward a communal interpretation. The words of the biblical text are voiced aloud for a shared hearing, and then the sermon expands upon the text, displaying and engaging its world aloud in shared space. The hermeneutical process that Ricoeur theorizes as belonging to private consciousness is intercepted by the sermon, which attempts to give voice to a shared hermeneutical encounter.

The sermon makes biblical interpretation communal in a second sense as well, namely, by joining the community's reception of the biblical text to the church's long history of reading. By gift, formation, and formal training, the preacher is grounded in the ecclesial tradition of reading. Ricoeur teaches us that every reader brings a prefigured understanding to the narrative text. In the case of the preacher, that preunderstanding has been shaped with unusual care by the church, which chooses and commissions its preachers to read in continuity with the tradition. For the later Frei, this is the definitive characteristic of all ecclesial hermeneutics. Ricoeur gives us resources for thinking about the church's history of reception as one important factor that must be integrated into a larger hermeneutical conversation that includes consideration of other contextual factors as well. But the key point here is that the sermon facilitates an encounter with the biblical text that is common to those gathered and in continuity with, if not conformity to, the interpretations of generations of ecclesial readers.

Preaching as Threefold *Mimesis*

The essential point for successfully appropriating Ricoeur's narrative theory for homiletics is that just as the preacher's engagement with the biblical text during sermon preparation can be grasped in three mimetic moments, so also the preached sermon in the hearing of the church will reflect these three mimetic moments.[1]

Formally, the sermon is an instance of mimesis$_2$. But because the sermon is a performed interpretation explicitly tied to the preacher's prior engagement with the biblical text on behalf of the church, it is a special form of mimesis$_2$ activity that will more or less successfully reflect each of the three mimetic moments of the preacher's encounter with the text. By analyzing a sermon through the lens of threefold *mimesis*, prescriptive criteria emerge for evaluating its capacity to navigate the demand for a discourse that is creative in its fidelity and faithful in its novelty. The sermon can be judged according to its ability to discern rightly and represent the congregation's narrative prefiguration (mimesis$_1$), its willingness to engage deeply and display the narrative world configured by this particular biblical text (mimesis$_2$), and its capacity to render seriously imaginable the new way of being made available through an encounter with this textual world (mimesis$_3$).

Mimesis$_1$: Debt to the Actual

Every hermeneutical encounter with a narrative text is a negotiation that begins with the reader's prefigured temporality. Our lives are inchoate stories in the sense that all the raw ingredients of an identity narrative (character, setting, motive, etc.) are already in place, awaiting the configuring influence of a plot. Typically, narrative prefiguration claims its role in the hermeneutical equation without the conscious effort of the reader. This is especially true of those aspects of mimesis$_1$ that constitute our basic competency in the practical field, that is, the reader's capacity for intuitively navigating the categories that make life narratable. This dimension of mimesis$_1$ is fascinating from a theoretical perspective, but not particularly instructive for guiding the text-to-sermon process. Concerning this core aspect of mimesis$_1$, there is little need for the preacher to take steps proactively intended to render her reading more authentically *for* others. In a given cultural context, there is likely almost perfect congruence between the preacher and the congregation with respect to this basic categorical matrix for construing what counts as meaningful human action.

[1] In *Preaching from Memory to Hope*, homiletician Thomas G. Long briefly explores the implications of Ricoeur's threefold *mimesis* for preaching (45–53). Up to this point, the argument of this book has been focused on explicating Ricoeur's claims about narrative in detail, situating them intelligibly in his larger hermeneutical project and relating them to Christian claims about the Bible. What follows will build upon Long's basic insight of relating Ricoeur's narrative theory to homiletics and attempt to work out this relationship in more detail.

But mimesis_1 can also encompass the reader's narrative self-understanding at a "higher" level than this basic proficiency with story. We do not come to new plots as narrative newborns possessing only unexercised capacities.[2] As appropriated here, therefore, mimesis_1 not only names our formal capacity for narrating our lives but also designates the sediment of our provisional attempts to do so through our history of encounters with various "texts."[3] On this reading of Ricoeur, mimesis_1 names the "baseline" for any new hermeneutical encounter. Narrative self-understanding is a process, and we are always negotiating our temporality in the flux between the narrative worlds we have inhabited and the ongoing contingencies of raw experience. The many and diverse engagements with narrative worlds that have shaped our lives are ingredient to the mimesis_1 we bring to each new reading situation.[4] We are the site of a contest, and each new story that would shape our sense of self must take its place alongside other contestants in a long and arduous "tournament of narratives" that is already in progress.[5]

It is this "higher" dimension of mimesis_1 that demands the preacher's conscious attention in the text-to-sermon process. In the first mimetic moment, the preacher who would read on behalf of others must make an explicit effort to identify imaginatively with the congregation's prefigured narrative self-understanding. When the preacher goes to the biblical text to listen and watch on behalf of the people, she must go as one well versed in their multiple narrative worlds. This plurality of worlds is increasingly complicated by media fragmentation in that story is now relentlessly "pushed" across hundreds of television channels, "pulled" from countless "blogs," and coauthored in "chat rooms" and other electronic forums that instantly and effortlessly assemble the most esoteric and ephemeral special interest groups composed of participants from every corner of the globe. Twenty-first-century North Americans enjoy or endure access to more stories told in more ways than ever before.

[2] See chap. 4, n. 34.

[3] This expanded definition of mimesis_1 clutters Ricoeur's generic and elegant theoretical scheme with the complexity of each hermeneut's cumulative narrative self-understanding, but it is essentially faithful to Ricoeur's account of the way threefold *mimesis* is a cyclical encounter that progressively climbs to new "altitudes." Ricoeur, *Time and Narrative*, 1:72.

[4] Though, as discussed in the section on the possibility of a "vicious" mimetic cycle in chapter 4, mimesis_1 should not simply be equated with the outcome of previous mimesis_3 engagements since the raw material of experience continuously pushes back against our attempts to emplot our lives, relentlessly problematizing and reframing past efforts at narrative self-understanding.

[5] James William McClendon, *Systematic Theology: Ethics*, 2nd ed. (Waco, Tex.: Baylor University Press, 2012), 149.

The preacher can neither pretend to be the arbiter of all the stories that shape the listeners nor imagine that there is a clearly circumscribed cultural canon common to all those in the pews. If she is to interpret convincingly on their behalf, she must be mindful that she is mediating a textual encounter for people who have been formed not only by the parable of the Good Samaritan and the ritual reenactment of "the night he was betrayed" but also by an eclectic cocktail of narrative material that may include (to name just a few North American examples from just one popular medium) stories of "spirit" and "redemption" narrated by Oprah, trickster narratives meticulously constructed from footage of the antics of *Survivor* contestants, "headline news" stories catering to and exacerbating a craving for the sensational—all punctuated by myriad thirty-second micro narratives optimized to construct identities and form appetites to the specifications of the purveyors of various goods and services.

Vicarious participation in the prefigured world of the listeners for whom the preacher seeks to mediate credibly an encounter with the biblical text does not end with fluency in the increasingly complex cultural narrative mélange. It also involves a sustained effort to know the storied history of a particular congregation, and the many individual experiences and subplots that are contributing to the next chapter of that history.

So to read for others and to mediate a hermeneutical encounter that will recognizably belong to the congregation, the preacher must know the many narrative worlds that have shaped them. But the relevance of mimesis$_1$ to homiletics goes beyond the preacher's conscious attempt to read the biblical text vicariously on behalf of the church. There is also a sense in which the sermon—though itself a mimesis$_2$ discourse—will have more or less explicit features traceable to this mimesis$_1$ aspect of the preacher's surrogate hermeneutical engagement during the sermon preparation process. Because the sermon is a performed interpretation that recapitulates the preacher's engagement with the biblical text on behalf of the congregation, specific features of the congregation's prefigured world will be reflected in the sermon in a variety of ways.

In particular, the sermon may explicitly deploy narrative material for the purpose of representing to the church a true depiction of its own prefigured sensibilities in order to set them in relief against the transformations the biblical text intends. In other words, one task of the sermon may be to narrate the congregation's prefigured self-understanding convincingly as part of the journey toward encountering a new configuration that will make a subsequent refiguration seriously imaginable.

The preacher's work in relation to mimesis$_1$ can be clarified with an organizing image.[6] In relation to mimesis$_1$, the task of the preacher can be helpfully imagined as that of a photographer, and perhaps most helpfully, a portrait photographer.[7] This image is appropriate to the first mimetic moment because, compared to other visual media, photography is remarkable for its dependence upon the actual.[8] The photographer works with what is given in the situation, not what can be invented. Likewise, preaching as mimesis$_1$ involves a *debt to the actual*. In other words, the preacher is constrained in this hermeneutical moment by the given narratives and circumstances that have shaped the people for whom she interprets. This is primarily descriptive work.

Of course, there are constructive dimensions to the work of a portrait photographer: decisions about lighting, perspective, and field of view. Likewise, the preacher is actively and, in a sense, creatively engaged as she attempts to frame the congregation's prefigured situation properly, in a way that is most appropriate in relation to the biblical story being interpreted.

Finally, we can note that the work of the photographer is not complete until the depiction is produced and presented to the subject. The portrait photographer's task is not simply to observe but to provide the subject with an image of herself for her own use. This is like what the preacher does in the mimesis$_1$ phase of the sermon itself. The text-to-sermon process begins with the preacher engaging the biblical text through the lens of the congregation's prefigured narrative self-understanding, but it moves toward presenting to the church a depiction of itself in light of this particular biblical text. The difference between the preacher and the portrait photographer is that the

[6] For a pedagogically generative discussion of homiletics presented in terms of various organizing images, see the section titled "Images of the Preacher" in Thomas G. Long, *The Witness of Preaching*, 2nd ed. (Louisville, Ky.: Westminster John Knox, 2005), 18–51.

[7] Taking a more directly descriptive approach, homiletician Nora Tubbs Tisdale has characterized this aspect of preaching as "amateur ethnography." See chap. 3, "Exegeting the Congregation," in Leonora Tubbs Tisdale, *Preaching as Local Theology and Folk Art*, Fortress Resources for Preaching (Minneapolis: Fortress, 1997), 56–90.

[8] I admit to intentionally assuming (as suits my purpose here) a fairly naïve posture toward photographic depiction as a reflection of the "actual" visual manifold. Pablo Picasso tells about having a bit of fun at the expense of such naïveté: "Right after the Liberation, lots of GIs came to my studio in Paris. I would show them my work, and some of them understood and admired more than others. Almost all of them, though, before they left, would show me pictures of their wives or girl friends. One day one of them who had made some kind of remark, as I showed him one of my paintings, about how 'It doesn't really look like that, though,' got to talking about his wife and he pulled out a tiny passport-size picture of her to show me. I said to him, 'But she's so tiny, your wife. I didn't realize from what you said that she was so small.' He looked at me very seriously. 'Oh, she's not really so small,' he said. 'It's just that this is a very small photograph.'" Carlton Lake, "Picasso Speaking," *Atlantic Monthly* 200, no. 1 (1957): 39.

preacher does not pose the subject at the most flattering angle, nor accentuate only the most comely features, but attempts to depict the subject from the perspective suggested by this particular biblical text.

Mimesis$_2$: Debt to the Real

Sermonic discourse is to be conformed to—funded and constrained by—the biblical text. If mimesis$_1$ calls for the preacher to go to the text on behalf of this particular ecclesial community, mimesis$_2$ reminds us that it is this particular text to which she is sent on the church's behalf. The second mimetic moment directs the preacher's attention in minute detail to the language of this biblical text and the world it displays. Preparing to preach calls for a close reading of the biblical text because the preacher is searching for a Word to the church that is more than an expression of her own best thoughts, or a heightened reflection of their own settled prospects.

If mimesis$_1$ means that the text-to-sermon process entails a "debt to the actual" (circumstances and prefigured temporality of the church), mimesis$_2$ points to the way the preacher's task is also and especially conducted under a *debt to the real*—namely, the reality of God that is the issue of the biblical text. God is not an object that can be referenced directly by descriptive discourse. But biblical faith confesses that God has given signs of God's self in history, and thus biblical poetics is a bid to bear witness to the reality that lingers beyond the horizon of all our significations in stories that give language to the mysterious reality of God's presence amid the contingencies of human history. These stories show the reader a world organized around the reality of God and invite her to explore the possibility of her own world transformed by that reality. Preaching is biblical only to the extent that it wrestles with the reality of God named in scripture.

Preaching as mimesis$_2$ highlights the way the preacher must attend to the biblical text with great care in the intensive reading that constitutes sermon preparation, but it also has implications for the shape of the sermon itself. "To read a narrative," says Ricoeur, "is to redo with the text a certain 'line' or 'course' (*parcourse*) of meaning."[9] There is a dynamism to the plot, and to read means to follow that movement under the guidance of the text. Preaching is simply an extension and expansion of the process of reading—a publicly enacted model reading. From the perspective of mimesis$_2$, to preach is not to talk about the biblical text, nor even to talk about what the text is talking about. Rather, to preach is to facilitate an encounter between a particular

[9] Ricoeur, "Bible and the Imagination," in Wallace, *Figuring the Sacred*, 150.

text and the community of faith such that the biblical text has its say in their hearing.

At the same time, preaching reconstitutes the text as more than mere text. Ricoeur shows us that discourse enjoys a remarkable promotion through inscription; but something is lost as well. Textuality corresponds to a contextually activated surplus of meaning and the advent of the textual world, but these gains come at the expense of the undeniable power of the *viva voce*. The human voice signals its own surplus of significance: an encounter with a living presence and its passion to communicate something. For this reason, a biblical text is reactualized as discourse through reading, but even more so through preaching. At its best, preaching honors the promotion that accrues to textuality during the text-to-sermon preparation process, even as it joins the power of the textual world to the compelling human presence of the living voice during the actual event of preaching:

> [T]he reconversion of writing into speech aims at recreating a relation not identical to, but analogical to, the dialogic relation of communication. Yet it does so precisely beyond the "scriptuary" step of communication and with its own character that depends on preaching's posttextual position.[10]

The process of reconstituting for the community the discourse that lies dormant in the marks on the page begins with the preacher at her desk, reading and considering well. But it is fully realized in the moment of preaching, in which the bid to name God becomes once again a living wager for the church. The text does not remain merely a text because "preaching brings back to living speech" what has been inscribed.[11]

In this way, the biblical text takes its place as a crucial link in a long "communicative chain."[12] God's gracious self-disclosure in the midst of the contingencies of human history is brought to speech as testimony. In the case of the biblical tradition, this testimony has become testament with the advancement in discursive power this promotion to textuality entails. Then comes the return:

> Writing, in its turn, is restored to living speech by means of the various acts of discourse that reactualize the text. Reading and preaching are such actualizations of writing into speech. A text, in this regard, is like a musical score that requires execution.[13]

[10] Ricoeur, "Naming God," 219.
[11] Ricoeur, "Naming God," 218.
[12] Ricoeur, "Naming God," 219.
[13] Ricoeur, "Naming God," 219.

Reading and preaching are part of the same movement in which a text is "reactualized" as discourse. The preacher reads on behalf of the church and then extends that toward a performed model reading in the hearing of the church. Ricoeur goes so far as to compare preaching to the performance of a musical score.

Ricoeur's notion of the biblical text as musical score suggests that with respect to the second mimetic moment, the preacher may be helpfully imagined as a music conductor. The conductor reads the score carefully before the performance. She studies it in anticipation of an event in which she will be responsible to facilitate the actualization of the static inscription into a living performance for a gathered community. Following the music in her head, she makes decisions about dynamics, tempo, and so forth. Unlike the individual musician who prepares by mentally tracing one isolated part, the conductor takes responsibility at a communal level, interpreting, planning, and imagining with an eye to the total effect of the music for the gathered community of listeners. In a similar way, the preacher attends to the biblical text in great detail, entering its world on behalf of others and experimenting with various strategies for displaying or enacting the total effect of that world in the sermonic event. The preacher studies the text in order to imagine possibilities for a performance that will make the text's claims and implications accessible to these listeners.[14]

The preacher as music conductor also provides a strong image for the way the biblical text should constrain the sermonic performance. Just as concertgoers justifiably demand fidelity to the particulars of the promised score, it is *this* text the sermon must actualize. Any preaching event that is not recognizably a performance of this "musical score" must be judged a failure, no matter how stimulating or winsome the result, for it is this particular music—this and none other—toward which the score points.

Shifting the focus to the preaching event itself, the image of preacher as conductor offers further insight. In the case of a concert, the listeners have not come to encounter the score (biblical text). They already have access to the score, and indeed some of them may be capable of performing (one part of) it with some degree of proficiency on their own. But it is not the score they have come for. Nor have they come primarily to encounter the conductor (preacher). Significantly, concert practice calls for the conductor's back

[14] We might even imagine the preacher's wrestling with the sermon manuscript during her preparation as comparable to the conductor's intense relationship with the performers who must be shaped through disciplined rehearsal into an "instrument" capable of giving life to the score as a compelling performance.

to be turned to the listeners, for she is not the focus of the performance. No doubt the conductor's presence is important, and her careful planning and rehearsal, her signaling of the tempo and dynamics, her skillful and passionate embodiment of the flow—all these will contribute in important ways to the encounter the listeners seek. But (with the exception of a few anomalous cases that distort the practice) it is not the conductor the people have come to experience. Rather, it is the music (world of the text) they have come together to experience. They have assembled as a community to share in what this music has to offer. All else is in service of this larger goal.

Mimesis$_3$: Debt to the Possible

The third mimetic moment emerges as a synergistic interaction between the first and the second. It is the site of a meaning event in which something new is generated that did not already exist in either the reading community or the inscribed text alone. The given prefigured temporality of the community meets the configured temporality of the plot to generate a third thing: the congregation's self-understanding reconfigured through an encounter in the world projected in front of this biblical text.

During the text-to-sermon process, the preacher's surrogate reading is the locus of the original sighting of this new world of possibilities. She has consciously taken up the prefigured temporality of the church as her own and approached the biblical text's configured plot on their behalf. As she reads there is an expectancy that something will be seen—something new and previously unavailable that will emerge from this particular reading, for this particular people, at this particular moment. We can speak of "going into" the world in front of the text to see this new possibility, but it is just as true that mimesis$_3$ marks the site of reentry into the domain of practice, for the adventure in the world in front of the text is at once a departure from the given, and a confrontation with new possibilities that are practicable in the everyday world of human affairs. The eventfulness of the third mimetic moment has the quality of a discovery for the reader/preacher. She knows when something has happened, when the spark of imagination leaps between the prefigured situation and the configuring plot, showing by its quick light the new thing that is possible.

Just as in mimesis$_1$ and mimesis$_2$, the third mimetic moment will also be reflected in the preaching event itself. The sermon will give voice to this new thing that the preacher has experienced in the world in front of the text. As performed interpretation and model reading, the sermon will facilitate the community's appropriation of the biblical text by pointing toward the new way of being it makes available.

The homiletical implications of threefold *mimesis* can be understood as a series of constraints on the preacher's interpretive task. If $mimesis_1$ entails a "debt to the actual" prefigured situation of the church, and $mimesis_2$ insists that the preacher work under a "debt to the real" referenced by the biblical text, $mimesis_3$ places the preacher under an obligation of equal seriousness, namely, a *debt to the possible*.[15] In other words, just as the preacher is liable for interpreting on behalf of this particular community, just as she is responsible for ensuring that it is this particular biblical text that receives her undivided and obedient attention, it is equally true that she must preach under an obligation to a new thing that for now only she has seen. In terms of $mimesis_3$, to preach is to keep faith with a hard-won vision of what is possible now for this church in light of its encounter with this text. The preacher must find language adequate to the new thing she has seen.

The preacher, who can be imagined as a portrait photographer in relation to $mimesis_1$, and a music conductor in relation to $mimesis_2$, can be imagined as a museum docent in relation to $mimesis_3$.[16] The role of the docent is to direct attention toward something and supply an interpretive lens so as to facilitate a richer encounter than would otherwise be possible. The good docent does not draw attention to herself but employs whatever linguistic resources are at her disposal to help others see for themselves. "Stand here," says the docent, "and look at it in this way in light of all that I have told you, and you will be able to see for yourself that. . . ." The experience is curated in the best sense of the term: the docent serves at the pleasure of those who have come with a desire and a willingness to be shown what they cannot as fully appreciate on their own.

To preach as a docent is to show something to the church that they cannot see as clearly, or appreciate as deeply, apart from the preacher's interpretive intervention. In the third mimetic moment, the preacher need not choose between rendering the biblical text or the hearers' context, for what comes into view through an encounter with narrative is the reader's own world refigured in light of the text. In one moment the preacher can point toward features of the church's ordinary experience and say, "Look at it in this way

[15] Ricoeur has described the moment when a reader confronts the new way of being disclosed by an encounter with narrative as "the shock of the possible." Ricoeur, *Time and Narrative*, 79.

[16] I first encountered the image of the docent in George R. Hunsberger, "The Newbigin Gauntlet," in *The Church between Gospel and Culture: The Emerging Mission in North America*, ed. George R. Hunsberger and Craig Van Gelder (Grand Rapids: Eerdmans, 1996), 23. Hunsberger employs the image in the context of reconceiving the practice of evangelism in the wake of the cultural changes outlined in the first chapter.

(made possible by this story) and you will be able to see for yourself that God is already present and articulate in our midst."[17] In the next, the preacher may indicate something in the biblical text and through a skillful "anachronistic" juxtaposition with some feature of ordinary experience bring its significance into sudden focus. The preacher serves as a practiced guide, helping the congregation navigate, explore, and appreciate the world projected between them and text. It is not a world generated by an "autonomous text" but a customized space that emerges in relation to this particular "reading." By knowing them well and accompanying them on their journey through this curated space, the preacher hopes to facilitate the richest encounter possible between the church and the text.

Threefold *Mimesis* in Action

The analytical power of a mimetic approach to preaching can now be demonstrated through application to concrete instances of practice. Ricoeur's threefold *mimesis* will serve as the theoretical framework for understanding and evaluating two sermons.

An Analysis of "Pain Turned to Newness"

The first analysis is of Walter Brueggemann's sermon on Mark 5:24b-34 titled "Pain Turned to Newness." This sermon is included and analyzed in *Preaching Jesus*.[18] Just as the homiletical approach proposed here has been worked out in dialogue with Campbell's postliberal proposal, so this first sermon analysis will be performed in relation to the detailed analysis of Brueggemann's sermon found in *Preaching Jesus*. In *Preaching Jesus*, Brueggemann's sermon is held up as an exemplar of postliberal preaching. A mimetic approach will also lead to a positive evaluation, but the categories of threefold *mimesis* fund a more robust and compelling account of what is happening hermeneutically "under the hood" of Brueggemann's sermon and why it succeeds in faithfully mediating a biblical word.

"Pain Turned to Newness" was preached at Columbia Theological Seminary on May 9, 1992 (line 5).[19] The sermon is based on the story of the

[17] The transformation is not merely one of perspective, for the docent discloses what is already present and awaiting "eyes to see." This is close to Mary Catherine Hilkert's notion of the preacher's task as "naming grace" for the church. Hilkert, *Naming Grace*, 44–57.

[18] The sermon is discussed extensively and included as an appendix to Campbell, *Preaching Jesus*), 197–201, 259–64.

[19] A full manuscript of "Pain Turned to Newness" is included in an appendix. Parenthetical references are to line numbers within the appendix.

woman with the flow of blood (Mark 5:24b-34). It is structured as a short introduction followed by four numbered sections. The introduction highlights the pericope's immediate literary context—it is an instance of Markan intercalation—as a clue to interpretation. The story of the woman "disrupts" (line 17) the story of the healing of Jairus' daughter (Mark 5:21-24a, 35-43). The first section describes the woman and her "desperate" (line 51) bid for healing: "Pain touches power and all things are new!" (line 73). The second section addresses Jesus' question: "Who touched?" (line 86). Section 3 is based upon Jesus' words to the woman by which he "authorizes her for a new possibility" (line 136). In the final section, the sermon names the new possibilities opened up for the hearers through the encounter with this story.

According to *Preaching Jesus*, Brueggemann's sermon is a good instance of practice because it pays close attention to the details of the story in Mark 5 and conforms itself to the "ascriptive logic" of that narrative. In other words, Brueggemann acknowledges that in the first place this is a story about Jesus—Jesus' identity is revealed through what the character Jesus says and does. Therefore, Brueggemann grasps that his first duty is to attend carefully to what the story is saying about the particular person of Jesus. In direct contrast to a negative assessment of a sermon by Wayne Bradley Robinson,[20] Campbell celebrates Brueggemann's willingness to "linger with the identity of Jesus before moving too quickly to his meaningfulness."[21] The analysis emphasizes that Brueggemann does not rush to show us how the story of Jesus fits neatly into an existing plausibility structure, perhaps as an illustration of some general truth about human nature. Rather, he "simply follows the movement of the biblical story itself, seeking a 'dramatic reenactment' of the story for the hearers."[22] Brueggemann's sermon is applauded in *Preaching Jesus* because it shows how this story about Jesus can be surprisingly helpful in recasting or "redescribing" the lives of the listeners in terms of the biblical narrative.

The analysis in *Preaching Jesus* points out that the sermon is structured as a brief opening followed by four "scenes" in which the "drama" unfolds.[23] It does not characterize the sermon's opening as an "introduction" (which might

[20] Wayne Bradley Robinson, "Angels, but Satan and Wild Beasts," in *Journeys toward Narrative Preaching*, ed. Wayne Bradley Robinson (New York: Pilgrim, 1990), 101–5. Campbell's brief analysis argues that in Robinson's sermon on Mark 1:9-15, Jesus is not "the subject of his own predicates, but is in fact the predicate of another subject: 'human experience.'" Campbell, *Preaching Jesus*, 196.

[21] Campbell, *Preaching Jesus*, 201.

[22] Campbell, *Preaching Jesus*, 197.

[23] Campbell, *Preaching Jesus*. Brueggemann's manuscript supports this claim in that it is divided into four sections headed by roman numerals.

suggest some received understanding of general human nature or experience as a "point of contact" for what follows), but rather as an "overview" of the pericope in context. The analysis emphasizes the way Brueggemann "begins with the story, not with human experience"[24] and suggests that Brueggemann simply begins by telling us about how this story of the woman with the flow of blood "intrudes upon" the framing story of Jairus' daughter, and then invites the hearers to "[l]isten to her story as a tale about your own life and our life."[25] Campbell alerts us that "Brueggemann's move is subtle here" because, rather than encouraging the hearers to find their own stories in the gospel story (as if they already knew their own stories and were simply looking for an affirming reflection of that settled narration in the biblical text), they are challenged to see whether this gospel story may function to "redescribe" their own lives on its terms.

A mimetic analysis affirms that Brueggemann's opening is effective, but Ricoeur's narrative theory helps us appreciate that it is even more subtle than the analysis in *Preaching Jesus* suggests. Campbell's analysis emphasizes that Brueggemann "begins with" the text, but this is not the case in the narrow sense claimed. Brueggemann's sermon does carefully engage the story from Mark 5, but his beginning is not "purely" textual. In fact, the sermon's first sentence opens onto a world that is as much about the prefigured situation of the hearers ($mimesis_1$) as the storied situation of Jesus and the woman ($mimesis_2$): "The woman in Mark 5 almost did not make the text, almost did not have a story" (line 7). This odd predication seamlessly blends a character from the storied world depicted in Mark 5 with second-order talk about "text" and "story" that are features of the world of an academic community well practiced in the interpretation of texts. From the start we are thrust into a peculiar narrative space in which a community of professional hermeneuts mingle with a character from one of their sacred stories. As the paragraph unfolds, we are told that the woman must "muscle her way" into the text in the midst of a "better, more impressive story about a more impressive character" (lines 11–12). Again, there is a juxtaposition of a character from the text with second-order talk about "characters" and "stories." Note also that the statement that Jairus is a more impressive character with a more impressive story is a window into Brueggemann's imaginative judgment about the prefigured world of his hearers. Brueggemann is interpreting out loud on behalf of his hearers, supplying them with a "portrait" of themselves in light

[24] Campbell, *Preaching Jesus*, 197.

[25] Campbell, *Preaching Jesus*, quoting Walter Brueggemann, "Pain Turned to Newness," in Campbell, *Preaching Jesus*, 260.

of this text just as surely as he is telling them the biblical story itself. And when Brueggemann promises that "her story might turn out to be our story as well" (lines 25–26), the hearers are on notice that what has already been happening will continue by design: not, as Lindbeck would have it, the perfect "absorption" of our world into that of the text, but a carefully negotiated interaction between those worlds that will yield new possibilities for living as yet unimagined.

Moving from the opening to the first "scene," we rejoin the analysis in *Preaching Jesus*, which describes this section as focused upon the character of the woman with the flow of blood, including her "desperate" (line 51) action of reaching out to touch Jesus. The analysis states that Brueggemann sums up the depiction of the woman by describing her as a "carrier of pain" and then observes that Brueggemann employs "anachronisms to give the story a contemporary ring."[26]

This description of Brueggemann's move does not fully appreciate what is masterfully achieved in these paragraphs because the homiletical approach in *Preaching Jesus* does not supply the theoretical resources needed to name what is happening. This section of the sermon should primarily be understood in terms of mimesis$_2$.[27] The preacher is the conductor here, skillfully reconstituting the dead score of the inscribed text as living music in the congregation's hearing. When Brueggemann unpacks how the woman had "endured much under many physicians" by describing days spent "helplessly in clinics, waiting rooms, emergency rooms, overwhelmed by technology, filling out endless forms, passed along through the medical bureaucracy" (lines 39–42), he accomplishes far more than a pleasing "ring," contemporary or otherwise. By this daring juxtaposition, he displays the world projected between this text and these readers. The woman inhabits their clinics even as they imagine her "smelly bandages" (line 36) and vicariously endures the displeasure of the crowd through which she pushes. If she has no "health insurance" (line 45), it is not because Brueggemann has indulged in a rhetorical bauble, for this is not empty ornamentation, but living and productive metaphor. When the preacher tells them that her touch from behind "is not a nice, innocuous suburban touch," but a "real touch, undertaken by an untouchable" (lines 58–59), the hearers are helped to see the woman in terms of their own lives,

[26] Campbell, *Preaching Jesus*, 197.

[27] I say *primarily* because, of course, all three mimetic moments are involved in this skillful performance of the text. The focus at this point in the sermon is on the "objective" textual world, but its compelling display is dependent on rightly discerning the prefigured situation of the hearers, and anticipating the refiguration this text points toward.

and their own lives in terms of hers. Finally, *contra* the singular focus of the homiletic in *Preaching Jesus*, it should be noted that what is accomplished here is not directly or exclusively a function of the identity of Jesus, for in this section it is the woman whose identity is rendered as her "pain touches [Jesus'] power."

Next, the analysis in *Preaching Jesus* notes that both the second and third "scenes" of the sermon are dedicated to the character of Jesus as he responds to the woman's touch. The sermon explores the new dynamic between "pain" and "power" worked out in the encounter between Jesus and the woman. The analysis rightly notes that Brueggemann guides the hearers to appreciate that Jesus is not a flat stereotype of generic power but "rather a person who embodies this power and healing in a unique way."[28] Jesus is depicted in the sermonic performance of this text as one who reacts to and is in turn shaped by this particular human encounter.

However, this aspect of the analysis in *Preaching Jesus* seems to contradict an earlier critique of a sermon by Robinson mentioned above. Robinson's interpretation of the story of Jesus' temptation in the wilderness is censured because, rather than focusing on Jesus' "enacted intentions," it engaged in textually unsupportable speculation about his "inner life" and on "what he surely must have learned from his 'experience' in the wilderness."[29] But how is this significantly different from Brueggemann's imaginative expansion on the moment when the woman touches Jesus and he feels power go out from him:

> Not only does the woman know she has gained new power for healing. Jesus is also aware that his body has been exposed to pain, and that exposure has redefined him as well as her. Jesus, the powerful one, is changed by contact with pain. He is changed in ways commensurate with her. He is not an unmoved mover or an unnoticing power. He is impacted decisively by her touch. (lines 93–98)

Robinson's sermonic performance of Mark 1 is no more psychologically speculative than Brueggemann's performance of Mark 5. The point is not that Campbell's analysis was wrong to criticize Robinson's sermon, or wrong to applaud Brueggemann's move, but simply that the analytical categories supplied in *Preaching Jesus* are not particularly helpful for distinguishing between these two instances of practice. Leaving aside Robinson's treatment of Mark 1:9-15, from a mimetic perspective the reason Brueggemann's move quoted above is good practice is not that he has detailed textual support proving the "enactment" of each of the thoughts, feelings, and attitudes he attributes to

[28] Campbell, *Preaching Jesus*, 198.

[29] Campbell, *Preaching Jesus*, 196.

Jesus but that he has first explored and then performed the world of this text in relation to these hearers in such a convincing manner that this creative expansion is seriously imaginable for them.

Proceeding to the sermon's "final scene," the analysis in *Preaching Jesus* notes that Brueggemann "carries the story into the time of his contemporary hearers" by inviting them to populate the story as one or another of its characters, "suggesting that there are various places they might stand in the story."[30] The discussion of this part of the sermon is concerned primarily with arguing that Brueggemann does make an ecclesiological move at the end, despite the sermon's obvious focus on highlighting personal appropriation through identification with one of the characters in the story.[31] The treatment of the sermon's conclusion is surprisingly brief, perhaps again betraying a scarcity of theoretical resources for explicating what is happening in this critical final section of the sermon.

A mimetic approach to this sermon has shown that in Brueggemann's skillful telling, the story has from the beginning been thoroughly integrated with the situation of the hearers, but in this last section appropriation does become the explicit agenda of the sermon as $mimesis_3$ moves front and center. Brueggemann plays the docent here, pointing his hearers toward new possibilities for their lives in light of this encounter with biblical narrative. The story, the preacher tells his hearers, has supplied "a new shape for social relations . . . that generates new possibility" (lines 176–77). Indeed, the "shock of the possible" is palpable as the preacher invites his hearers to be "dazzled" (line 179) by the new "patterns of social power" (line 178) that come into view, the "totally new model of life and reality" (lines 182–83) indicated by the trajectory of this narrative. The docent helps us see that we no longer need to "settle" for the "old, weary patterns of 'haves' and 'have-nots,' for the usual arrangements of strength and weakness, power and powerlessness" (lines 184–86) because the story displays "a different option, a different life" (line 187). Brueggemann points the hearer toward a possible future, a reconfigured way of being that was not available before the hearer's encounter with this biblical story.

[30] Campbell, *Preaching Jesus*, 199.

[31] See especially Campbell, *Preaching Jesus*, 199 n. 35.

An Analysis of "Lost"

The second analysis is of a student sermon based on Luke 15:1-7 titled "Lost."[32] This sermon is representative of the preaching that takes place in introductory preaching courses where homiletical theory serves to support a pedagogical agenda. After briefly sketching the structure of the sermon, an evaluation and critique will demonstrate the value of threefold *mimesis* as an analytical tool in the classroom.

The sermon begins with a short introduction (lines 5–19) in which the preacher offers an interpretive gloss on the parable of the lost sheep—it is described as a story "about the forgiving nature of God" (line 7)—and promises to explore "how this sheep became lost, and, by extension, discover how we become lost" (lines 18–19).[33] In the next section, the preacher tells a contemporary story about a childhood experience of becoming lost at Disneyland (lines 20–35). The sermon then proposes two ways of understanding who was at fault in the childhood experience story and draws analogical connections to who is at fault when people become "lost" at church (lines 37–60). Building on the second possible interpretation (it is the child's/sheep's/churchgoer's fault for intentionally withdrawing), the sermon offers a psychological account of withdrawal, tying it to depression and ultimately to fear as a pervasive feature of the contemporary cultural context (lines 61–103). The sermon concludes by announcing the "good news" that Jesus is the shepherd who seeks us out despite our withdrawal (lines 105–112) and points toward a number of ways for the hearer to appropriate this message, including the possibility of enacting the community's resistance to fear and isolation through liturgical practice (lines 114–132).

In the following analysis, the categories of threefold *mimesis* will prove useful both descriptively and prescriptively when applied to this sermon. The sermon's introduction makes brief reference (lines 5–6) to Luke's framing narrative (vv. 1-2) but turns quickly to the parable proper (vv. 3-6) and begins to display its world (lines 9–16). Here we are entering the domain of "conducting" mimesis$_2$, but even from the beginning there is reason for some concern about the care with which the biblical text is being performed. The parable is set in "the wilderness" (v. 4), but in the preacher's telling the textual world opens onto a "pasture" (line 9). Is this an intentional anachronism designed to intermingle productively the world of the text with that of the congregation, a

[32] This sermon was chosen anonymously from a list of sermons submitted to the author by master of divinity students over the past five years.

[33] A full manuscript of "Lost" is included in an appendix. Parenthetical references are to line numbers within the appendix.

calculated echo of the twenty-third psalm, or simply a failure to attend closely to the language of the text and so an early indication that the debt to the biblical text may go unpaid? We will see. Next, the sermon turns to the question of how one of the sheep "becomes separated from the rest of the flock" (lines 10–11). The preacher tells us with great candor that although this is not a concern of the biblical text itself (lines 11–12), it will nevertheless become the explicit focus of the sermon (lines 17–19). A lacuna in the textual narrative invites this question during the preacher's surrogate reading on behalf of the congregation, and now that same eventful interaction is being recapitulated in the hearing of the church in order to set the agenda for a shared hermeneutical encounter. Finally, already in this introduction we see a hint of how the preacher will supply the church with an image of its prefigured narrative self-understanding (mimesis$_1$) since the separated "sheep" is attributed not only "family" and "loved ones" but also "feelings, pain, sorrow, and fear" (line 15).

The sermon's next move is to introduce another narrative: a story about the preacher becoming lost at Disneyland as a child (lines 20–35). Note that there are now three mimesis$_2$ depictions explicitly in play. There is the mimesis$_2$ of the emplotted biblical text to which the preacher is obliged to conform the sermon, the mimesis$_2$ of the sermon as an oral "text" configured according to the conventions of the sermonic genre, and the mimesis$_2$ of the story about the preacher as a child.[34]

The introduction of this new narrative about becoming lost has at least two important functions in the sermon. First of all, it transposes the story of the lost sheep into the realm of contemporary human experience and so allows the preacher to evoke and even personally testify to the "petrifying fear" (line 26) of being lost. Second, and more crucial, it serves to fill the lacuna in the biblical text. The parable does not speak to the question of how one becomes lost, but the childhood story does. In the preacher's telling of this experience, there are exactly two ways that a sheep/child can become lost. Either those responsible for caretaking are negligent (lines 37–43) or the one who becomes lost "runs away" (lines 49–51). Since the sermon turns explicitly on this issue of how one becomes lost, from this point forward in the sermon the childhood story will effectively replace the parable as the instance of mimesis$_2$ that is most determinative for the sermon.

The remainder of the sermon is oriented primarily around the second explanation for how one becomes lost.[35] The preacher is now freely

[34] Technically, there is a fourth mimesis$_2$ event since the biblical text is itself a story about the telling of a story.

[35] The first explanation (i.e., that it is negligence on the part of those responsible for

interchanging talk of the "sheep" (lines 52–57) and "someone" (line 60) in the contemporary context. Now that the explanation of the "sheep" willfully "making a decision" to "leave the flock" is preferred, the sermon begins to explore exactly how and why such a "scary situation" could come about: "What could possibly cause someone to make this decision? Most of the time it is fear" (lines 59–60).

Exploring this "fear" becomes the sermon's primary vehicle for supplying a "portrait" to the hearers of their own prefigured narrative self-understanding (mimesis$_1$). The hearers are prone to fear because their world is a frightening place. It is the site of a "multitude of traumatic events" (line 63) including terrorism (line 64), the war responding to terrorism (line 64), a tsunami (line 64), and Hurricane Katrina (lines 64, 69). Furthermore, the church and the individuals within it have "faced innumerable difficulties" of a more local nature, including illness, death, divorce, arguments, and financial problems (lines 70–73).

The sermon then explores the psychological dynamics of the hearers' prefigured situation, charting a progression from the fear caused by these many traumas to "depression" (lines 74–75), and from depression to "withdrawal from friends, . . . family, . . . loved ones, and . . . faith" (lines 76–77). This depiction of pervasive fearfulness leading to isolation reaches its climax with the description of a new consumer product tailored to this way of being: an armed SUV that encourages us to "hunker down" and "blow each other up" (lines 88–89). Such is the situation with people "all around us" (lines 92, 117), and perhaps even the hearers themselves (line 114). The temptation is very great "to pull back" and "go at it alone" (lines 96–97). Finally, the tendency to withdraw from others is compared analogically to yet another terrifying event in which "things begin to fall apart" (line 99): "Like in that terrible disaster with the Space Shuttle Columbia, when one shingle pulled away others followed and soon the whole ship came flying apart" (lines 99–101).

Having supplied this bleak portrait of the hearer's prefigured narrative self-understanding, the sermon turns now toward mimesis$_3$—the new possibility for being in the world made available in the encounter with the biblical text as mediated by the sermon.

---

caretaking) is explored very briefly when the preacher suggests that some in the church may become distracted and so leave others behind. I expect that this "first" explanation is not explored in detail because the most natural analogue to a negligent family in the Disneyland story would be a negligent shepherd in the parable, and this presents obvious difficulties because of the strong traditional association between Jesus and the shepherd. In this sense, the church's traditional reception of the parable may actually constrain the telling and explication of the Disneyland story.

The first move the sermon makes in this direction simply announces the "good news" made available in the parable: the rescue of the lost does not depend on some self-awareness or effort on the part of the sheep but on the shepherd who alone realizes that the sheep is missing, leaves the ninety-nine, and searches out the one that is lost (lines 105–110). If the future is governed by God's unconditional and sacrificial love initiated in Christ (lines 110–112), and not our own performance, then the biblical text really has offered us a new way to imagine our lives in the presence of the reality of God. This new option for imagining our lives is properly conformed to the biblical text, but unfortunately nothing in the sermon up to this point has laid the groundwork for it. The world of the parable has not been convincingly displayed, and therefore this mimetic "shock of the possible" is not as seriously imaginable as it might have been. Rather than the parable, it is the story about getting lost at Disneyland that has occupied the hearers' imaginations up to this point.

As a result, it is not altogether surprising that the sermon then turns abruptly to a different vision of the new future made available to the hearer. The preacher suggests that perhaps the hearer has at last "come to realize that you are lost" (line 114). The hearer is assured that "Christ is searching for you now," but something more is required: "you have to prepare yourself" (lines 117–118). This second mimesis$_3$ in which everything depends on the lost one realizing and correcting the withdrawal is explicitly connected to the Disneyland narrative that originally supplied the explanation of how the lost one became lost (lines 119–124). In this alternative mimesis$_3$ vision, restoration depends upon being "ready and willing to allow him to lead us" (lines 123–124).

The sermon concludes with a striking proposal about how the new possibilities for living proffered by the encounter in the world in front of the text (mimesis$_3$) will begin to be realized in the congregation's shared life (lines 125–132). The people are invited to "come to the altar for prayer"—evidently a customary practice. But in light of the encounter with this text, a revision to the practice is suggested. The hearers are invited to show their resistance to isolation by taking the hand or shoulder of their neighbor (lines 127–128)—a sign of vulnerability, of unity, and of hope for the finding of the many in the world who are lost. By this embodied practice, the worshipping community is encouraged to enact the alternative future made available in the gospel.

The categories of threefold *mimesis* have proved helpful in exposing the underlying dynamics of the hermeneutical encounter facilitated by this sermon. Especially important in terms of critique is the way the Disneyland story displaces the biblical story as the guiding narrative influence on the sermon. It is interesting that this leads to a split mimesis$_3$ move at the sermon's conclusion. The proffer of a ritually enacted resistance to the forces of fear, depression, and withdrawal is compelling, but the prior articulation of its significance is confused. Are the hearers invited to embrace a future in which God in Christ finds them despite their frailty, or does all depend on their ability to become conscious of their withdrawal and return willingly? These may not be mutually exclusive options, but the sermon is not clear about how the hearers can imagine these two possibilities together as part of the same future.

Conclusion: Toward a Mimetic Homiletic

This discussion of threefold *mimesis* has not ventured a comprehensive homiletic. Several important topics are not directly or extensively addressed—issues of sermon structure, delivery, the language of the sermon, and so forth. Rather, the focus has been on what is traditionally designated the text-to-sermon process, and specifically on a cluster of hermeneutical issues related to the preacher's encounter with biblical narrative and how the sermon may be properly conformed to that encounter.

The decision to privilege the hermeneutical encounter with the biblical text is not accidental but grows out the conviction that, to borrow Barth's language, the great need of Christian preaching is met in the promise of the Bible. The moment of engagement with the biblical text is not just one among many equally weighty entries in the homiletical encyclopedia but is singularly decisive for preaching. All the other significant aspects of preaching are latently present in that crucial event and should be judged by the criterion of fidelity to that initial encounter. By deploying Ricoeur's hermeneutics to map the contours of the preacher's encounter with the biblical text, this project may show the way forward for further appropriation of Ricoeur's threefold *mimesis* as a theoretical resource for other aspects of preaching.

With respect to sermon form, for example, this account of Ricoeur's hermeneutical theory in relation to preaching has important implications. The three mimetic moments of the preacher's surrogate encounter with the biblical text provide guidance for how the sermon should be shaped. This is not to suggest that the sermon's structure should rigidly, sequentially, or superficially reflect the three moments in Ricoeur's phenomenology of reading—as if the three points of the classic propositional sermon could now be replaced by a one-size-fits-all tripartite mimetic sermon form. The structure of the sermon takes shape in response to the communicative tasks it must accomplish, and good sermon form will be as diverse as the manifold ways God's word confronts, comforts, inspires, and challenges the church. What threefold *mimesis* offers is a set of categories for thinking more clearly and at a finer level of granularity about the different tasks of the sermon. Every sermon must pay against three debts, and therefore the structure of every sermon must robustly support the preacher's obligation to the actual prefigured situation of the congregation, the reality of God depicted by the configuring action of the biblical text, and the new possibility that is the church's narrative self-understanding reconfigured in light of its encounter with that reality. At the same time, the preacher must not lose sight of the sermon's own character as a $mimesis_2$ event with its own configurational demands. Ricoeur's narrative theory clarifies that sermon form is worked out in this tension: it must reflect a debt to the preacher's surrogate hermeneutical encounter in each of its three mimetic moments, and it must also be emplotted according to the demands of the sermonic genre.

Ricoeur's hermeneutical approach is also suggestive for future reflection on sermon delivery or, better, "performance." Recent homiletical literature on preaching as an embodied oral/aural event has rightly emphasized the importance of moving beyond the image of the preaching moment as the conveyance of informational freight.[36] Sermon delivery is not merely another "step" to be negotiated independently after the preacher has successfully completed the prior step of determining what should be said. Ricoeur's understanding of preaching as a link in a long communicative "chain" provides resources for theorizing the moment of preaching not as a separate task but as the culmination of biblical language's long destiny as discourse. As a spoken event, preaching is a "performed interpretation" in which the biblical text comes to fruition as a timely word in the hearing of the church. Like reading for the individual, preaching is for the gathered community a moment in which the eventfulness of discourse is reconstituted from the lifeless, inscribed artifact. In preaching, the remarkable promotion in semantic power that accrues to discourse through inscription is synergistically joined to the engaging presence of the embodied voice as vital new testimony emerges out of the preacher's adventure in the world projected in front of the biblical text.

Using Ricoeur's hermeneutics to understand the preacher's interpretive task is also generative for thinking about the language of preaching. By clarifying the nature of biblical discourse, Ricoeur helps us appreciate what it would mean for sermonic language to be conformed to it properly. The Bible is poetic testimony forged under a debt to the reality of God's self-disclosure

[36] For a concise discussion and brief bibliography, see Jana Childers, "Introduction: The Preacher's Performance," in *The New Interpreter's Handbook of Preaching*, ed. Paul Scott Wilson (Nashville: Abingdon, 2008), 213–15.

in history. The importance of this realization for sermonic language can scarcely be overstated. The Bible is not a deposit of revealed propositional truth about objects in the world. The preacher needs to appreciate that biblical discourse labors to bring forth something beyond the ken of ordinary descriptive discourse. Its revelatory character abides in its ability to redescribe human reality in accord with the reality of God. Ricoeur teaches the preacher that to interpret such discourse is, first of all, to display its world. As performed interpretation, the sermon itself must take up this challenge in language most appropriate to the task. Preaching is prose, but if it is to do justice to the biblical text and the transformations it intends, it must not be prosaic. If preaching is to recapitulate the fruits of a reading that is sensitive to the metaphorical nature of biblical discourse, it must strive to do so in language appropriate to such discourse. Guided by Ricoeur's insights into the Bible as poetic discourse, the preacher will summon all the linguistic resources at her disposal in a bid to bear faithful testimony to the new possibilities glimpsed in the world in front of the text. This is not to insist or even recommend that preaching be always lyrical, but preaching dare not attempt to do justice to a world disclosed through poetic discourse by exclusive recourse to linguistic strategies from another discursive domain—especially one that is oblivious to precisely those dimensions of reality the Bible seeks to disclose.

Finally, Ricoeur's narrative theory points toward a compelling account of preaching viewed not only as a discreet act on a given Sunday but as an ongoing ministry of ecclesial transformation over the course of a lifetime.[37] This is a subject that deserves more attention, and its neglect is indicated by the absence of any common shorthand to identify it as a locus of homiletical reflection. Ricoeur's notion of the mimetic "spiral" helps explain what happens in a preaching ministry over the long term. On a given Sunday, the church's prefigured narrative self-understanding (mimesis$_1$) is shaped by the configuring influence of the biblical text mediated by the sermon (mimesis$_2$) such that seriously imaginable new options for being in the world come into view (mimesis$_3$). Then come the experiences of the week, in which this refigured identity narrative is tested and challenged by the contingencies of experience. But the rhythms of worship call for a constant return to the configuring power of biblical narrative. Sunday by Sunday, the church comes

[37] Richard Lischer has named this aspect of preaching with particular force: "Every day, Christians are sorting through their narrative options and claiming an identity as followers of Jesus Christ. On Sunday, the preacher helps them in this task by means of a poetic activity. The preacher makes (*poiein*) words, approximately fifteen-hundred of them, on a Sunday morning, three-million in a career, and over the long haul of ministry, he or she speaks into existence an alternative world." Lischer, *End of Words*, 104.

back "around" to a fresh encounter with mimesis_2 and the new self-understandings (mimesis_3) provoked by the preaching of the gospel. Yet this return is not on the same "plane" as it would be in a vicious cycle. Rather, it is always at "a new altitude" resulting from the progressive and productive interaction of biblical narrative and the ongoing story of the church's life. Imagining this ascending hermeneutical "spiral" can give conceptual clarity to our attempts to understand the ongoing ministry of preaching as it participates in God's work of transforming God's church "from one degree of glory to another" (2 Cor 3:18).

Ricoeur's theory of narrative as threefold *mimesis* has been appropriated for homiletics to identify a series of obligations that define the task of preaching. The preacher works under a debt to the actual prefigured situation of the church (mimesis_1), a debt to the reality of God referenced by the biblical text (mimesis_2), and a debt to the new possibility for the church that the preacher has glimpsed in light of the text (mimesis_3). This final debt—the preacher's responsibility to give voice to the new thing God makes possible in our midst—is the ultimate challenge of preaching both in and out of season. My hope is that this theoretical exploration will prove fruitful not only for those who think about preaching, but ultimately for those they teach—those who, week in and week out, must stand before the church and speak under the burden and privilege of this profound commission. For it is not in second-order theoretical reflection but in the many ordinary and faithful acts of preaching that the "transfer from text to life" is wagered anew each Sunday "in the hope that . . . what [we] have risked will be returned a hundredfold as an increase in comprehension, valor, and joy."

Appendix

"Pain Turned to Newness"

"Pain Turned to Newness"

Mark 5:24b-34

Walter Brueggemann
Columbia Theological Seminary
May 9, 1992

The woman in Mark 5 almost did not make the text, almost did not have a story. She is at the edge of the crowd as Jesus approaches. Even in the larger gospel narrative, she has to muscle her way into the text. She is an intruder who does not belong there, for her action takes place in the middle of a better, more impressive story about a more impressive character. In the verses just before her intrusive narrative (vv. 21-24a), a leader of the synagogue, a big, impressive, influential man, persuades Jesus to make a sick call on his ailing daughter. And just after this woman's intrusive narrative, the story of the big synagogue man is resumed and completed (vv. 35-43). This story of the woman is an inconvenience that disrupts only briefly the better story of the man. I will wager that not only is her Bible story an inconvenience, she herself was endlessly an inconvenience as well to those around her.

But then, the Bible and life itself are like that, little stories of insignificant people who are unworthy, who crowd in upon better stories and demand their fifteen minutes of fame, and if not fame, then fifteen minutes of well-being. The wonder, of course, is that the woman made it into the text at all. As we shall see before we finish, we may be very glad she made it in, because her story might turn out to be our story as well. Listen to her story as a tale about your own life and our life.

I

The woman is a pitiful character, a surplus member of the crowd, a "non-person." She stands at the edge of the crowd and watches. The first thing we learn about her, the most important fact about her, the fact that establishes her identity, is that her body is a mess. She is a carrier of pain. Her pain comes at us in three layers:

- She has been hemorrhaging for twelve years. That's a lot of blood that has been lost, as the life ebbed out of her. We can imagine her all in bandages, in smelly bandages, unattractive, for a bleeder in a crowd is at best unwelcome.
- She had "endured much under many physicians." She had been in frantic pursuit of health, spending her days helplessly in clinics, waiting rooms, emergency rooms, overwhelmed by technology, filling out endless forms, passed along through the medical bureaucracy, poked at and questioned by lots of medical experts and a few medical students, some gentle, some uncaring.
- The end result is, she had spent all that she had. She had no health insurance, so that all her wherewithal was used up in a futile pursuit of health care, but still she bled. Now she is bloody and broke.

She is like lots of folks at the edge of the crowd, carrier of pain, pain from bleeding, pain from medical indifference, pain from economic exhaustion, without health, without hope, pitiful!

She makes one last, desperate effort for her future. She still has the imagination and courage to try one last option. Her desperate action is fueled by faith. She reaches out to touch power. Her frail, extended hand enacts the drama of *pain touching power*. She said, "If I can only touch his clothes, I will be made well." She enacts bold, body-to-body, person-to-person contact that cuts through her poverty, brokenness, despair, and shame. She is indeed "reaching out and touching someone," but it is not a nice, innocuous suburban touch. This is a real touch, undertaken by an untouchable, that shatters the neat division between the well and the sick, the acceptable and the disreputable. She overrides all the categories that belong to her disability. Her eagerness to touch is an act of desperate hope, like the eagerness of a child to touch, extending hands in order to be safe with mother. It is like the heavy-veined, pulsating hands in a nursing home, reaching out to touch the child that has just entered. It is exhausted, forlorn life touching full, powerful life, and power is transferred by the touch from the one to the other. This is the human act of "laying on of hands" that transfers possibility. This is the real "apostolic succession," as the continuity of human power and human possibility is enacted.

The outcome happens just as she had hoped for the woman. She touches, and immediately (this is Mark's favorite word, *euthus*, straightway, promptly, in this very moment), immediately, the bleeding stops, and she is healed. Pain touches power and all things are new!

II

Only now does Jesus speak, only after he has been touched. The healing happened by his presence, without his knowing it. He is so saturated with the power for life that the power spills over into those around him. Immediately (the same preferred word of Mark again), Jesus knew power had been transferred from him. This was a bold, concrete human transaction. We cannot tell if Jesus is upset at the intrusion of the woman, or anxious for his own body, or compassionate toward the needy one. He wants to identify the one with whom he has been coupled in a holy transformation from sickness to health.

Jesus has a quick conversation with his entourage. He asks his disciples, "Who touched?" Maybe his word is a command, "find her." But his disciples resist. They are not as intense about the matter as is he. They give a casual response, as though the touch did not matter. They do not know how important the touch is between pain and power, even if Jesus knows. They say, "It's a big crowd, it could have been anyone. It is foolish to try to locate the toucher in this mass." They think in generalities. Jesus, however, is much more intense, caring, concerned, and specific than his best friends. Not only does the woman know she has gained new power for healing. Jesus is also aware that his body has been exposed to pain, and that exposure has redefined him as well as her. Jesus, the powerful one, is changed by contact with pain. He is changed in ways commensurate with her. He is not an unmoved mover or an unnoticing power. He is impacted decisively by her touch.

While his disciples have no concern or interest in the matter, because they are not direct players in this drama of pain and power, Jesus continues to notice, to wonder, and to care. He looks. He surveys the crowd. Even in all his power, however, he is not able to identify the woman.

She takes the initiative. She announces herself, which reflects her new-found courage and freedom, which comes from being healed. The narrator says, ". . . knowing what had happened to her, the woman came in fear and trembling, fell down before him and told him the whole truth." It is an amazing moment between this pained woman and this powerful healer. She knows irreducibly what had happened to her. By his power she had been healed. But she also knows she has taken an inappropriate initiative on her own behalf. She had pushed in where she did not belong. She had touched him when one does not properly touch the powerful. She told him about her pain and the truth about his power, which had now become power for life, truth about the transformation that her courage had instigated, about which he knew nothing.

She comes in fear and trembling. How odd. Why is that? Because she knew she had intruded upon him improperly. Because she expected to be shamed or scolded, because she was used to being abused and "manhandled" by men, for pain is always frightened in the presence of power.

III

Now Jesus speaks to her for the first time. He finally has found his partner in creating a new possibility. This is a confrontation between power and pain, out of which something new can be wrought. He speaks as the powerful one. He surprises her and no doubt the onlookers as well. He does not scold or shame or abuse her. He acts out and models a new way of power towards pain. He is not unhappy that they have converged in this uncommon way. He does not measure if his power has been diminished or trivialized by her touch. His mind is completely off himself and his own authority. He is able to think not of his own interests, but of "the interests of others" (cf. Phil 2:4).

He is focused fully and intensely upon her and upon her future. She had hardly dared entertain the thought that she might have a future. But he authorizes her for a new possibility:

He addresses her: "daughter." It is close to a name, as close as she has ever been to a real identity. He gives her a title of regard and acknowledgment, perhaps even of affection. He counts her a full member of his family of faith and obedience. He names her in a way that honors her.

He celebrates her faith. "Your faith has made you well." He does not even claim to have done anything for her. Her faith was in part her passion for Jesus and her confidence in his lordly capacity. But her faith was also about herself, refusing to accept the sorry state in which the doctors and bankers had left her disabled. Her faith is the courage and freedom to take an initiative for well-being. She had faith in her capacity to reach out, to touch, to take, to receive, to be changed, to benefit from the touch of power. Her faith is her conviction that her future did not need to be only more of the same dreary past tense.

Finally he dismisses her with a blessing: "go in peace." Go in holiness, go in *shalom*, no more bleeding, no more hemorrhaging loss of life, no more manhandling by doctors who would not help her, no more poverty from exhausted finances, but now full, healthy, joyous human life. She has become a full, liberated character in her life story.

End of story. That is enough. Now Mark, in his telling, goes back to the better, bigger story of the leader of the synagogue. Even then, however, Jesus does the same for the powerful man and his daughter as he did for this pitiful woman. Nothing more. The nameless woman is given her life as well as is the leader of the synagogue. The woman is now forever a key character in the story of Jesus, because of her need, and her fear and trembling, and her courage and caring. She becomes someone she was not, as she moved into the circle of Jesus' life-giving power.

IV

You recognize, do you not, your own place in this story. We are all hemorrhaging women, with life bleeding out of us, tired of being abused, with exhausted resources, scarcely able one more time to reach out for a touch. We are all of us part of the busy disciples, too busy with numbers to notice, too important and preoccupied. We are not Jesus but we do as baptized folk share in his power and in his capacity to heal, to let ourselves be touched so that some of our God-given power can flow to the lives of other bleeding outsiders. We are also the by-standing folk who watch in astonishment. We watch because this hurting woman and this caring agent of God, this odd text, provide a new shape for social relations. It is a shape that generates new possibility, new chances for communion, and new patterns of social power.

We are dazzled. Who would have thought

a) that we would be here so many years later, talking about one feeble reach for new life that succeeded?
b) that this pitiful woman would generate a totally new model of life and reality?

Those who trust this story do not willingly settle for the old, weary patterns of "haves" and "have-nots," for the usual arrangements of strength and weakness, power and powerlessness. This story offers to us a different map of reality, a different option, a different life. This is a new life we receive by touching and sharing power. It is a new life we give by being touched. The word is for us and for all our fellow bleeders: "Go in peace, be healed of your disease, by your faith be whole."

“Lost”

“Lost”

Luke 15:1-7

Anonymous student preacher

This morning, our scripture lesson comes from the gospel of Luke where we read the parable of the lost sheep. In this story Jesus teaches a group of tax collectors and sinners about the forgiving nature of God. He uses this illustration of God as a shepherd tending his flock.

The story opens with a flock of sheep in a pasture—one hundred sheep to be exact. At some point, one of the sheep becomes separated from the rest of the flock. Here is where I have a question (because the scripture doesn’t tell us): how in the world does this sheep get separated from its flock . . . its family . . . its loved ones? How does it become LOST? See, I don’t think this separation is as simple as it sounds. This is a serious thing. It involves feelings, pain, sorrow, and fear. How DOES this sheep become lost?

This morning, we are going to take a closer look at this parable and try to begin to understand how this sheep became lost, and, by extension, discover how we become lost.

Have any of you ever become lost? I mean really and truly LOST! The type of being lost where there is a petrifying fear that sets in. I have had, thankfully, only one experience where I have become really and truly lost. Back when I was a young child my family and I went to Disneyland in California. All I can remember from this experience is looking up and realizing that my family was nowhere to be seen. All I could see was a sea of strangers. This image is frozen in my mind.

In that instant I was struck with such a truly petrifying fear that I couldn't move, I could not think . . . all I could do is cry.

That's a terrible spot to be in. There were literally hundreds of strangers all around but no sign of my family. I was truly LOST. (Perhaps an interesting note to add here is that there is NO indication that the lost sheep was by herself. No, she may have been surrounded by hundreds of lost sheep. She has simply become lost from her flock.) I stood there frozen in fear until my father came and took my hand and led me back to my family.

Now trust me, there are two sides to this story when it comes to explaining how I became lost. One is that I was separated from my family by a crowd or by something that caught my attention and my family walked on ahead. From this perspective, I was left behind by my family. Here, my family was careless. They were not concerned with me and they left me behind and that's how I became lost. (By the way, this is the story I prefer to believe.)

For some of our lost folks, they have fallen victim to neglectful churches and sheep. For some, we have worked so busily to build churches, or our lives, that we have left others behind. Is this how we become lost?

The second opinion, the one my brothers insist is true, is that I saw something cool like Donald Duck or Mickey Mouse and I ran away toward whatever it was— away from my family where I got separated.

Maybe the sheep, that day, was young and naïve and got distracted in some way from the rest of the flock (maybe he found a nice new patch of grass to eat) and got separated. Maybe a larger crowd separated the sheep from her family. Maybe the flock failed to teach him to follow the shepherd and stay alert.

This second way the sheep may have become lost is a far more scary situation. In this case, the sheep, for some reason, makes a decision to leave the flock, to turn away and go at it alone. What could possibly cause someone to make this decision?

Most of the time it is fear.

Would you agree that over the past years our world has experienced great struggle? There has been a multitude of traumatic events including 9/11, the global war on terrorism, the tsunami, Katrina, and so many more things.

Would you also agree that this nation, our country, has faced some of the greatest tragedies of its time: terrorism has struck fear in are hearts, drugs and crime have grown more devastating, and tragic events like Hurricane Katrina have impressed the true uncertainty life brings?

Finally, would you agree that our very own church and our families have faced innumerable difficulties: illness, deaths, divorces, arguments, pain, struggles, and financial problems? We all have faced so much.

When we face such tragedy, such uncertainty, fear sets in and we can easily become depressed and afraid. Do you know what the leading symptom is for depression? It's withdrawal: withdrawal from friends, withdrawal from family and loved ones, and withdrawal from faith. It seems that when things get hard—maybe real hard—we begin to pull away from the flock and go at it alone.

Just recently I read in a journal about a fearful new product that a U.S. company has begun to produce. The Ibis Tek Corp. of Pennsylvania has begun production of a new SUV—one that I believe encompasses this fearful decision to go at life alone. This SUV has the available option of a sunroof that opens allowing a platform to raise that can hold your choice of weapons: a fully automatic machine gun or a grenade launcher!

Hey, if our world is getting too scary we can just hunker down in our new SUV and blow each other up. This is truly the mentality that many people have in these times of uncertainty.

Do you know that we have people all around us who feel like that sheep—feel that they might be better off going at it alone? There are people right now, that you know, who are feeling so much pain and struggle and fear and turmoil—yes even within our own church and our own homes—that they believe that it would be best to pull back from this world, to pull within a bunker and go at it alone. And when people pull out of life—when we stop working and living together and following the Great Shepherd—things begin to fall apart. Like in that terrible disaster with the Space Shuttle Columbia, when one shingle pulled away others followed and soon the whole ship came flying apart. Folks, these people are lost and are hurt and are lonely and we need them and Christ wants them.

Here's the good news: the parable doesn't end with that sheep realizing he's lost. I guess it could, I suppose. No, it goes on to tell of the shepherd realizing the sheep is lost and it tells of how the shepherd leaves the 99 other sheep to go and search for the one lost sheep. (Understand the significance and sacrifice of a real shepherd leaving 99 sheep to search for one.) That's how much Christ wants us. That's how much he wants to find us when we become lost. He would sacrifice his own life to save us, to rescue us.

Maybe this morning you have come to realize that you are lost; either because you have never been told about the great shepherd or maybe you thought you could go at life alone. Maybe you know of someone who is LOST. Christ is searching for you now. But you have to prepare yourself.

Have you ever tried to grab the hand of a child who doesn't want their hand to be grabbed? Or tried to take a child somewhere where he or she doesn't want to go? It's nearly impossible. See, we are like that child. Christ is ready to grab hold, like my father did at Disneyland, and lead us back to the flock. But we have to be ready and willing to allow him to lead us.

This morning, as we prepare to come to the altar for prayer, I ask you to grab a hold of someone around you. Maybe as you come to the altar or remain in your pew you can hold your neighbor's hand or shoulder. By doing this we show that we are unable to handle this world by ourselves and that we are uniting here today for the millions in this world who are lost, that they may be found.

The altar is open.

Bibliography

Aristotle. *On Rhetoric: A Theory of Civic Discourse.* Translated by George Alexander Kennedy. 2nd ed. New York: Oxford University Press, 2007.

Auden, W. H. "For the Time Being: A Christmas Oratorio." In *Collected Poems*, edited by Edward Mendelson, 347–400. New York: Modern Library, 2007.

Auerbach, Erich. *Mimesis: The Representation of Reality in Western Literature.* Princeton, N.J.: Princeton University Press, 1953.

Barth, Karl. *Church Dogmatics.* 4 vols. New York: T&T Clark, 2009.

———. *Deliverance to the Captives.* New York: Harper, 1961.

———. *The Epistle to the Romans.* London: Oxford University Press, 1968.

———. *Evangelical Theology: An Introduction.* New York: Holt, 1963.

———. *Homiletics.* Translated by Geoffrey William Bromiley and Donald E. Daniels. Louisville, Ky.: Westminster John Knox, 1991.

———. "The Need and Promise of Christian Preaching." In Barth, *The Word of God and the Word of Man*, 97–135.

———. "The Strange New World within the Bible." In Barth, *The Word of God and the Word of Man*, 28–50.

———. "The Word of God and the Task of the Ministry." In Barth, *The Word of God and the Word of Man*, 183–217.

———. *The Word of God and the Word of Man.* New York: Harper & Row, 1957.

Bartlett, David Lyon. *Between the Bible and the Church: New Methods for Biblical Preaching.* Nashville: Abingdon, 1999.

Brueggemann, Walter. "Pain Turned to Newness." In Campbell, *Preaching Jesus*, 259–64.

Buttrick, David. *A Captive Voice: The Liberation of Preaching*. Louisville, Ky.: Westminster John Knox, 1994.

Campbell, Charles L. *Preaching Jesus: New Directions for Homiletics in Hans Frei's Postliberal Theology*. Grand Rapids: Eerdmans, 1997.

Childers, Jana. "Introduction: The Preacher's Performance." In *The New Interpreter's Handbook of Preaching*, edited by Paul Scott Wilson, 213–15. Nashville: Abingdon, 2008.

Comstock, Gary. "Truth or Meaning: Ricoeur versus Frei on Biblical Narrative." *Journal of Religion* 66, no. 2 (1986): 117–40.

———. "Two Types of Narrative Theology." *Journal of the American Academy of Religion* 55, no. 4 (1987): 687–717.

Craddock, Fred B. *As One without Authority*. Revised and with new sermons. St. Louis: Chalice Press, 2001.

———. *The Cherry Log Sermons*. Louisville, Ky.: Westminster John Knox, 2001.

Crites, Stephen. "The Narrative Quality of Experience." In Hauerwas and Jones, *Why Narrative?*, 65–88.

Crossan, John Dominic. *The Dark Interval: Towards a Theology of Story*. Niles, Ill.: Argus, 1975.

DeHart, Paul J. *The Trial of the Witnesses: The Rise and Decline of Postliberal Theology*. Challenges in Contemporary Theology. Malden, Mass.: Blackwell, 2006.

Diamond, Jared M. *Guns, Germs, and Steel: The Fates of Human Societies*. New York: Norton, 1997.

Dibelius, Martin. *From Tradition to Gospel*. Library of Theological Translations. Cambridge: James Clarke, 1971.

Ellingsen, Mark. *The Integrity of Biblical Narrative: Story in Theology and Proclamation*. Minneapolis: Fortress, 1990.

Fant, Clyde E. *Preaching for Today*. Cambridge: Harper & Row, 1987.

Fiddes, Paul S. *Past Event and Present Salvation: The Christian Idea of Atonement*. 1st American ed. Louisville, Ky.: Westminster John Knox, 1989.

Frei, Hans W. *The Eclipse of Biblical Narrative: A Study in Eighteenth and Nineteenth Century Hermeneutics*. New Haven: Yale University Press, 1974.

———. *The Identity of Jesus Christ: The Hermeneutical Bases of Dogmatic Theology*. Philadelphia: Fortress, 1975. Reprint, Eugene, Ore.: Wipf & Stock, 2000.

———. "The 'Literal Reading' of Biblical Narrative in the Christian Tradition: Does It Stretch or Will It Break?" In *The Bible and the Narrative Tradition*, edited by Frank McConnell. New York: Oxford University Press, 1986.

———. "Of the Resurrection of Christ." In Hunsinger and Placher, *Theology and Narrative*, 200–206.

———. "Response to 'Narrative Theology: An Evangelical Appraisal.'" In Hunsinger and Placher, *Theology and Narrative*, 207–12.

———. "Theological Reflections on the Accounts of Jesus' Death and Resurrection." In Frei, *Identity of Jesus Christ*, 1–49.

———. "Theology and the Interpretation of Narrative: Some Hermeneutical Considerations." In Hunsinger and Placher, *Theology and Narrative*, 94–116.

Frei, Hans W., George Hunsinger, and William C. Placher. *Types of Christian Theology*. New Haven: Yale University Press, 1992.

Gilkey, Langdon. "Cosmology, Ontology, and the Travail of Biblical Language." *Journal of Religion* 41, no. 3 (1961): 194–205.

———. "An Appreciation of Karl Barth." In *How Karl Barth Changed My Mind*, edited by Donald K. McKim, 150–52. Grand Rapids: Eerdmans, 1986.

Girard, René. *The Scapegoat*. Baltimore: Johns Hopkins University Press, 1986.

Gross, Nancy Lammers. *If You Cannot Preach Like Paul. . . .* Grand Rapids: Eerdmans, 2002.

Hauerwas, Stanley, and L. Gregory Jones, eds. *Why Narrative? Readings in Narrative Theology*. Grand Rapids: Eerdmans, 1989.

Hays, Richard B. *First Corinthians*. Interpretation: A Bible Commentary for Teaching and Preaching. Louisville, Ky.: John Knox, 1997.

Higton, Mike. *Christ, Providence, and History: Hans W. Frei's Public Theology*. London: T&T Clark, 2004.

———. "Hans Frei and David Tracy on the Ordinary and the Extraordinary in Christianity." *Journal of Religion* 79, no. 4 (1999): 566–91.

Hilkert, Mary Catherine. *Naming Grace: Preaching and the Sacramental Imagination*. New York: Continuum, 1996.

Hunsinger, George. "Afterword." In Hunsinger and Placher, *Theology and Narrative*, 235–70.

———. "The Newbigin Gauntlet." In *The Church between Gospel and Culture: The Emerging Mission in North America*, edited by George R. Hunsberger and Craig Van Gelder, 3–25. Grand Rapids: Eerdmans, 1996.

Hunsinger, George, and William C. Placher, eds. *Theology and Narrative: Selected Essays*. New York: Oxford University Press, 1993.

Husserl, Edmund. *Idées directrices pour une phénoménologie*. Translated by Paul Ricoeur. Paris: Éditions Gallimard, 1950.

Imbens, Annie, and Ineke Jonker. *Christianity and Incest*. Minneapolis: Fortress, 1992.

James, Henry. "The Art of Fiction." In *The Future of the Novel: Essays on the Art of Fiction*, 3–29. New York: Vintage, 1956.

Kafka, Franz. *The Great Wall of China: Stories and Reflections*. Translated by Willa Muir and Edwin Muir. New York: Schocken, 1946.

Kay, James F. "Review of *Preaching Jesus: New Directions for Homiletics in Hans Frei's Postliberal Theology*." *Theology Today* 56, no. 3 (1999): 403–5.

———. "The Word of the Cross at the Turn of the Ages." *Interpretation* 53, no. 1 (1999): 44–56.

Kelsey, David H. *The Uses of Scripture in Recent Theology*. Philadelphia: Fortress, 1975.

Lake, Carlton. "Picasso Speaking." *Atlantic Monthly* 200, no. 1 (1957): 35–41.

Lampe, Peter. "Theological Wisdom and the 'Word about the Cross': The Rhetorical Scheme in 1 Corinthians 1–4." *Interpretation* 44, no. 2 (1990): 117–31.

Lindbeck, George A. *The Nature of Doctrine: Religion and Theology in a Postliberal Age*. Philadelphia: Westminster, 1984.

Lischer, Richard. *The End of Words: The Language of Reconciliation in a Culture of Violence*. Lyman Beecher Lectures in Preaching. Grand Rapids: Eerdmans, 2005.

Long, Thomas G. *Preaching and the Literary Forms of the Bible*. Philadelphia: Fortress, 1989.

———. *Preaching from Memory to Hope*. Louisville, Ky.: Westminster John Knox, 2009.

———. *The Witness of Preaching*. 2nd ed. Louisville, Ky.: Westminster John Knox, 2005.

Luther, Martin. *Luther's Works*. Vol. 36, American ed. Edited by Jaroslav Pelikan and Helmut T. Lehmann. St. Louis: Concordia, 1955.

MacIntyre, Alasdair C. *After Virtue: A Study in Moral Theory*. Notre Dame, Ind.: University of Notre Dame Press, 1981.

Marsden, George M. *Understanding Fundamentalism and Evangelicalism*. Grand Rapids: Eerdmans, 1991.

McClendon, James William. *Systematic Theology: Ethics*. 2nd ed. Waco, Tex.: Baylor University Press, 2012.

Metz, Johann Baptist. "A Short Apology of Narrative." In Hauerwas and Jones, *Why Narrative?*, 251–62.

Moltmann, Jürgen. *The Crucified God: The Cross of Christ as the Foundation and Criticism of Christian Theology*. London: SCM Press, 1974.

Mudge, Lewis Seymour, ed. *Essays on Biblical Interpretation*. Philadelphia: Fortress, 1980.

Neuger, Christie. *Counseling Women: A Narrative, Pastoral Approach*. Minneapolis: Fortress, 2001.

O'Connor, Flannery. *The Violent Bear It Away*. In *Collected Works*, Library of America 39, 329–480. New York: Library of America, 1988.

Placher, William C. "Hans Frei and the Meaning of Biblical Narrative." *Christian Century* 106, no. 18 (1989): 556–59.

———. "Introduction." In Hunsinger and Placher, *Theology and Narrative*, 3–25.

———. "Paul Ricoeur and Postliberal Theology: A Conflict of Interpretations?" *Modern Theology* 4, no. 1 (1987): 35–52.

Reagan, Charles E. *Paul Ricoeur: His Life and His Work*. Chicago: University of Chicago Press, 1996.

Resner, André. *Preacher and Cross: Person and Message in Theology and Rhetoric.* Grand Rapids: Eerdmans, 1999.

Ricoeur, Paul. "The Bible and the Imagination." In Wallace, *Figuring the Sacred,* translated by David Pellauer, 144–66.

———. "Biblical Hermeneutics." *Semeia* 4 (1975): 27–148.

———. *The Conflict of Interpretations: Essays in Hermeneutics.* Edited by Don Ihde, translated by Willis Domingo et al. Northwestern University Studies in Phenomenology and Existential Philosophy. Evanston, Ill.: Northwestern University Press, 1974.

———. *Freedom and Nature: The Voluntary and Involuntary.* Translated by Erazim Kohak. Northwestern University Studies in Phenomenology and Existential Philosophy. Evanston, Ill.: Northwestern University Press, 1966.

———. *Freud and Philosophy: An Essay on Interpretation.* Translated by Denis Savage. New Haven: Yale University Press, 1970.

———. "The Function of Fiction in Shaping Reality." In *A Ricoeur Reader: Reflection and Imagination,* edited by Mario J. Valdés, 117–36. Toronto: University of Toronto Press, 1991.

———. "The Hermeneutics of Testimony." In Mudge, *Essays on Biblical Interpretation,* 119–54.

———. *Interpretation Theory: Discourse and the Surplus of Meaning.* Fort Worth: Texas Christian University Press, 1976.

———. "Naming God." In Wallace, *Figuring the Sacred,* translated by David Pellauer, 217–35.

———. "Narrative Identity." In *On Paul Ricoeur: Narrative and Interpretation,* edited by David Wood, 188–200. London: Routledge, 1991.

———. *Oneself as Another.* Translated by Kathleen Blamey. Chicago: University of Chicago Press, 1992.

———. "Philosophical Hermeneutics and Biblical Hermeneutics." In *From Text to Action,* translated by Kathleen Blamey and John B. Thompson, 89–101. Evanston, Ill.: Northwestern University Press, 2007.

———. "Philosophy and Religious Language." In Wallace, *Figuring the Sacred,* translated by David Pellauer, 35–47.

———. *The Rule of Metaphor: Multi-Disciplinary Studies of the Creation of Meaning in Language.* Translated by Robert Czerny. University of Toronto Romance Series 37. Toronto: University of Toronto Press, 1977.

———. *The Symbolism of Evil.* Translated by Emerson Buchanan. Boston: Beacon, 1969.

———. *Time and Narrative.* Vol. 1. Translated by Kathleen McLaughlin and David Pellauer. Chicago: University of Chicago Press, 1984.

———. "Toward a Hermeneutic of the Idea of Revelation." In Mudge, *Essays on Biblical Interpretation,* 73–118.

———. "Toward a Narrative Theology: Its Necessity, Its Resources, Its Difficulties." In Wallace, *Figuring the Sacred,* translated by David Pellauer, 236–48.

———. "Truth and Falsehood." In *History and Truth*, translated by Charles A. Kelbley, 165–91. Evanston, Ill.: Northwestern University Press, 1965.

Ricoeur, Paul, Charles E. Reagan, and David Stewart. "The Critique of Religion." In *The Philosophy of Paul Ricoeur: An Anthology of His Work*, 213–22. Boston: Beacon, 1978.

Robinson, Wayne Bradley. "Angels, but Satan and Wild Beasts." In *Journeys toward Narrative Preaching*, edited by Wayne Bradley Robinson, 101–5. New York: Pilgrim, 1990.

Ryle, Gilbert. *The Concept of Mind*. Senior Series. London: Hutchinson's University Library, 1949.

Sangster, William Edwin. *The Craft of Sermon Construction*. Philadelphia: Westminster, 1951.

Scholes, Robert E. *Textual Power: Literary Theory and the Teaching of English*. New Haven: Yale University Press, 1985.

Springs, Jason. "Between Barth and Wittgenstein: On the Availability of Hans Frei's Later Theology." *Modern Theology* 23, no. 3 (2007): 393–413.

Stendahl, Krister. "Biblical Theology, Contemporary." In *The Interpreter's Dictionary of the Bible*, vol. 1, edited by George Arthur Buttrick et al., 418–31. Nashville: Abingdon, 1962.

Strawson, Galen. "Against Narrativity." *Ratio* 17, no. 4 (2004): 428–52.

Taylor, Barbara Brown. *The Preaching Life*. Cambridge, Mass.: Cowley, 1993.

Tisdale, Leonora Tubbs. *Preaching as Local Theology and Folk Art*. Fortress Resources for Preaching. Minneapolis: Fortress, 1997.

Tracy, David. *Blessed Rage for Order: The New Pluralism in Theology*. New York: Seabury Press, 1975.

———. *Dialogue with the Other: The Inter-Religious Dialogue*. Louvain Theological and Pastoral Monographs 1. Grand Rapids: Eerdmans, 1991.

Wallace, Mark I, ed. *Figuring the Sacred: Religion, Narrative, and Imagination*. Minneapolis: Fortress, 1995.

———. "Introduction." In Wallace, *Figuring the Sacred*, 1–32.

———. *The Second Naiveté: Barth, Ricoeur, and the New Yale Theology*. Studies in American Biblical Hermeneutics. 2nd ed. Macon, Ga.: Mercer University Press, 1995.

Webb, Stephen H. *Re-Figuring Theology: The Rhetoric of Karl Barth*. SUNY Series in Rhetoric and Theology. Albany: State University of New York Press, 1991.

Wilder, Amos Niven. *Early Christian Rhetoric: The Language of the Gospel*. Peabody, Mass.: Hendrickson, 1999.

Willimon, William H. "Answering Pilate: Truth and the Postliberal Church." *Christian Century* 104, no. 3 (1987): 82–85.

———. *Conversations with Barth on Preaching*. Nashville: Abingdon, 2006.

Wills, Garry. *St. Augustine*. New York: Penguin, 1999.

Zahrnt, Heinz. *The Question of God: Protestant Theology in the Twentieth Century*. New York: Harcourt, Brace & World, 1969.

Index